Wits, Wenchers
and Wantons

Wits, Wenchers and Wantons

London's Low Life: Covent Garden in the Eighteenth Century

by

E. J. BURFORD

ROBERT HALE · LONDON

Robert Hale Limited
Clerkenwell House
Clerkenwell Green
London EC1R 0HT

To my dear wife
for all her help
and encouragement

British Library Cataloguing in Publication Data
Burford, E. J.
Wits, wenchers and wantons: London's low life:
Covent Garden in the eighteenth century.
1. Covent Garden (London, England)—Social life
and customs   2. London (England)—Social life
and customs—18th century
I. Title
942.1'32   DA685.C7
ISBN 0-7090-2629-3

Photoset in Palatino by
Rowland Phototypesetting Ltd, Bury St Edmunds, Suffolk
Printed in Great Britain by St Edmundsbury Press
Bury St Edmunds, Suffolk
Bound by WBC Ltd

Contents

List of Illustrations   vii
Acknowledgements   x
Preface   xi

 1 The Abbot's Garden   1
 2 The Flowering Years   24
 3 Mother Elizabeth Whyburn and Sally Salisbury   42
 4 Tom and Moll King's Coffee-House   53
 5 The Bagnio-keepers   65
 6 The Charming Betsy Careless and the Marvellous
    Fanny Murray   76
 7 The Places of Resort   85
    Carpenter's Coffee-House – 'The Finish'   85
    The Rose Tavern   89
    The Shakespeare's Head Tavern   94
    The Covent Garden Cyprians   102
    The Bedford Head Coffee-House   107
    The Bedford Arms   112
    The Ben Jonson's Head   117
    Nancy Dawson and Friends   122
 8 Mother Jane Douglas, 'The Empress'   128
 9 Pharaoh's Daughters   135
10 Mrs Phillips' Sex Shop   144
11 The Heyday   150
12 The Theatrical Connection   169
13 Mrs Elizabeth Gould   185
14 The Adventures of a pair of Rakes   195
15 Betsy Coxe and other Votaries   200

16 More Lists of Cyprians   209
17 The Nurseries of Naughtiness   223

Bibliography   238

Index   241

List of Illustrations

1	The Strand at Charing Cross, 1547	2
2	Detail from Ralph Agas' map, 1572	4
3	Detail from J. Braun & F. Hogenburg's map, 1572	5
4	A group of English bawds, c. 1615	7
5	St Paul's Church, Covent Garden, 1640	9
6	Portrait of Jean Le Becq	12
7	Bridewell Prison, c. 1666	20
8	Bridewell Prison, c. 1700	20
9	Plan of eighteenth-century Covent Garden and its notable inhabitants	22–3
10	Will's Coffee-House	25
11	Button's Coffee-House	27
12	Tom's Coffee-House	31
13	View of Covent Garden, 1720. Sutton Nicholls	38–9
14	The Carting of Bawds in Paris, c. 1730	40
15	Constables arresting a *Cyprian* in Covent Garden	43
16	*Le Mauvais Lieu*. Jan Steen, 1678	46
17	Sally Salisbury	47
18	Sally Salisbury's attack on the Hon. John Finch	51
19	Moll King in 1739	54
20	Drunken rakes rioting in Covent Garden	56
21	*Covent Garden Morning Frolick*, 1739. J. Boitard	57
22	Beadles evicting trouble-makers	59
23	Constables arrest a gentleman in Covent Garden	61
24	Elegy on the death of Tom King, 1737	63
25	The Strand at Charing Cross, c. 1700. J. Maurer	66
26	Mother Elizabeth Needham meets the York wagon. Hogarth	69
27	Betsy Careless attended by *Little Cazey*. Hogarth	77
28	Miss Fanny Murray, 1756	81
29	Carpenter's Coffee-House	87
30	The Rose Tavern. Hogarth, 1735	91

31 The Shakespeare's Head, 1768   95
32 Thomas Davies' bookshop in Russell Street   99
33 Soliciting in the Piazza   101
34 Harris's List of Covent Garden Ladies, 1764   104
35 A kiosk under the Piazza portico   113
36 Miss Nancy Dawson   123
37 Mother Jane Douglas and her *Cattery*. Hogarth, 1735   129
38 Kind and Tender Usage at the Old Calf's Head   139
39 Lord Andrew Archer's mansion in King Street   142
40 Pharaoh's Daughters beware. Gillray, 1797   143
41 Miss Constantia Theresa Phillips   145
42 A sale of English Beauties in the East Indies. Gillray   148
43 View of Covent Garden *c.* 1730–40 – looking west. J. Maurer   151
44 View of Covent Garden *c.* 1749 – looking east. J. Maurer   151
45 Bridewell Prison *c.* 1740. Hogarth   153
46 Thomas de Veil, magistrate, in Bow Street court   155
47 John Rich opens his King's Theatre in Bow Street, 1732. Hogarth   158
48 Bow Street Runners *c.* 1800. Rowlandson: detail   161
49 Sailors from HMS *Grafton* threaten the Star Tavern in the Strand   163
50 *The Tars' Triumph*: burning down the Star Tavern   164
51 David Garrick's Old Theatre in Drury Lane   170
52 View of the Piazza. J. Maurer, 1753   180–1
53 W. Stow's *Mapp of the Parish of St Paul's*, 1755   183
54 The *Hummums* destroyed by fire, 1769. W. Grimm   189
55 Sir John Fielding in his court in Bow Street   191
56 The Bow Street Public Office, 1792   192
57 *The Reforming Constable*   193
58 Mr Samuel Derrick   202
59 Mrs Jane Lessingham   203
60 Interrogation in the Watch-House   207
61 A gallant propositioning a *Cyprian* in the Piazza   210
62 Miss Isabella Wilkinson the Sadler's Wells dancer   213
63 Mrs Margaret Cuyler   215
64 Mrs Mary Corbyne, 'the White crow'   215
65 *A Peep at Christies*. Lord Derby and Miss Elizabeth Farren. Gillray   218
66 *Le Cochon et les deux Petits*. The Duke of Norfolk and 'the Royal Sovereign'. Gillray   222
67 The Sausage Woman in Covent Garden Market. Martin, 1772   224
68 *Dividing the Spoil*. Cruikshank, 1796   226

69 *Beau Mordecai Inspir'd*. Carington Bowles, 1772   229
70 Mr Hewitt's new *Hummums Hotel*   235
71 The Old Cider Cellar in Maiden Lane   236

Credits

Acknowledgements

I should like to express my sincere thanks and appreciation for the help given in my researches for this work. Firstly to Miss M. J. Swarbrick, Archivist at the Westminster City Council's Library and all of her assistants who were tireless in their help, in particular in the discovery and choice of the illustrations; to Mr R. E. Samways, Principal Assistant Archivist at the Greater London Council, and particularly to John Philips Keeper of Prints and his colleague Raphael Hart likewise for their help in choosing many illustrations.

My thanks are also expressed to Mr Thomas Shaw, Keeper of Printed Books at the Guildhall and Mr Ralph Hyde, Keeper of Prints and Maps and to Mr James R. Sewell, Deputy Keeper of Records at the Corporation of London Records Office, for supplying information about many of the characters whose names and activities appear in this work.

Especial thanks are due to Catherine Jestin, Librarian of the Lewis Walpole Museum of Farmington, USA, and her colleague Mr Frank Sussler, Curator of Prints for information supplied about Jack Harris's *Cyprians* and to Miss E. Talbot Rice, Librarian of the National Army Museum for details of the many military gentlemen involved in Covent Garden's diversions. I must also express appreciation of the co-operation of the staff at the British Museum Print Room.

I am mindful of the help given in this effort of mine to the authors of the works listed in the bibliography for the enormous amount of detail even if only small parts are here incorporated: I should like this to be a small tribute and memorial so their names should not be forgotten.

E. J. BURFORD
London

Preface

The very name of Covent Garden evokes differing thoughts in different people. To the musically minded it is the splendid Opera House in Bow Street. To thousands of others it is the theatreland of Drury Lane, the Aldwych and the Strand. To those of religious mind it is Inigo Jones' little masterpiece, St Paul's, Covent Garden, in which so many famous – and infamous – persons are buried. And before its marvellous fruit, flower and vegetable market was removed a few years ago over the River Thames, it was visited by hundreds of thousands of people lured by the fame of the hall in which the world's produce was displayed.

Over and above all, however, Covent Garden was for close on three hundred years London's principal pleasure garden, the Mecca of pleasure-seekers of every kind from the most simple to the most villainous, the most elegant to the most rough, reaching its peak – or, according to one's viewpoint, its nadir – in the eighteenth century, when it became London's 'sin city'.

The greatly altered Covent Garden of today is once more designed to lure the pleasure-seeker, albeit in a somewhat quieter and cleaner and more sophisticated ambience, and certainly not at the level of its eighteenth-century depravity.

Although there is a plethora of books about different aspects of 'the Garden', there is not one which gives a full account of the lives and actions of the men and women who created the attractions – the taverns, the coffee-houses and chocolate-houses, the *bagnios* and 'houses of resort' – which made it the magnet for all sections of society from dukes to dustmen, peeresses to prostitutes, the upright to the depraved, the wit to the ignoramus, in the process creating the new class of courtesans who became the 'Toasts of the Town'. This is the first book to shed light on their activities in full, 'warts and all'.

1. The Abbot's Garden

Covent Garden comprises that area of about thirty acres bounded by the Strand, along St Martin's Lane to Long Acre, then down Drury Lane back again to the Strand. In olden days the muddy, dirty, ill-kept highway now known as the Strand followed the River Thames to the Eleanor Cross at Charing (now Charing Cross), thence through a leafy path by the church of St Martin-in-the-Fields until it met another track through the 'long acre', at the end of which it reached an even more ancient track called Drewerie Lane, which was the continuation of a footpath from the City of London's gate at the end of Fleet Street, called Wych Strate. A *wych* or *wyke* in this connection was most probably a dairy farm. It is recalled today by the name of Aldwych – the old *wych* – leading into the Strand at what was once known as 'the backside of St Clement's Church'.

From at least Anglo-Saxon times all the land outside the City walls as far as Chelsea, then westward to Kensington and Bayswater, round to the ancient Ty Bourne and swinging eastwards along the course of the Olde Bourne formed part of the vast holdings of the Abbey of St Peter at the West Mynster, built originally on the then island of Thorney by the King of the East Saxons known as Seberht after his conversion to Christianity about the year 600.

The earliest record is of a grant of land about the years 1200 'near the wall of the garden of the Abbot of Westminster', and there is a record of 'a quit rent . . . for a garden between the churchyard of St Martin's and the garden of the Abbey' during the reign of King Henry III. The first mention of Covent Garden as such is a record (dated between 1250 and 1283) of a 'quit rent from messuages in Aldewichestrate on the south part of the gate of the garden of the Abbot and Convent of Westminster'. This is taken to mean that there was a Benedictine monastery or convent then on the site.

The abbey must have been leasing out small parcels of land for

1

pasturage and small market gardens as well as for inns and taverns along the north side of the Strand, which was the principal highway, although it was for centuries 'verie jepardous to all people . . . on horsebacke as on foote . . . in winter and in summer, by nyghte and by daye . . . noxious and foule'. Even as late as 1756 a French visitor observed that, '. . . the middle of the road was garnished with a thick muddy liquid three or four inches deep so that pedestrians were bemired from head to foot . . . [and] the centre kennel was constantly stopped-up because . . . lazy servants threw offal and dust and rubbish into it . . . the heavy overhanging signboards of houses and taverns . . . were wont to fall on pedestrians' heads in very bad weather.' In 1475 a parcel of land thereabouts was leased to 'that vpryghte and knowinge man' Chief Justice Sir John Fortescue.

In 1515 there is the lease of 'a garden called Covent Garden in St Margaret's parish' (*sic*), and as such it is referred to in the accounts of the churchwardens of St Martin-in-the-Fields in 1525; in 1530 there is an 'Aquittance of rent' for Covent Garden. Some time before 1536 one Richard Weston held some land by a grant from the abbot. In that year he transferred his grant to one Henry Dingley, who then leased it to Richard Browne. Mr Browne was unlucky because in that year Henry VIII swapped some land in Berkshire for Covent Garden and Long Acre – which actually comprises seven acres. King Henry wanted the freeholds, so Dick Browne, wily enough not to tangle with such an adversary, surrendered his rights. Henry Dingley was made of sterner stuff – or was perhaps more obtuse – and refused the offered compensation, taking proceedings against Browne for having forfeited his rights to the King. King Henry ended all such disputes when he dissolved the monasteries in 1539, thus acquiring all rights to all lands and properties about Charing Cross and north of the long acre. By this one act he catapulted England out of the Middle Ages, laying the foundations *inter alia* for Covent Garden's bright and prosperous future.

His son, Edward VI, in 1547 granted both Covent Garden and Long Acre to his maternal uncle Edward Seymour, Duke of Somerset, then the most powerful man in the kingdom. When he was beheaded for treason in January 1552, the property was given to one of the architects of his ruin, John Russell, first Earl of Bedford. His equally unlucky cousin, the brave soldier Sir John Palmer who was executed with him, had built a small house on the site.

On that part abutting on the Strand John Russell built a small house which was thenceforth to be known as Bedford House.

(Opposite) The Strand in the time of Edward VI

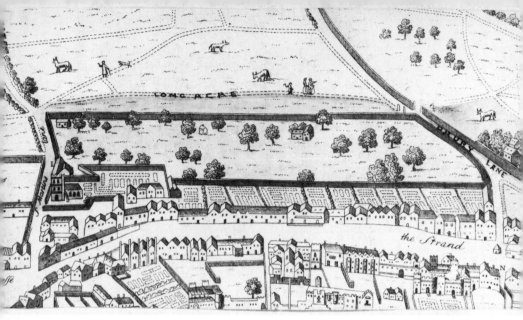

Detail from Ralph Agas' map of 1572 based upon the Surveigh of 1560: the earliest view of Covent Garden, showing a small shed at the left-hand corner and a wall enclosing the whole area

When he died in 1556, he was succeeded by his son Francis, whose main contribution to the Russells' fortunes was the adoption of the motto '*Che sará sará*' ('What will be will be'), perhaps because of the unpredictable actions of Queen Elizabeth I towards her courtiers. In her reign house-building all over London was unchecked, and property values increased enormously. Braun and Hogenburg's map of 1572 depicts a row of small dwellings and taverns along the north side of the Strand and behind them a large pasture with a small structure on it which some think may have been a chapel, but it may well have been a cowshed. This is the earliest representation of Covent Garden.

Queen Elizabeth's great minister William Cecil, later Lord Burghley, had a lease in 1570 from Lord Bedford which gave him 'the right to enter and walk within the eastern part of the garden through one gate or door'. It was a very low door. When the Queen visited the old courtier lying ill abed, she had to stoop to go through, which occasioned her remark that she would not have bent for Philip of Spain but she would do so for her old mentor.

Lord Burghley transformed this house into a most splendid mansion, run by a household 'of more than eighty persons . . . at a cost of more than forty pounds the week'. It was known as Burghley House until his son was created Earl of Exeter, when the name was changed to Exeter House. Next door was Cecil House, built for Burghley's other son. These mansions dominated the

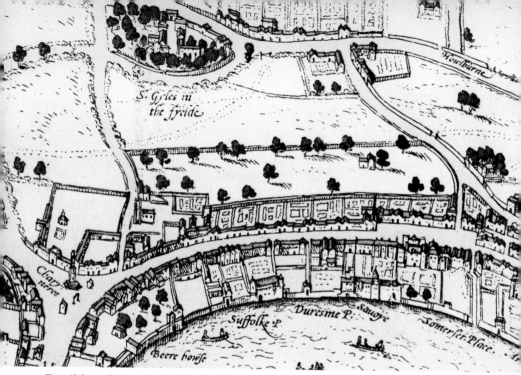

Detail from Braun and Hogenburg's map of 1572. The shed has disappeared but there is a more substantial building in the right-hand area near Drury Lane

Strand frontage of Covent Garden, dwarfing the adjoining houses and shops. The garden then 'had posts and rails running as far as Drury Lane . . . from which it was separated by a mud wall'.

Drury Lane marks the line of the ancient field-path from the City of London to Olde Bourne (Holborn) and is reputed to have been named after Sir Roger de Drury of Thurston in Suffolk, who died in 1408, because when his grandson Robert built a substantial mansion about 1495 the site was known as 'Drury Place . . . in the then Wyche Strete an eastern way to Temple Bar'. However, it is just as likely to have been an ancient 'drewerie lane' for about 1225 the word 'drewerie' or 'drowerie' meant 'a litel luste, a drory that ys but a duste', or carnal copulation. Since the nearest 'assigned place' for fornication licensed by the City of London was in Snow Hill just outside Newgate (under the same regulations which governed the eighteen licensed brothels on the Bankside in Southwark belonging to the Bishop of Winchester), there can be little doubt that a country lane only a short stroll outside the gates, allowing amorous pursuits free of interference from any authority, was a sure invitation for lovers. That Drury Lane was even then neither morally nor physically clean is demonstrated by its nickname 'Turnshite Alley', by which it was still popularly known in 1722.

The Garden was not completely devoid of other inhabitants: the churchwardens' accounts for 1580 and 1581 record the burials of 'poore women . . . oute of ye covent garden', and in 1600 record 'Mr Jeames Russell . . . who was slaine in Bedforde House'. At this time the only entrance to the Garden was in a small lane at the back of St Martin's Church, which was still 'in the fields'. In 1639 St Martin's Lane was still built up only on its eastern side as far as Long Acre, and in 1593 it was still 'the leafy lane . . . on the waye unto Saint Giles' – St Giles still being regarded as a distant country village.

John Stow's *Surveigh* (1598) does not even mention Covent Garden but Strype's revision observes that it was probably called Covent Garden because '. . . it was the Gardens and Fields to that large Convent or Monastery where Exeter House formerly stood . . . those grounds being all encompassed with a Wall'. John Norden's map of 1593 depicts a pasture with what look like sheds for sheep or cattle and a large 'common garden' divided into small plots for cultivation.

When Francis, second Earl of Bedford, died in 1585, the contents of his house at Chenies and some of the furniture in Bedford House had to be sold to defray the costs of his funeral. His grandson, Edward, third Earl, completely reconstructed Bedford House, whose courtyard now had an entrance from the Strand. He also created the formal garden at the back of the mansion, whose wall later became the southern boundary of the market. He was on the point of selling his Woburn lands as well as Covent Garden to pay his debts when his cousin Francis intervened and successfully petitioned King James I to prevent his alienating any part of his estates.

Francis Russell succeeded to the earldom and estates in 1626. He was a keen and thrifty businessman; he also had the good sense to marry in 1609 a great heiress, Katherine, daughter of Giles Brydges, third Baron Chandos. They were a well-matched pair who produced ten children. One of Francis' first actions was to clear the property of all the rough sheds and broken-down hovels and other detritus which cluttered up his London estate, as well as cleaning out the open sewer which ran through it. A number of poor-quality tenements had already been erected on the site by a man named John Ward, who now proposed to build another seventeen in an alley 'with only a nine foot alley exit into Long Acre'.

Inigo Jones, at this time a member of the Commission for Buildings set up by Charles I in 1625, surveyed the property when

A group of English bawds and their gallants in the reign of James I. (By an unknown Flemish painter)

Francis offered him the chance to develop it. He reported in October 1638 that this proposed alley 'led through the garden of My Lady Stanhope and several other Persons of Quality . . . with alleys of mean houses . . . having no other way to go out'. These were breaches of the Proclamation for Buildings, which required that all houses be built of brick, without overhanging storeys.

As early as 1631 Francis had leased to John Powell, Edward Palmer and John Barrodale 'all that . . . parcel of land . . . called Covent Garden . . . for thirty-four years at a yearly rental of £17.0.6d . . . payable quarterly in the Dining Hall . . . of Bedford House'. The lease mentioned parcels of land reserved for a vestry house and a 'street or passage fifty feet broad on the south side for a churchyard'. This was the later King Street.

Francis had to pay the King the enormous sum of £2,000 for the special licence, which provided that these new buildings must provide 'a distinguished Ornament . . . stately houses for Persons of Quality'. This accorded with Inigo Jones' original idea of an Italian-style piazza. However, after paying out £2,000, the Earl was somewhat short of ready cash, and it was agreed that there should be arcades on two sides only, and a church on the third side, leaving the boundary wall of Bedford House on the south side. The arches were to be built of stone and the buildings of brick stuccoed over.

On the north side each house had two bays, each twelve feet wide, with a frontage of thirty feet, but the sixth house had three bays and a frontage of thirty-nine feet. All were fifty feet high with a pitched roof of eleven feet. The arcade was twenty-two feet high with a walkway twenty-one feet wide. Each house had a mezzanine floor for use as a drawing-room or living-quarters, the bedrooms being above. Some had a parlour and study on the ground floor, using the first floor as the dining-room. All the principal apartments had 'shuttynge windowes', and most doors had 'stocklocks'. There were coach-houses and stables at the rear.

The tenants had the right to walk under the portico and turn away anyone who caused a nuisance or a trespass. More fundamental problems were the supply of water and of waste disposal; there was, however, a clause in the lease which provided that if the tenant 'could not occupy his house for want of a correct sewer' he could give six months notice to quit without incurring any penalty. At this time in Covent Garden there was 'a greate Gutter whiche rendereth itselfe into the Strand sewer'. Water had been supplied from the time of James I. Indeed, in 1608 the Lord Mayor cut off supplies to Lord Burghley's house 'because

St Paul's Church, Covent Garden in 1640. Inigo Jones called it 'The handsomest barn in England'

he wasted water'! Piped water was to be conveyed 'to the house of every man who will take it . . . at a certain rental' but it was piped only into basements. The Worshipful Company of Plumbers had been incorporated only in 1612 and they had not yet got around to plumbing in houses.

In 1635 a new sewer was constructed 'in front of the houses to carry away refuse water . . . into the Strand sewer' but it was not connected up with Covent Garden because the Earl was unwilling, or more likely did not have the money. In 1683 he secured a licence to build 'a sewer lined with brick'.

These splendid modern houses lacked bathrooms, lavatories or facilities for ablutions – indeed, there were no bathrooms in any London house until late in the eighteenth century. Hot water had to be carried upstairs in buckets or ewers for bathtubs – usually of metal – which were quite small. Hence home bathing was infrequent, which may account for the popularity of the 'hummums' (bathing establishments) which were built in the Strand from about 1675; this luxury was to be enjoyed only by those with time and money. Personal ablutions were usually done in a china bowl with water poured out from a pitcher or ewer; the water was drawn from either a cistern of rainwater on the roof or a cistern of piped water in the basement.

Locally made soap was of very poor quality. In the sixteenth century it was usually imported from Castile. The Soapmakers' Company was incorporated only in 1638. Soaps were taxed under

Oliver Cromwell, but these taxes were abolished with the Restoration, when the importation of good soaps from France began, which made ablutions more pleasant. But fresh drinking-water still had to be bought from water-carriers.

The disposal of waste water and human waste was an awkward problem. At a convenient time chamberpots and night commodes would be carried down into the basement and emptied into the cesspit or thrown onto a compost-heap in the garden. More often than not the servants would save themselves the drudgery of this unpleasant job by emptying the contents out of a window into the 'kennel' (gutter), which would be blocked in dry weather or flood the noisome contents away in winter. It was then the custom in English civilized society to keep the chamberpots in a cupboard or sideboard in the dining-room. According to the Duc de la Rochefoucauld, it was the 'common practice to relieve oneself while the rest are drinking . . . without concealment'.

Most of these modern houses had a small hut built over the cesspit; these were called 'houses of easement' or 'the jakes' (referring to Sir John Harington their inventor). There was not much ease about it – there was a wooden board with a hole in it. Dr Johnson opined that a jakes was a place for reading or thinking. He opposed the Dutch idea of a quilted seat: 'No, sir! there is nothing so good as the plain board.' These cesspits were cleared out only occasionally, by night, by gong-farmers, who had had a closed shop from time immemorial; the noise and smell from their wagons were a source of frequent complaint. (Not until 1783 was the first water-closet to be built in London by Robert Adam for the Earl of Derby's mansion in Grosvenor Square; it was connected by a brick drain to the public sewer.) The more affluent households had a commode or even the old-fashioned 'schetinge-pan': ladies at Court were wont to urinate in an obscure corner of one of the innumerable passages. Pepys relates that a Great Lady relieved herself in his chamberpot while still conducting a conversation with him.

The original tenants of the new Piazza were of the best 'quality' – only the nobility and very rich gentry could afford the rentals anyway. There was no commercial activity under the arches other than temerarious hucksters and importunate Drury Lane prostitutes; these were active from about 1640. There was a tavern in the north-east corner called the Lyon's Head, on the site occupied later by the Shakespeare's Head. Commerce was confined to the new fine shops in Russell Street.

There was trouble over St Paul's Church, which had been

commissioned in 1631 – the first new Anglican church built in London since the mid-sixteenth century. Inigo Jones called it 'the handsomest barn in England' – it had to be simple because the Earl could not afford more money at the time. Apart from the vociferous criticisms of the local ratepayers, the vicar of St Martin-in-the-Fields, the Reverend William Bray, claimed that it lay within his parish and was therefore within his rights of patronage. The Earl dissented and took the dispute to the Privy Council, which decided in 1641 that a new parish of St Paul's, Covent Garden, be established with all rights of patronage vested in the Earl of Bedford. The enabling Act was not passed until 1645, by which time Francis Russell was dead and the Civil War had begun. In 1660 King Charles II declared all Commonwealth legislation invalid, so the fifth Earl had to start all over again, and not until 1667 were the new boundaries established.

The principal streets were King Street (after Charles I), Henrietta Street (after his Queen) and Russell Street, which immortalized the family. It was then described as 'a broad thoroughfare with many fashionable shops and places of refreshment, constantly thronged with shoppers as well as pickpockets, prostitutes and other predators'.

Russell Street was crossed by Bow Street, whose southern extension was then known as Charles Street (now part of Wellington Street), and there was a 'very short but well-built and inhabited street called York Street formed in 1636' (and named after James, Duke of York) which linked Charles Street with Brydges Street, which was built in 1637 to commemorate Giles Brydges, 3rd Baron Brydges. Catherine (sometimes spelt Katherine) Street was the continuation of Brydges Street and led into the Strand. These two streets, says Strype, were 'well-built and of greate resort for the theatre there'; in 1675 it was described as 'a new-made street into Covent Garden'. A notoriously evil tavern, the Fleece, stood at its corner with York Street. By 1700 both streets had become dens of iniquity: John Gay in 1712 mentioned the site 'where the harlots stand in Catherine Street where it descends into the Strand'. It was then regarded as the eastern boundary of Covent Garden, although this was later stretched to Drury Lane.

The western boundary was St Martin's Lane, connected in 1636 by a short extension, New Street, with King Street. In 1737 Bedford Street was constructed to join up with Half-Moon Alley and thence into the Strand. In 1666 it was described as 'a very pleasant and spacious street taken up by eminent tradesmen such as Mercers, Lace-men, Drapers . . . the West side is the best'.

The portrait of Jean Le Becq over the doorway of the Lebeck's Head the coffee-house on the corner of Half-Moon Street and Chandos Street which was named after him long after his death. He had been cook at the Half-Moon Tavern in the Strand, at the other end of the street

At the south-west corner of Half-Moon Alley at the junction with the Strand stood the ancient Half-Moon Tavern – indeed, Half-Moon Alley had been cut through its spacious grounds originally as a footpath into the Garden. About 1690 it was managed by a French Huguenot, Jean Le Becq, who was famed for his cooking. The dining-room stretched some seventy feet up Half-Moon Alley. It maintained its high repute even after Le Becq's death about 1730, when the new proprietor, Thomas Key, renamed it 'The Key'.

Bedford Street ran into Chandos Street, named after William Brydges, 7th Baron of Chandos. On the corner stood White's Coffee-House, a notorious gambling resort for the rich and famous. After about 1740 it was known as the Lebeck's Head. At the nearby Caesar's Head lived the bookseller-publisher William Sare.

Maiden Lane was originally a noisome alley 'behind the Bull Inn' – Bull Alley was one of the many alleys connecting the Strand with Maiden Lane and Covent Garden. Bull Inn Court still exists – the Café American stands on the Strand corner. At the western end of Maiden Lane stood the infamous enclave known as the Bermudas (near today's National Gallery) after the poem by Andrew Marvell who lived there in 1677. Its real name was Round Court, 'one of the *Rookeries* full of Town-Pyrates and a hotbed of Robbers' who could sometimes be accommodated in the Round House on the site. A couple of doors away from today's Rule's restaurant, further east, was the White Wig (or White Peruque) in which Voltaire once stayed. At No. 20, on the corner with Half Moon Alley, was the infamous Cyder Cellar but of greater interest was the Hand and

Pen, a 'Marriage-shop' established about 1700 which arranged 'marriages without Imposition' – that is, without any tiresome interference from authority.

Three other alleys still exist: Lumley Court (next to Stanley Gibbons' stamp emporium); Heathcock Court, on the Strand corner of which lay the Heathcock Tavern (Barclay's Bank is now on the site), and Exchange Court, now a cul-de-sac. Denmark Alley, Marygold Court and Oliviers Alley have all gone.

Long Acre was to develop into a spacious street marking the northern boundary of Covent Garden, becoming later a very fashionable shopping centre. Oliver Cromwell lived there from 1637 until 1645, and after the battle of Naseby he moved over to Bow Street.

As early as 1632 Bow Street was coupled with Drury Lane as 'troblinge the adjacent areas . . . by lewdest *Blades* and female *Naughty-packs*' but it was commonly known as Thieving Alley, although (*vide* Strype) it was in 1637 'built up with good houses, well-inhabited and resorted unto by the Gentry for Lodgings'. It probably got its name because it was bent like a bow.

The area's subsequent decline can in part be attributed to the Civil War, during which many of the fine houses owned by Royalists were left empty and subjected to vandalism and burglary with consequent deterioration. When the new Earl of Bedford, William, returned to Bedford House for the funeral of Francis in 1641, he found himself in deep trouble because of his support for the King. An angry Parliament fined him £800 and sent in commissioners to sequestrate enough valuables to cover the fine. They found plenty of furniture and tapestries but no money or gold and silver valuables, so that on 16 September 1645 they ordered that all goods and chattels in Bedford House be sold. This caused the Earl to change his allegiance, and in the following December he surrendered to the Earl of Essex and thereafter concentrated his energies on improving his properties, in particular draining his Norfolk fenlands for which he has become famous.

Evidence of serious deterioration in morals comes from the tract entitled *Saint Hilaries Teares* (1642): 'If you step aside into Covent Garden, Long Acre and Drury Lane, where these *Doves of Venus*, thos Birds of Youth and Beauty – the Wanton Ladies – doe builde their *Nestes*, you shall finde them in suche a *Dump* of Amazement to see the Hopes of their Tradeinge frustrate. . . . [Before 1642] Ten or Twentie Pound Suppers were but *Trifles* to them . . . they are nowe forc'd to make doe on a diet of Cheese and Onions . . . the ruination of Whoreinge was why the London Bawds hated 1641 like an old Cavalier. . . .' It is an indication of the wealth of the inhabitants and frequenters of the Garden that before the Civil War they could spend such immense sums on such pleasures.

The King's supporters had to flee and many never returned. Many Roman Catholics tried to hide in the Garden and were arrested when celebrating secret Masses; in 1657 John Evelyn, the diarist, was apprehended as a suspected Papist and confined to his house during one of the raids.

In February 1644 the first little shop appeared under the portico of the Piazza, thus breaching the residential qualification, and a further decline was noted in 1656 when 30 shillings were paid for 'painting the benches in the market place'. The Civil War could not, however, stop men and women frequenting the notorious Cockpit theatre in Brydges Street, although its activities were illicit. With the restoration of the monarchy, in 1663 King Charles' friend and crony Tom Killigrew was permitted 'to build a theatre . . . neere the site of the Cockpit'. It was constructed mainly of wood but was very elegant. There were two tiers of boxes, including a splendid Royal Box. The front of the stage projected into the auditorium, as in Elizabethan days. Candle-lit chandeliers were suspended from the proscenium arch for the evening performances, but the walls were pierced with many windows because most performances were then held in daylight hours. The seating capacity was only seven hundred.

It became known as the Theatre Royal, or Covent Garden Theatre and on 7 May 1663 opened with a performance of Beaumont and Fletcher's *The Humorous Lieutenant*. Since all the employees, including actors and actresses, were considered members of the royal household – they were His Majesty's 'Comoedians' – taking an oath of allegiance and wearing a special livery when not on stage, they acquired a certain recognition which helped sweep away the contemporary image that players were all itinerant rogues and vagabonds.

Success was immediate. While the upper tiers were crowded with the nobility and gentry and their ladies – often masked so that licit and illicit could not be distinguished – *hoi polloi* crowded the pit. Wit and badinage, not usually of a high order, were exchanged between pit and circle. Elegantly dressed beaux would invade the stage to ogle the actresses as well as the demi-reps and prostitutes in the audience or haggle loudly with the orange-girls less about the price of the fruit than about the after-sales services required. The crowds were a source of great profit to the adjacent taverns and coffee-houses and bagnios. Here it was that the pretty little Nell

Gwyn put her foot on the first rung of the ladder that was to bring her great success as an actress and into the King's bed later on, to become the mother of two dukes.

The theatre had to be closed because of the Great Plague of 1665. It was re-opened after eighteen months and resumed its glory until January 1672, when it was completely destroyed by a fire, so fierce that neighbouring houses had to be blown up to prevent the conflagration spreading. The second building was designed by Christopher Wren and was much more substantial and twice as large; it lasted another 117 years. The entrance was moved to Drury Lane, the building occupying a whole block reaching back into Brydges Street, in which the original entrance had been situated.

This second theatre was more rowdy and noisy than the first one. The audience was heard more often than the actors. People of all ranks went in their finery to be seen and heard; quarrels and fights were frequent. The plays would be disrupted by beaux and Mohocks. The actors were stretched to make themselves heard above the disturbances, although stars always secured a hearing. A bad performance would cause the audience to express disapproval both vociferously and physically. Criticism of the players' private lives was by no means gentle: one of the bitterest critics was John Dryden. In *Poor Pensive Punck* (1691) he exploded:

> The *Play-house Puncks*, who in a loose undress
> Each Night receive some *Cullies'* soft address;
> Reduc'd perhaps to the last poor *half-Crown*
> A tawdry *Gown* and *Petticoat* put on
> Go to the House where they demurely sit
> Angling for *Bubbles* in the noisy *Pit* . . .
> The *Play-house* is their place of *Traffick*, where
> Nightly they sit to sell their *Rotten-ware*:
> Tho' done in silence and without a *Cryer*
> Yet he that bids the most is still the Buyer:
> For while he nibbles at her *Am'rous Trap*
> She gets the *Mony* but he gets the *Clap* . . .

Very few actors escaped Dryden's spleen: he called Thomas Betterton a 'Stage-Ape' and 'Brawny Tom', whose 'chief prerogative was swiving each *Drabbe'*. The great actress Elizabeth Barry was stigmatized as a 'mercenary Whore'; Mary Lee (who married Sir Charles Slingsby and was thereafter always billed as Lady Slingsby) was damned as 'having a Lady's *Honour* with a Player's *Purse'*, and Dryden reminded her that he had known her when she was just a whore. Most savage, however, was his attack upon the popular comedian James Noakes:

15

Ye smock-fac'd Ladds, secure your gentle Bums
For full of *Lust* and *Fury* – see! he comes:
'Tis bugg'ring NOKES, whose damn'd unweildy *Tarse*
Weeps to be buried in his Foreman's *Arse* . . .

From about 1645 Russell Street, with its fine shops, became the centre of fashion. There were mercers and wig-makers, barbers and booksellers, and there were also the discreet milliners' and mantua-makers' boutiques wherein comely young maidens offered not only their wares but also themselves, if the price or the promise was right, to the swaggering young beaux and 'bloods'.

Amid all this the market people, as yet not legally recognized, were selling fruit and vegetables 'under the garden wall of Bedford House' and outside the row of posts and railings which marked off the Piazza square, whose ground was dusty in summer and muddy in winter; not until 1667 were the first 'three loads of gravell . . . layed and spread'. Water was also available from the parish pump.

The Great Plague of 1665 and the Great Fire of London in the following year gave a tremendous fillip to Covent Garden. Affluent Londoners fled the plague, forsaking their beloved narrow, dirty City streets for the open ground outside. The rural market-gardeners who had been forbidden to enter the City now set up their stalls within the Piazza; first came the vendors of fruit, then of vegetables, and then the flower-sellers much in demand for nose-gays to offset the dreadful stenches. With the coming of the Dutch, Flemish and Huguenot refugees, the marketing became more orderly.

The Great Fire likewise caused the immigration of City merchants whose premises had been gutted. A contemporary report is revealing: '. . . and as shopkeepers in Villages are a verie great Injury to those in Market-towns . . . even so are they to the City of London that hath [since the Fire] set up in Covent Garden . . . by whiche many houses and shops [in the City] are not tenanted and those which are . . . are exceedingly fallen . . . for want of the Trade they had formerly'. The shopkeepers in the Garden were free from the straitjackets of the City Guilds and Livery Companies, with their ancient restrictive regulations. The Russells, good businessmen, had few restrictions. Among the greatest beneficiaries were the Jews, who up to that time had been forbidden to trade within the City of London. The Russells had no such inhibitions. Covent Garden was well able to absorb all these newcomers, who provided jobs for many new hands.

Realizing that there was a lot more money to be made, the Earl secured a charter from Charles II in 1670 giving him the right 'to hold a Market for fruit vegetables and other produce in the place commonly called the Piazza . . . within the rails . . . every day in the week except Sundays and the Feast of the Nativity . . . for the buying and selling of all manner of fruit flowers roots and herbs whatsoever . . . for ever'. In addition he had all Liberties and was free of all tolls tallages and customs.

Eight years later Bedford came to an agreement with two Londoners, Adam Pigott, a cutler, and Thomas Day, a tallow-chandler (who had already been putting up small shops outside the garden wall, and leasing them to market gardeners), giving them the right to carry on and charge rents. They were to pay his Lordship £80 a year, and he stipulated that the shops must be uniform as to frontages, the roofs must be a foot lower than the garden wall, there were to be no chimneys, and there had to be 'free passage' between shops and the rails for horses, carts and coaches, the whole to be kept clean and in good repair. Their leases were to run until 1699.

So much for the market. In 1689 the churchwardens and overseers of St Martin-in-the-Fields attended certain Justices 'concerning the suppression of Bawdy-houses existing in several by-alleys and other places in Covent Garden and Drury Lane'.

In Drury Lane there were 'Professional Stallions in discreet Drury Lane brothels for married Women', and (according to Tom Browne of Shifnal) these bawdy-houses 'were fain to go in disguise as Coffee-houses . . . when in fact they are taverns selling spirits'.

In 1681 the first bagnio was opened in a basement at the rear of the then Piazza Tavern in the Little Piazza, by Robert Lazenby, who gave way two years later to Henry Harris, who by 1690 had leased it to John Small. By then these Turkish baths had become known as hummums and had built up large clienteles, usually of dissolute people. John Small, however, was to stress that his basement 'in the last house of the Little Piazza' (later to be famous as the Bedford Arms Tavern) was utterly respectable. Women were not admitted except on specified Women's Days. His charges were quite high: 5 shillings single and 4 shillings per person if 'Double or more'. Parties of young gentlemen would make an occasion of their visits. The other houses in the Little Piazza soon adapted to this new fad – indeed, the Little Piazza soon became known as 'the Hummums'. It was not long before they all admitted men and women without discrimination: from places of assignation they became real brothels – so much so that from about 1700 brothels became popularly known as bagnios, an Italian word for the very ancient Anglo-Saxon institutions known as 'Stewes' – hot baths.

The Piazza itself was not far behind in this ancient trade, and its clientele was very wide. In 1680 appeared the poem 'The Pious Prelate', an attack upon Nathaniel Crew, who was not only Bishop of Durham but also the third Baron Crew, not noted for his continence or honesty in religious matters:

> Fools, Fucksters and Knaves in Piazza doth dwell
> Who in Parliament and Counsels his Country doth sell!

When the leases expired in 1699, the Duke of Bedford leased his whole estate for building purposes, insisting that it should be properly laid out. The estate then included 'all the Inns and Tenements . . . neare the back gate in Charles Street', one of which was the Cock, a notorious brothel run by 'Mother' Wilkinson – the first mention of a brothel in Covent Garden. To complete the building plan, Bedford House was demolished in 1705.

While the buildings were being erected, the Duke charged only a peppercorn rent, but thereafter £100 a year for sixty-one-year leases, stipulating that all the rebuilding must be completed by midsummer 1707, by which date '. . . the Herb Market . . . would be leased for seven years at £300 a year with a four per cent increase every year thereafter'. Fourteen houses were built on the line of the demolished wall of Bedford House. The new street was called Tavistock Row, the last house abutting upon the hummums (eventually being incorporated into the Bedford Arms); at one time every house in Tavistock Row was a brothel.

All sorts of tradesmen and journeymen now began to move into the new market. They included potters, tinsmiths, basket-weavers, cutlers and knife-grinders, carpenters and coopers and all ancillary trades needed for a market. There were, of course, inns, taverns and ale-houses – mostly illicit, and coffee-houses and chocolate-houses selling 'Spanish chocolate'. There were other chocolate-houses and milliners selling neither chocolate nor fashionable hats.

There was never a dull moment because there were so many diversions. There were occasional hangings on a specially erected gallows in Catherine Street, cartings of rebellious scolds or obstinate harlots, assaults and drunken brawls sometimes leading to mayhem and murder, exceptional events like the arrest of the famous highwayman Claude Duval in the Hole-in-the-Wall Tavern in Chandos Street, and even greater excitement when, after being hanged at Tyburn, his body was brought back for burial in St Paul's

Church in the Piazza. There were muggings galore as well as murderously inclined gangs of pickpockets, and homosexual prostitutes who would attack unappreciative gentlemen who refused their services. And of course there were the throngs of colourful and sometimes raucous female prostitutes at all times of the day and night.

There was also a variety of offensive smells from sewerless alleys from countless chamberpots being emptied into the kennels, as well as from rotting fruit and vegetables and unwashed bodies. There were other useful amenities such as marriage-shops, advertised by itinerant 'marriage-cryers' – usually down-at-heel and unfrocked clergymen who still had authority to perform marriages. In those days too, it was still possible for a man to sell his wife or even auction her in the market. By an Act of 1642, taking a woman to wife before witnesses was considered a good and lawful marriage, without a licence or banns. These first so-called 'Fleet marriages' – Fleet Street being the main centre of this activity – are recorded as early as 1674, the parties being brought in by 'marriage-players', usually clad in white aprons. (A blue apron was the sign of a Fleet Street prostitute.) In 1689 an Act of William III made it compulsory to register births, marriages and deaths – but this did not stop the trade. Not until the Marriage Act of 1752 was it necessary to have a Marriage Licence.

There were naturally frequent complaints by respectable citizens at such iniquities. In 1690 the Society for the Reformation of Manners was founded – albeit several of the noble founders were themselves not too respectable – and spent most of its endeavours in harassing bawds and poor prostitutes, who were then sent to the houses of correction, otherwise known as Bridewells, there to be redeemed by savage whippings at a whipping-post, or hemp-picking until the fingers were bloody and torn to pieces, or walking upon the treadmill or, in many cases, being mutilated by having their noses slit.

There were frequent raids by posses of constables or beadles ordered 'to beat-up the Vermin . . . which too much infest the Hundreds of Drury'. John Strype, the historian, remarked on the spacious mansions well inhabited by nobility, gentry and wealthy tradesmen in Covent Garden but also mentioned 'the mean courts and alleys', where lived the multitude of 'verie poore' artisans, labourers, porters and servants who were needed to keep the gentry comfortable. There were also 'Drury's many courts and dark abodes . . . where Harlots nightly pursue . . . their guileful paths . . . down Catherine Street to the Strand'. And there was the

The Bridewell Prison. Originally a palace of Henry VIII, which his son Edward VI turned into a House of Correccion for beggars, bawds and fallen women. By about 1600 it had deteriorated into a hell-hole of a prison. It was destroyed in the Great Fire of London in 1666. (The illustration is of the rebuilt establishment)

The Bridewell Prison in the Fleet, about 1700. This is a sanitized impression. The reality was a filthy rundown place of incarceration for men and women of evil life

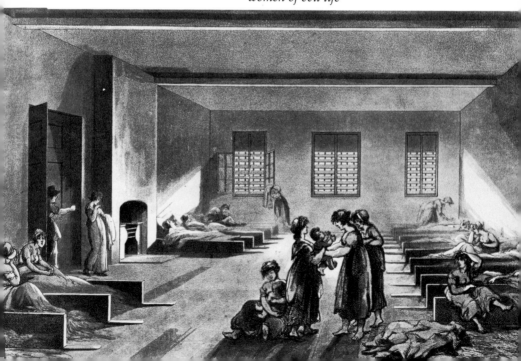

Infants' Office in nearby St Giles where young children 'stood at livery' ready to be hired out by the day to 'town mendicants'.

The general decline in manners and morals really started with the restoration of King Charles II to his throne in 1660. He cast a very tolerant eye on all manifestations of pleasure, however bizarre or vicious, and interfered very little in his subjects' pleasures. He encouraged the theatre, which in his day produced plays of the most obscene content, and indeed he chose many of his ephemeral mistresses from the ranks of Covent Garden beauties and actually patronized Mother Cresswell's brothel on at least one occasion. He also averted his eyes from the iniquities of the gambling-houses and 'Mollies houses'. His own Court was considered one great brothel, wherein a number of Court bawds pursued their business, while his own sexual activities caused many of his courtiers to serve as pimps in order to ingratiate themselves with him.

Small wonder then that at the beginning of the new century *The Tatler* could report of the Piazza that, 'Every house from Cellar to Garrett is inhabited by *Nymphs* of different orders, so that Persons of every Rank can be accommodated.' Small wonder too that such a 'sin city' as Covent Garden could thrive within such an atmosphere.

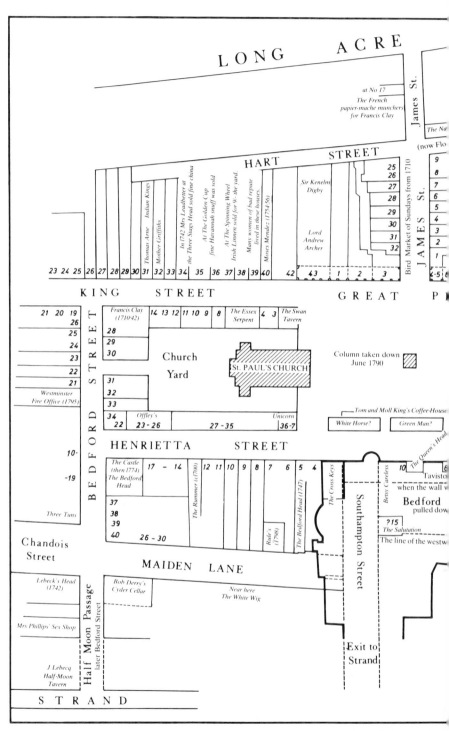

LONG ACRE

at No 17
The French
papier-mache munchers
for Francis Clay

James St.

The Na

(now Flo

HART STREET

Thomas Arne

Indian Kings

Mother Griffiths

In 1742 Mrs Leadbetter at
the Three Stags Head sold fine china

At The Golden Cup
fine Havannah snuff was sold

At The Spinning Wheel
Irish Linnen sold for 9/- the yard.

Many women of bad repute
lived in these houses

Moses Mendez (1754-56)

Sir Kenelm
Digby

Lord
Andrew
Archer

25
26
27
28
29
30
31
32

Bird Market of Sundays from 1710

JAMES St.

9
8
7
6
5
4
3
2
1

23 24 25 26 27 28 29 30 31 32 33 34 35 36 37 38 39 40 42 43 1 2 3 4-5

KING   STREET   GREAT   P

21 20 19
26
25
24
23
22
21
Westminster
Fire Office (1795)

BEDFORD   STREET

28
29
30

31

32

33

34
22

Francis Clay
(1710-42)

14 13 12 11 10 9 8 The Essex
Serpent 4 3 The Swan
Tavern

Church
Yard

St. PAUL'S CHURCH

Column taken down
June 1790

10-

-19

Three Tuns

Chandois
Street

Offley's
23 - 26

27 - 35

Unicorn
36-7

Tom and Moll King's Coffee-House

White Horse?

Green Man?

HENRIETTA   STREET

The Castle
(then 1774)
The Bedford
Head

17 - 14

The Rummer (c1700)

12 11 10 9 8 7 6 5 4

The Cross Keys

Southampton Street

Betsy Careless

The Queen's Head

10

Tavisto
when the wall w

Bedford
pulled dow

37
38
39
40

26 - 30

Rule's
(1798)

The Bedford Head (1747)

?15
The Salutation
The line of the westw

MAIDEN   LANE

Lebeck's Head
(1742)

Half Moon Passage

later Bedford Street

Bob Derry's
Cyder Cellar

Near here
The White Wig

Exit to
Strand

Mrs Phillips' Sex Shop

J Lebecq
Half-Moon
Tavern

S T R A N D

A plan of Covent Gar

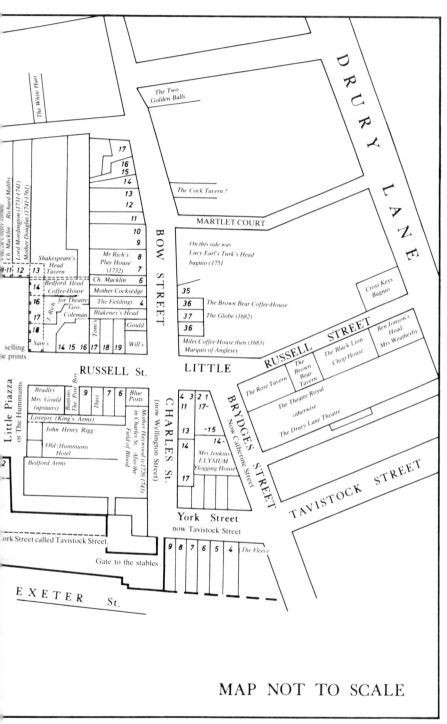

DRURY LANE

The White Hart

The Two
Golden Balls

The Cock Tavern ?

MARTLET COURT

On this side was
Lucy Earl's Turk's Head
bagnio c1751

17
16
15
14
13
12
11
10
9
8
7

BOW STREET

Ch. Macklin Richard Maltby
Lord Mordington (1731-1741)
Mother Douglas (1741-1761)

Shakespeare's
Head
Tavern

Mr Rich's
Play House
(1732)

Ch. Macklin   6

Mother Cocksedge

-11 12   13

Bedford Head
Coffee-House
for Theatre
Geo.
Coleman

The Fieldings   4

Blakeney's Head

Gould

Tom's

Will's

L. Rich

14
16
17
18

Sam's

selling
e prints

14 15 16 17 18 19

35

36   The Brown Bear Coffee-House

37   The Globe (1682)

36

Miles Coffee-House then (1683)
Marquis of Anglesey

Cross Keys
Bagnio

RUSSELL STREET

Ben Jonson's
Head.
Mrs Weatherby

The Black Lion
Chop-House

The Rose Tavern

The
Brown
Bear
Tavern

The Theatre Royal

otherwise

The Drury Lane Theatre

RUSSELL St.

LITTLE

Little Piazza
or The Hummums

Bradley
Mrs Gould
(upstairs)

Lovejoy (King's Arms)

John Henry Rigg

Old Hummums
Hotel

Bedford Arms

Buttons
The Post Box

9

Davi

7 6

Blue
Posts

Mother Haywood (c1720 1743)
in Charles St. Also the
Field of Blood

CHARLES St.
(now Wellington Street)

2

4 3 2 1

11   17-

13   -15

14   14-

17

Mrs Jenkins
ELYSIUM
Flogging-House

BRYDGES STREET
Now Catherine Street

TAVISTOCK STREET

York   Street

now Tavistock Street

ork Street called Tavistock Street

Gate to the stables

9 8 7 6 5 4   The Fleece

EXETER   St.

MAP NOT TO SCALE

he eighteenth century

2. The Flowering Years

Early in the eighteenth century the magnificent Piazza was the principal attraction. The aristocratic residents could enjoy by right of tenure all the amenities of a reasonably quiet and modern habitat to enable them to walk and talk under the portico. The unwelcome presence and attentions of the general public were discouraged – at least to some extent – by the absence of taverns and places of refreshment, always excepting the Lyons Head tavern.

The noise and hurly-burly of commercialism were to be found in adjacent Russell Street with its bright modern shops and coffee-houses which drew people of all walks of life to enjoy the lively scenes. The street was thronged from morn till night with customers for the shops, mainly to the fine new milliners' shops, each with its bevy of young and pretty female assistants, and to see and perhaps even to drink with the wits, writers, poets and beaux.

There were also the actors and actresses and famous actor-managers from Drury Lane who could be stared at with wondering or critical eyes, and the lovely, lively 'Toasts of the Town' to be admired or envied. And of course there were the pickpockets, pimps and prostitutes from nearby Drury Lane and its swarming alleys.

The oldest and by far the most famous establishment was Will's Coffee-House founded about 1670 by William Urwin on the first floor of 21 Russell Street, at the north-west corner with Bow Street – indeed, it was often called No. 1 Bow Street. The ground floor was occupied as early as 1637 by a haberdasher under the sign of 'The Three Roses' or 'The Roses' although John Twigg says that it was originally known as 'The Red Cow' and even as 'The Rose' – not to be confused with the scabrous hostelry of that name further up the street. Will Urwin's occupancy by 1674 is attested by his advertise-

(Opposite) Will's Coffee-House at No. 1 Bow Street

Fred.ᵏ Adcock

Nᵒ 21 Russell Street, Covent Garden

ment for the apprehension of a runaway servant whom he had accused of theft.

On 3 February 1664 Samuel Pepys stopped at 'the great Coffee-house where I never was before . . . where Dryden the Poet whom I knew at Cambridge . . . was sitting with all the Wits of the Town'. It was John Dryden who was to make Will's famous. He always occupied the big armchair by the fire in winter and always sat on the balcony in full view in summer – indeed he was known as 'The King of Will's. John Dennis, however, in his satire 'A Day's Ramble' (*c.*1698) remarks:

> To *Will's* I went, where Beauty and Wit
> In mutual contemplation sit . . .
> But which were *Wits* and which were *Beaus*
> The Devil's sure's in him who knows . . .
> To make amends I there saw DRYDEN
> Whom *Pegasus* takes so much pride in. . . .

From 1669 until 1687 Dryden lived nearby in Long Acre (in what is now No. 137). On 18 December 1679 he was assaulted by a gang of ruffians on his way home from Will's and seriously injured. (He blamed John Wilmot, Earl of Rochester, as the instigator, whom he had lampooned savagely.) The poet Alexander Pope noted in 1699 that Dryden was 'plump of fresh colour with a downcast look and not very conversible'. Richard Steele and Joseph Addison were regular *habitués* – Steele was later to say that *The Tatler* was written in White's Coffee-House (in Chandos Street) and poetry in Will's. William Urwin, who was said after 1680 'to have lapsed in his fortunes' died in 1698, in which year one Thomas Urwin's name appears as the ratepayer.

The club still flourished, Steele and Addison now being the leading lights, closely followed by Tobias Smollett and William Congreve. In 1712 the Urwin connection ceased. After several changes in ownership the premises became known from 1730 to 1751 as Chapman's Coffee-House.

After Will's had closed, most of the devotees transferred their custom to a newly opened coffee-house on the opposite side of the street managed by Daniel Button at the sign of the Post Boy. This tavern, previously run by two ex-actors, Peter Duncombe and a friend, had fortuitously been vacated on 1 January 1711. Button was reputed to have been an 'old servant' of Charlotte, Countess of

(Opposite) Button's, No. 10 Russell Street. The original façade still standing in 1859 when it was known as the Caledonien Coffee-House

Warwick, who had set him up in business 'under Addison's patronage' to woo him away from Will's. Charlotte Middleton, 'then worth £20,000', had married Edward Rich, Earl of Warwick, in 1696 and had been widowed in 1701, her husband dying 'verie penitent', probably because he had whittled away much of her fortune. She was still 'a gracious Beauty' and was Addison's mistress until she married him in 1716.

Henceforth this establishment was known as Button's, and it was to become famous through the patronage of Addison and Steele, both lively politicians and journalists who between them founded *The Tatler* and *The Spectator*, on which basis their niche in history is firmly secured. They used Button's for their social life, and it was remarked of Addison that 'he gave too much to the ordinary drinking habits of the time, by excessive use of Canary Wine and Barbados Water'; it was difficult to get him to leave a tavern even after his last pint of wine. His fame as essayist and poet was matched by his modesty and sweetness of temper, and he was moreover a superb and charming conversationalist. In sharp contrast Pope was not so welcome at Button's because not only was he very argumentative but he had a bitter invective and 'an itch for provocation'.

Richard Steele, born in Dublin, was one of Addison's most fervent admirers as well as a close friend. At one time he had been a captain in the army. In 1705 he married Margaret Stretch, a rich widow with extensive estates in Barbados, but she died within eighteen months of the marriage and left him a considerable fortune. Notwithstanding this inheritance, he was 'continually and constitutionally Improvident and Impecunious' and perpetually in debt to Addison. He was knighted in April 1715. Another famous patron was Sir Godfrey Kneller, the painter, who lived in the Piazza (where now the Floral Hall stands) until he died in 1723, when the house was taken over by yet another painter, Sir James Thornhill.

Button's has come down in history as a place famous for the wits and beaux who frequented it, but at least one contemporary dissented. 'The Town Assembly' in 1717 observed:

> I now proceed, to famous BUTTONS go:
> Here's *LION* rampant with his glittering Show . . .
> and many an *ASS* surveys the tawdry Sight . . .
> the STATER, OWL, BUFFOON and WIT. . . .

There had been an effigy of a lion outside the original tavern in the north-east corner of the Piazza from very early on but this clearly cannot be the lion mentioned above, because in *The Guardian* of 13 July 1713 Addison stated that it was his intention to erect a lion's head 'in imitation of those in Venice . . . whatever the Lion swallows I shall digest for the use of the Publick . . . it is now erected at Button's Coffee-House in Russell Street where it opens its mouth at all hours for the reception of all such intelligence as shall be thrown into it . . .'. Aspiring writers and poets were encouraged to thrust their manuscripts into the lion's gaping mouth in the hope of their being published in *The Tatler* or *The Spectator*. There was a curious report in *The Guardian* (No. 71, 2 June 1713) about a Mr Ironside 'who within the past five weeks muzzled three lions, gorged five and killed one [and] . . . was on the following Monday to hang *ad terrorem* the skin of a dead one at *Button's*, over against *Tom's* in Covent Garden'.

Little is known of Button's private life. In the parish register of St Paul's church under 16 April 1719 it is recorded that he paid 2 guineas for two places in no. 8 pew on the south side of the north aisle. He died on Sunday 3 October 1731 after a very painful illness and 'in a penurious condition'. His death occasioned a witty epitaph:

> Odds Fish and fiery Coals!
> Are Graves become Button-holes.

His customers deserted the establishment. The coffee-drinkers went to the Bedford Coffee-House and the diners to the Shakespeare's Head. The premises were taken over by a cheese-monger named Edmund Gore who was followed by a number of undistinguished tenants until the building was destroyed in the dreadful conflagration of March 1769. By the turn of the century the house had once again become a coffee-house under the sign of the Caledonien.

Across the road at 17 Russell Street was the bookshop of Thomas Lewis, who had published Pope's *Essay on Criticism*, which contained such immortal lines as 'To err is human, to forgive, divine' and (perhaps more apposite to what was going on upstairs) 'Fools rush in where angels fear to tread.' On the first floor was Tom's, founded in 1698 by Captain Thomas West, 'morose in his character but popular with Seamen'. (This should not be confused with Tom King's or Tom's Tavern in St Martin's Lane, in which in 1717 the Westminster Fire Office was established.)

Its popularity is measured in Mackay's *Journey Through England* (*c.*1722): 'After the Play the best Company generally go to Tom's and Will's Coffee-houses near adjoyning where there is playing of

Picket, and the best of Conversation 'til Midnight. Here you will see Blue and Green Ribbons and Stars sitting familiarly with privat Gentlemen and talking with the same Freedom as if they had left their Quality and Degrees of Distance at home . . . and a Stranger tastes with Pleasure the universal Liberty of Speech with the English Nation. . . .'

Tom West was also a hard drinker so that it occasioned little surprise when in a fit of intense gout compounded with *delirium tremens* he threw himself out of a second-floor window in 1722. The club was taken over by John West – presumably his son – who greatly expanded the private gambling rooms which by 1730 had some seven hundred subscribers. The place was much frequented by sea-captains who came to drink, to swap stories and information, and to gamble at 'hazard'.

When John died in 1735, Anne West carried on until 1739, when the club as a going concern was taken over by Richard Haines. His son Thomas changed the gaming-rooms, until then private, into a public subscription, thus expanding the business very greatly, but when he died on 11 February 1808 his obituary called him 'the Master of Tom's Coffee-house'. (Fanny Burney called it in 1798 'an accommodation address'.) The premises were pulled down in 1865.

While these clubs as well as the hostelries and the two theatres played an important role in attracting the crowds, the principal magnet was the ready availability of numerous pretty ladies of easy virtue, and places in which their company could be enjoyed. There were also a great many males of easy virtue for those so minded, and for these there were special clubs and taverns available for the indulgence of their particular activities. These were known as 'Mollies houses' or 'houses of male resort', mostly taverns situated in the environs of Covent Garden and the Strand and particularly in Clare Market adjacent to Drury Lane.

Ned Ward's famous book *The London Spy* (*c*.1700) has a chapter headed 'Of Mollies Clubs': 'There are a particular Gang of Sodomiticall Wretches in Town who call themselves *Mollies* and are so far degenerated from all Masculine Deportment . . . that they rather fancy themselves as Women, imitating all the little Vanities . . . of the Female Sex . . . not omitting the *Indecencies* of lewd Women . . . to commit those odious Bestialities that ought for ever to be without a name!' The nickname 'Mollies' clearly derives from the Latin word *mulieres* (females) and was often corrupted to 'Moggies' to imply that the practitioners were as quiet and as sly as cats.

(Opposite) Tom's Coffee-House at No. 17 Russell Street, Covent Garden

The Clare Market (on ground originally belonging to the earls of Clare) was at first a flesh market but by 1708 just a row of sleazy tenements and taverns. The principal one was the Bull and Butcher, owned by a man named James Spiller and better known as the Spiller's Head; others were the Fountain, the Sun and the Bull Head. At all of these young catamites were easily available and much patronized by City magnates. There were also 'nocturnal assemblies at *Bog-houses*' or public lavatories. That homosexuality was very prevalent may be seen from a street ballad *The Long Vocation* (1700) – the period when Court and courtiers left London in the summer:

> When *Sodomites* were so impudent to ply on th'Exchange
> And by *Daylight* the Piazzas of Covent Garden to range.

Ned Ward describes the Fountain Tavern in Russell Street, Covent Garden (he omitted the name in the original version because 'he was unwilling to bring Odium upon the house'), where homosexuals 'met every evening in the week' to entice 'unwary Youth into the like Corruption'. They dressed up as women of various occupations and played practical jokes upon one another. Ward was much taken with the charade of a woman in childbirth, using a doll which was 'Christen'd and the Holy Sacrament of Baptism impudently prophan'd'. Other charades mimicked girls losing their maidenheads or quarrels between husbands and wives. Every one in his turn 'would make a *Scoff* and a *Banter* of the little effeminate Weaknesses of Women gossipping o'er their Cups all for the Purpose to extinguish that natural affection due to the Fair Sex . . .'.

There was always plenty to eat, and a very great quantity of liquor was dispensed, which accounted for the drunken riots which ensued and which ended only when the constables were called. It was a dangerous diversion because the penalty if found *in flagrante delicto* was death in accordance with the Act of Henry VIII. In 1721 after a raid in Covent Garden a man named George Duffus was charged in the same court as Mother Needham and remanded till the following January, when a Special Verdict was handed down for 'this horrid Crime . . . [because] he had attempted to *indorse* another person'. Juries were very reluctant to pass the death sentence and required incontrovertible proof of 'penetration'. On this occasion Duffus was sentenced to a fine of 10 marks and a spell in the pillory in Hart Street (now Floral Street). In three raids on Covent Garden in December 1724 'some twenty Persons supposed to be sodomites' were rounded up; several had already 'been stood in the Hart Street Pillory for the like offence of this filthy crime'.

In the series of trials that ensued as a result of the raid on Mother Margaret Clap's Mollies house in February 1726 (Ned Ward had mentioned it as early as 1707), it transpired that the Three Tobacco Rolls run by 'one Jones, a Tallow Chandler' in Drury Lane was also a Mollies house. Jones, 'had absconded himself' and could not be found, but a man named Martin Mackintosh (otherwise 'Orange Deb'), an orange-seller, was put in the pillory. Several of the frequenters at Mother Clap's place were eventually hanged. The public reaction was summed up by Ned Ward:

'Tis strange that in a Country where
Our Ladies are so kind and fair
Gay and lovely to the Sight
So full of Beauty and Delight,
That Men should on each other doat
And quit the charming Petticoat . . .
Who could Women's Charms refuse
And such a beastly Practice use?

For those who sought other diversions there was of course the theatre. Queen Anne was shocked at the extent of obscenity in speech and bawdiness which obtained there, and, it was then said that, 'The theatres are just more commodious Brothels in which the Play was incidental to the main business of prostitution.'

In January 1704 the Queen ordained that there must be 'reform of the Indecencies and Abuses of the Stage'. Censorship was imposed on playwrights, and gentlemen were forbidden to climb on the stage and go backstage to meet the actresses. The noise and the cross-chat between people in the upper and lower parts of the house sometimes drowned the voices of the actors. Ladies of 'the Quality' vied with demi-reps to attract attention from beaux or likely looking high-spenders. The theatres opened at 4 p.m., and the plays started at 6 p.m., but as there were no orderly queues for tickets and seats there was always a free-for-all jostling and a dreadful jam at the doors. If any part of the audience was dissatisfied, their criticism was raucous and practical – they booed the actors off the stage or threw missiles, most frequently oranges – and it was said that the pit ruled the theatre.

After dark a linkboy with a flaming torch must be employed to escort play-goers home or to any rendezvous they preferred, although that was no guarantee against robbers or pickpockets. The elderly watchman with his bell and cries gave evil-doers plenty of warning to disperse and reform after he had passed. Tavern waiters were in league with local doxies to help waylay likely 'gulls' and 'cullies', reeling drunk and with gold in their pockets, and they got a commission on the tip-off. There would be noisy and vicious quarrels fomented by swindlers and swindled alike, swords would be whipped-out in a trice, and often murder committed immediately and unwittingly.

There were other alarums and excursions. On 21 July 1708 the Muscovite Ambassador Andrei Artamonovitch Matveyev was forcibly arrested while sitting in his coach in Covent Garden, 'at the instance of Mr Morton, a Lace Man . . . and other creditors . . . the bailiffs thrust themselves into the coach, took away the Ambassador's sword and cane, and carried him to *The Black Raven* Spunging House . . . the debt was only fifty pounds but [the Ambassador] was compelled to put up bail for three hundred pounds . . .'. There was a terrific row next day when all the other ambassadors protested vigorously to the Privy Council, which immediately ordered the arrest not only of Mr Morton and the other creditors but of the attorney who had acted for them and of the bailiffs who had assaulted the Ambassador.

Matveyev was no barbarian foreigner; his father was a rich Ukrainian *boyar*, a personal friend of the Tsar, and the young man was a brilliant linguist and a trained diplomat who had already filled a number of posts abroad. The fatuous verdict of the magistrates, who discharged all the prisoners because they 'could not discover any Law that they had offended' caused international friction. The consequent recall of the Ambassador (who was posted to Paris) eventually compelled Parliament to pass the Act which formally confirmed diplomatic privileges. Andrei Artamonovitch was created a Count and went on to a brilliant and long diplomatic life in Paris and Spain but never again visited Britain.

These continual disturbances often led to mayhem by Mohocks', gangs of aristocratic hooligans pledged to create as much trouble as possible merely for the sake of amusement. One of their favourite diversions was assaulting elderly women around Covent Garden and bundling them into empty barrels which were then rolled down the nearest incline. They regarded all women outside their own class as legitimate prey, and many a respectable girl and woman was raped in Covent Garden streets after nightfall. Their activities became so outrageous that in 1712 Queen Anne issued a 'Proclamation Against Vice' 'for the suppressing of Vice, Profanation and Immorality'. This demanded that '. . . all Persons who frequented Bawdy-houses, Musick-houses, Gameing-houses . . . be effectually prosecuted and punished'.

On 11 March 1712 five Mohocks, all 'Peers and Persons of Quality', caused an affray in a tavern in the Strand in the course of which they killed the landlady: '. . . the Gentlemen laughed and ordered that she should be added to their Bill.' The Queen, shocked and angered beyond endurance, ordered an enquiry. The High Constable, John Salt, who had released the culprits from custody when they had 'pulled rank', was removed from office, but in the subsequent trial all five Mohocks were acquitted. This shocked the Queen even more, and she issued an edict 'Regarding Great and Unusual Riots and Barbarities', which included a reward of £100 and immunity to informers. The magistrates then complained that, although bawds had been taken in the act in their own bawdy-houses, many had to be acquitted because nobody could be found to testify against them.

The onset of the eighteenth century also witnessed the emergence of another group of pleasure-seekers – the Jews. The street-ballad *The Long Vocation* (*c*.1700) includes the stanza:

> When the Season was too hot for the Goggle-Ey'd Jews
> To exercise their Faculties in Drury Lane *Stews*. . . .

At about the same time Thomas Brown of Shifnal in his *Amusements Serious and Comic* included 'A Letter to Madam Lucy, kept by a Jew in Covent Garden' chiding her because she had 'thrown off her old Christian acquaintances and revolted to the Jews'. Other contemporary references observe that the Jewish beaux and 'sparks' sought their pleasures in Covent Garden and in particular Drury Lane. Most of these observations reflect curiosity rather than anti-semitism since there were then so few Jews (in 1730 there were only four thousand in all England) that all aspects of their lives, appearance and behaviour excited considerable interest.

In 1653 Oliver Cromwell had invited the *savant* Menasseh ben Israel and about a dozen companions to come in and form the new community. They were anxious to seek a new haven from the murderous Spanish Inquisition. King Charles II encouraged further immigration partly because he owed the Jews some favours for their financial and political help during his exile. These were Sephardim, the 'western' Jews who had taken refuge in the Netherlands when the seven Dutch Provinces had broken the Spanish yoke under Prince William of Orange, under whom they had enjoyed complete religious liberty. Others had been invited to Britain by William III and helped to reorganize the nation's finances. By 1700 many had become very wealthy as brokers and import-export merchants. Nearly all of the original settlers had in

Spain and Portugal been compelled to live as *Marranos*, crypto-Jews, and had reverted to their ancient faith as soon as they were in a free country. Many were not even circumcised, which created some tense problems later for the leaders of the settled British community.

Their children, born in Britain, were completely anglicized, naturally adopting the manners and dress of their new friends. They also adopted some of their sexual morals. Visits to brothels and intercourse with Christian prostitutes were frowned upon by Jewish law, but in Spain and in Holland brothels were licensed and regular visits to bordellos were a way of life. The chapbook *A Trip Through the Town* (c.1730) refers to 'young Jews . . . of the Tribe of Mordecai' frequenting the Covent Garden whore-houses 'three or four times in a week particularly on Sundays . . . with upright Gait and morose Speech and pretty smooth Countenance . . . wearing Swords, except upon their Sabbath (and no whit inferior to their Gentile friends in Foppery and Lechery) . . . and spending freely money on loose Women on Saturday evenings . . .'. (The Jewish Sabbath ends at sundown on Saturday.) These young *Levites* were generally popular in the bawdy-houses because they were invariably kind and courteous to the womenfolk and were always good for 'a Gold Piece'. They were not heavy drinkers and thus not prone to drunken brawls or attacks on women – and they were good lechers.

There is no record, so early, of any Jewish bawd, although on 1st August 1724 one Ruth Marks was charged with keeping a disorderly house in Duke's Place and 'causing a great disturbance'. (Marques, or Marks, was a common name amongst Sephardic Jews.) She pleaded guilty but extreme poverty and was fined 13s.4d. and 'bound over to find Security for good behaviour for one year in the sum of two thousand pounds'.

By about 1730 it was estimated that some twenty-five per cent of Jews were 'working mainly as footmen and servants in the houses of their richer co-religionists', and a smaller group was earning a living as petty pedlars, handicraftsmen and small shopkeepers. Assistance from community funds was granted to all in need to prevent anyone descending into crime or destitution.

In 1710 the young German baron Zacharias von Uffenbach, while on a five-month tour of England, was informed that in London alone there were some 25,000 prostitutes, but he was most intrigued 'by the great quantity of Moors of both sexes . . . hawking their bottoms about the Strand and Covent garden . . . the Females in European dress with uncovered black bosoms'. Most of these black people had been brought into the country as slaves and then either abandoned or sold when their masters returned to the West Indies. The day of the black bawd was yet to come.

In 1725 'The front windows of the Piazza were filled from seven at Night until four or five o'clock in the Morning with Courtezans of every description . . . who in the most impudent Manner invite the Passengers from the theatres into Houses where they were accommodated with Suppers and Lodgings, frequently at the expense of all they possessed. . . .'

Nor had the reckless behaviour of the gentry been curbed. In June 1735 three young army officers stormed into a Covent Garden brothel at three o'clock in the morning and when the frightened bawd refused them admission one of them thrust his sword through the wicket, wounding the doorkeeper in the face. Amidst great uproar a dozen watchmen and unarmed constables came up, but when all the officers drew their swords and threatened to spit them, they retreated and the officers marched off. At times troops had to be called in to quell the disturbances.

Much of this deterioration took place after the accession of George I in 1714. He had not wanted to leave his comfortable Hanover to come and rule a country – in his opinion – full of king-killers. He was a brave soldier and honest in his own financial affairs, but he was as lecherous as a goat. He had brought over an entourage of some seven hundred, and the subsequent immorality of the Court was matched only by the cupidity and rapacity of almost every functionary. The King, his two German mistresses and his Court remained unpopular throughout his reign – the degree of their unpopularity is shown by the anecdote in which 'the Maypole', the beautiful but humourless and very slender Countess Ehrengard Melusina von der Schulenberg, was mobbed and booed by a crowd while riding in her splendid carriage. Frightened, she cried out, 'Goot peoples, ve haf come only for your goots!' and the crowd riposted 'Yes! and for our chattels too!' The other lady, Sophia Charlotte, Countess von Platen also beautiful but very fat, was known as 'the Elephant and Castle'. Both were created peeresses and both died very rich.

On 11 January 1727 King George I died suddenly of apoplexy. He had cared little for his British subjects and they in turn had cared little for him, so that his passing was unmourned. His son ascended the throne at the age of forty-three as George II – a

(Overleaf) View of Covent Garden, 1720, by Sutton Nicholls. Tom and Moll King's three shacks are in the foreground

C

St Anns

St Giles's

St Pauls

King

GARDEN

In Paris in the early eighteenth-century bawds and whores were taken in tumbrils to special houses of correction where they might be redeemed. In Covent Garden these women were dragged at the cart-arse and whipped all the way to the Bridewells, cursing and swearing and being pelted with stones and refuse by the onlookers

bad-tempered, lecherous little man from whom bawdry had nothing to fear. One of the first things he did was to revive the Court and encourage brighter functions and more gaiety, causing (according to one sardonic observer) 'Gallantry to become a Science'. One of the side effects was that 'man's Mistress more counted than the Prime Minister' since the royal favourites 'could confer Mitres as well as Titles'. Many a nobleman owed his title to judicious bribery, and some bishops secured preferment by the same means.

The Court might be gayer, but the King's gross manners took some stomaching. In a letter to Stephen Fox in 1727 John Hervey mentioned that he had been at Court the previous night: 'There was Dice Dancing Sweating and Stinking in abundance, as usual!' The peppery little King used to show his displeasure to even the highest in the land by turning his backside to them when they were speaking to him – indeed, a Rump Club was later formed of those to whom His Majesty had turned his arse.

40

Small wonder then that courtiers sought their relaxation elsewhere, and Covent Garden offered them the chance to 'get away from it all'. True there was also stinking and sweating and dicing and gambling in the Garden's establishments, but one could make one's own choice and be free of royal constraint or disapproval. All could enjoy themselves under the porticos, in any way they pleased, including, if they so wished, a visit to the excellent establishment founded in the reign of James II still carried on by the famous bawd Mother Elizabeth Whyburn, and the delights offered by her fabulous sexpot, Sally Salisbury.

3. Mother Elizabeth Whyburn and Sally Salisbury

Elizabeth Wiseborne (Mother Whyburn or Whybourne) was by far the most notorious bawd in the reign of Queen Anne and was a worthy successor to that greatest of Jacobean bawds, Mother Cresswell, from whom she undoubtedly learnt the trade. She was born in the City of London in 1653, her father being a respected Anglican clergyman. Theirs was a comfortable home much frequented by theologians of different faiths – she claimed that one visitor was the eminent Jew Dr Fernando Mendez, Court Physician to Charles II who had accompanied Catherine of Braganza to England in 1669.

As a teenager the young Elizabeth was sent to Italy to complete her education. There she acquired a taste for luxury and elegance, and 'after being seduced . . . she made some study of the customs obtaining in the best Italian *seraglios'*. She also acquired some knowledge of medicine and in later years was to boast of the efficacy of the anti-arthritic and anti-venereal concoctions which she had given to many a noble lecher. After her return to England she married one Edward Brook, in 1677, but no more is heard of him. By 1679 she was operating 'a discreet Business from a considerable Premises near the theatre in Drury Lane'.

Mrs Whyburn's connections with the Court and the aristocracy were many and close. She was very friendly with Moll Davis, one of King Charles II's old mistresses, who had a discreet villa in the salubrious village of Knightsbridge, where the gravelpits were deemed particularly healthful, especially to ladies recovering from inconvenient diseases and pregnancies. She claimed that the famous Royalist poet Sir John Birkenhead ('of sweete dispositions but not very grateful unto his benefactors') had been a client as

*The constables arresting a
Cyprian outside Sam's Coffee-
House at the corner of the Piazza
and Russell Street, about 1730*

early as 1679, when she was but twenty-seven. Another was the
Bishop of Bath and Wells, Dr William Beveridge, 'who was inclined
to flagellation'. A more esteemed client was Dr Richard Meade
MD, with whom she could discuss medical matters and gain useful
information about the latest treatments of venereal disease, while
he would be 'dallying with two Wantons at the same time'.
Alexander Pope and John Gay were friends as well as customers.
Two of King Charles II's bastard sons, the Dukes of Richmond and
St Albans, were welcome guests too – she used to call Richmond
playfully 'Rich World', both the young men being besotted with
the charms of Sally Salisbury.

Only the *crème de la crème* of harlotry could make use of Mrs
Whyburn's establishment. Her charges were so high that, 'Altho'
she kept a House of Free Hospitality she made Folks pay vastly
Deere for what they had, but her Customers paid the highest Price
with the greatest Pleasure.'

A contemporary chapbook, *Crazy Tales*, describing the amatory exploits of a young rake roaming Covent Garden and the Strand, gives some first-hand information about her:

> A good old *Trot* that chanc'd this Youth to spy
> Survey'd his Person with a wistful Eye.
> Six times At least she had seen Winters ten
> And in her youth great Judgement had in Men. . . .

She approached him saying:

> My name is WISEBOURN: from all parts repair
> to my fam'd Roof the discontented Fair.
> Rich City Wives, and some not far from Court
> Who loath their Husbands and who love the Sport:
> Brides match'd with Impotence that wants an Heir:
> Numbers of these I succour ev'ry Day
> Who keep their *Stallions* well in Pay . . .
> To gratify the *Nymph*, if tales say true
> The famous WISEBOURN often lay *perdu*
> And rang'd all corners of the Town
> To find sound handsome Youths,
> Well-limb'd and strongly chinn'd. . . .

These youths were invited to go to her house in Drury Lane 'before the clock strikes eight' to satisfy themselves that her arrangements were as promised. This is but another aspect of her wide-ranging services. All the time, however, she maintained a façade of deep religiosity, attending St Martin's Church regularly, ostentatiously carrying a large brass-bound prayer book. She always kept good order in her house 'as in a nunnery': a Bible was always open on the hall table, and good and edifying works were scattered around so that 'for every Minute they sinned they might repent an hour' – if their leisure intervals permitted. Her house chaplain read prayers twice a day, and she boasted that she had always 'a parcel of honest religious girls about her . . . and as many Scripture texts at command as any Presbyterian parson'. Many of the rooms had a picture on the wall of some grave clergyman 'to demonstrate her veneration for the Cloth'. Clutching her Bible, she would make the rounds every morning of all local inns and taverns 'to see what Youth and Beauty the Countrey had sent to London'. She also visited the Bridewells in the Fleet and Clerkenwell 'to cull out the finest kitlings', and those found suitable would be sprung out by a consideration to the jailer. She visited the Lock Hospitals in Southwark and Kingsland as well as St Thomas' Hospital, asserting that through her medical knowledge even slightly poxed youngsters could be cured. Lost maidenheads were restored by Mrs Lydia

Bennett at her clinic-cum-convalescent home at the Knightsbridge gravelpits, and when the girl was restored to health she could be offered as a virgin to wealthy local gentry before being returned to the Drury Lane headquarters.

Mother Whyburn also inspected the children who were offered for sale or for hire daily outside St Martin-in-the-Fields; suitable ones would be cleaned up and examined 'as a Butcher might chuse a Mare at Smithfield . . . then they were drest up with Paint and Patches . . . and let out at extravagant Prices . . . she always calling them young milliners or Parson's daughters . . . their virginities were restored as often as necessary' to make them acceptable to 'Persons of the Quality'.

About the year 1705 she made the acquaintance of John Jacob Heidegger, son of a prominent Zurich clergyman, a man of great charm, wit and good breeding but so ugly that he was known as 'Count Ugli'. He took it in good part. He was *persona grata* in the highest circles of society and was then introducing Italian opera to London at the Haymarket Theatre. He lived in the environs of the Garden and by 1707 was Mrs Whyburn's paramour and also a full partner in her Drury Lane bordello. The partnership was nourished by the support of his patron and friend the dissolute young Philip, Duke of Wharton, who gave them considerable protection from the minions of the law.

Heidegger's concerts and masquerades at the Haymarket were a huge success but by 1713 had become so outrageously pornographic that he had to turn to opera and serious music to avoid prosecution. Indeed, in 1729 the Middlesex Grand Jury castigated him as 'a principal Promotor of Vice and Immorality'.

In 1713 the quiet tenor of Mother Whyburn's establishment was broken by a fracas caused by her madcap protégée Sally Salisbury, in a drunken spree which ended with Sally's arrest and the apprehension of some of her coterie. Mother Whyburn was charged with disorderly conduct, and only by the expenditure of a very large sum in bribes did she manage to avert a charge of keeping a disorderly house. Matthew Prior, the poet, then called Mother Whyburn 'the antiquated *She-Captain of Satan*'.

Nevertheless, the antiquated She-Captain had some good traits. Another critic observed that, '. . . although she did a World of Mischeif . . . no Beggars were turn'd away from her house without some help.' She had perhaps convinced herself that she was demonstrating practical Christianity by taking destitute and helpless girls off the streets, feeding them and clothing them and giving them a roof over their heads, even though their eventual means

Le Mauvais Lieu, *Jan Steen, 1678. A scene in a brothel with a drunken cull
being robbed while his companions look on and laugh*

of earning a living was not quite in accord with Christian ethics.

Sally Salisbury's career was so bizarre and brilliant that it is a
story on its own. She was the first of the 'Toasts of the Town' to rise
to great fame from common stock. Before her, all the courtesans
had come from the ranks of the ladies of the quality. Sally's beauty,
wit and dare-devil exploits caught the popular imagination and
turned her into a star.

She was born in 1692 in Shrewsbury, her father, Richard Pridden
(or Prydden), being a bricklayer and her mother Margaret a house-
wife. They were very poor and constantly being harassed by
bailiffs, but Pridden was regarded as an honest artisan although
feared for his vile temper. Her parents came to London when Sally
was three years old, bringing with them their other girls Margaret
(Peggy), Mary (Molly) and Jenny, who was the youngest and later
blinded by smallpox. Sally was the prettiest, with a quick wit and a
trigger-like temper. They lived in an alley off St Giles.

Sally Salisbury: the first of the Great Impures

When she was nine she was apprenticed to a sempstress in Duke's Place but one day her mother, who had by now taken to drink, created a disturbance at her workplace for which the child was so badly beaten that she ran away and was fortunate to be taken in and sheltered by a kind-hearted couple in Covent Garden, Peter Garth, a hatter, and his wife Teddy. By this time her father had become a volunteer in the Regiment of Guards, and life had somewhat improved, but Sally did not go back home but helped at an orange-barrow in Covent Garden, where she was seduced and 'frenchified' – infected with a venereal disease – which turned the Garths against her. It was at this point that she was picked up by Mother Whyburn, who promptly sent her to Lydia Bennett's health farm at Knightsbridge gravelpits where she was cured and re-virginized. She was then fourteen years old!

Prior to this, while in Covent Garden, the famous actress Elizabeth Barry had taken a liking to the little orange-seller, who had 'a sweet voice', but her uncouth behaviour – picked up from the local roughs – and her quick temper caused the actress to lose interest. Sally claimed to have attended a dancing school where she had become friendly with 'a little Jewish boy, heir to a Jew's great estate' but no more is heard of this encounter. Then Mrs Needham introduced her to the vicious Colonel Charteris, who quickly abandoned her in Bath. Having made her way back to London, she was next heard of as 'the beautiful little wench that sells pamphlets to the schoolboys and apprentices . . . in Pope's Head Alley in

47

Cornhill in the City of London'. Here she supplemented her income by a little juvenile prostitution with the apprentices at 'half-a-crown for half-an-hour'.

Sally was taken off the alley by 'a rich Dutch Merchant' who treated her well but pestered her to say she loved him. Her quick temper betrayed her and after one such occasion she burst out, 'Damn ye and your broken Tongue: how can I love rotten Teeth and stinking Fifty!' She fled from his house with some clothes and money but was soon picked up after a raid on a bordello in St Martin's Lane. Because of her age she was bailed out.

By 1708 Sally was firmly in Mother Whyburn's benevolent embrace and being taught some semblance of manners by the other star boarders, Elizabeth Minshull, Diana Cadogan, Elizabeth Stanley and Diana Brainsborough. She had immense charisma and was sought after by some of the greatest in the land. One of the first was the 'ageing and wither'd' Lord William Bentinck, who was followed by the very young Viscount Bolingbroke. She had a brief *affaire* with Charles Fitzroy, Duke of Richmond, which broke up when she was told that Richmond 'had slandered her, asserting that she . . . being a woman of infamous character ought not to be admitted to Public Rooms where Ladies frequented'. She tackled him head on and he 'swore great Oaths' that he had never said any such thing, but it cost him a tongue-lashing and £150. She was also courted by his half-brother the Duke of St Albans, who competed with Lord Bolingbroke and the Earl of Cardigan for her favours. Sally claimed also to have lain 'with the noble Augustus just over from Germany' – the Prince of Wales, later George II. Richmond, who was a Knight of the Garter, seems to have remained a favourite despite all ups and downs. She used to twit him that 'As a Whore she was good enough for a Garter', but her most famous crack was 'Ay, my lord! Whores and bastards are always lucky!' Another close friend was the poet Matthew Prior who wanted to marry her; he was often to be seen with her at the Rose Tavern in Russell Street.

In 1713 occurred the drunken riot in Mother Whyburn's house which involved the apprehension of Sally and Robert Henley (later Lord Northington and Lord Chancellor), the Earls of Scarborough and Ossory, Mrs Elizabeth Marsham (later Lady Marsham), a French nobleman the Baron Antoine de 'F . . . g' and a rich young gentleman known as 'Beau B . . .' whom Sally's exactions eventually ruined. Sally was sent to Bridewell at Tothill Fields by Mr Justice Blagney (who was later to be reprimanded for his perversions of the course of justice) who sent a messenger to the jailer 'not to have her punished . . . because he had other plans for her'. He turned out to be her 'limberham' – a devoted, slavish person. Another was Mr Justice 'S', who had once sent her to the Marshalsea debtors' prison. It was arising out of this unpleasantness that Sally had the temerity to tell Mother Whyburn that 'she kept only a common bawdy house', which caused some temporary estrangement, but Sally was soon using her benefactress' place for her entertainments.

Apart from such business hazards she spent the next years in every manner of frivolity and debauchery, for a while being one of the Duke of Buckingham's harem, where she indulged in an ancient form of depravity, as spelt out in a contemporary satire about *Belle Chuck*:

> Between two marble Pillars, round and plump
> With Eye intent, each Sportsman, with his Aim,
> The *Money-Chuck-Hole*, bordered by the Rump,
> And from this play, Sally derived a Name . . . [Belle Chuck]
> Within her tufted *Chuck* the Guineas shone.

It was about this time that she adopted the name of Salisbury, when, having her hair dressed at Bath, the attendant remarked upon her remarkable resemblance to Lady Salisbury. Thereafter Sally claimed to be a natural daughter of one of the Salisburys who had sent her out to be fostered 'for Milk and Pancakes . . . by the Priddens'. She gave herself airs and graces, refusing to admit that she had been a barrow-girl. By this time her parents were unashamedly sponging off her, and in all this she maintained a close friendship with her sister Jenny, who acted as a foil and frequently as a duenna.

To Sally's dismay, Mother Whyburn died suddenly on 20 November 1719. She was buried in the church of St Martin-in-the-Fields, being then described as 'an elderly churchgoing woman'. There were a number of posthumous 'tributes', one of these *Memorials* being constrained to comment:

> *MUSE*, stop awhile, for thou hast cause to mourn
> And shed a Tear o'er pious Wisebourne's Urn . . .
> Within thy walls the Rich were ever pleased:
> From thy Gates no *Lazar* went unfed.
> *South Sea* Directors might have learned from thee
> How to pay debts, and wear an honest Heart!

She died intestate and her very considerable estate had to be administered by the Registrar of Probate, who recorded that she was 'Elizabeth Whyborne, Widow, otherwise Percy'. Nothing is known of Mr Percy, who was seemingly her second husband. The final accolade was an advertisement in the *London Journal* of 13 May 1721 for a book entitled *The Life of the late CELEBRATED Mrs Elizabeth Wisebourne vulgarly called Mother Whyburn*, and her name was kept alive by the fame of her nymphs, especially Sally Salisbury. (Curiously enough the satire *Crazy Tales* was reprinted in 1783 in a chapbook entitled *New Crazy Tales, or Ludicrous Stories*.)

In the following twenty years there are occasional references to harlots claiming to have been trained by Mother Whyburn as a *cachet* testifying to the excellence of their performance.

After Mother Whyburn's death, Sally entered into a relationship with Mother Needham although maintaining considerable freedom of movement; it was in this period that the famous escapade occurred which involved one of Needham's nymphs and Sally at Newmarket races, to which the two girls went with George Brudenall, Earl of Cardigan. Getting him blind drunk, they put him to bed at a local hostelry and decamped to London with his clothes and jewellery. On his return the two madcaps restored his clothes and property, and the old Earl treated the matter as a great joke. During this time too, 'Beau B . . .' (possibly Lord Buckingham) set her up in a snug residence in Shepherds Fields (now Shepherd Market) and settled 8,000 crowns a year on her – but shortly afterwards he died, a ruined man. So Sally fell into the welcoming arms of the 'Baron de F . . g', who soon parted from her, alleging that she had given him the pox. She was never short of lovers, but she always showed open contempt for them all, even when they were lavishing money and gifts upon her.

Then Nemesis caught up with her. Lady Mary Wortley Montagu wrote in a letter dated 25 December 1722: 'The freshest News in Town is the fatal accident happened three Nights ago to a very pritty young Fellow, brother to Lord Finch who was drinking with a dearly beloved *Drabb* whom you may have heard of by name of Sally Salisbury. In a jealous *Pique* she stabbed him to the Heart with a Knife. He fell down dead immediately but a Surgeon being called and the Knife being drawn out of his Body, he opened his Eyes and his first words were to beg her to be Freinds with him, and he kissed her.'

Lady Mary's vivid account is not quite true: Jack Finch had arrived at the Three Tuns Tavern in Chandos Street just after midnight on 22 December. He was quite drunk but demanded drink from the landlord, who gave him a bottle of wine to keep him quiet. At two in the morning Finch called the potboy for more drink. Sally arrived with her sister Jenny at about four o'clock in a

Sally Salisbury's attack on her paramour, the Hon. John Finch in the Three Tuns Tavern in Chandos Street on 22 December 1772. She was convicted of assault, fined £1000 and a year in Newgate, but she died of consumption there three months later

51

raging temper because Finch had given some opera tickets to Jenny and not to her. Both women were quarrelsome drunk, created a scene outside the tavern, got the landlord out of bed and demanded 'a glass of Frontenac', which he served reluctantly. Then in a drunken fury Sally rounded on the befuddled Finch and stabbed him. She was immediately quite distraught, crying out 'Jacky! you are not so bad as you imagine!' The surgeon Dr Colhart was called and staunched the wound, by which time Sally almost fainting was calling out, 'Jacky, forgive me!' Finch then replied, 'I die at pleasure by your hand.' She wanted to go home with him and care for him, but he decided that she should go to her own house instead, and there she was arrested, charged with attempted murder and sent to Newgate to await trial.

At the Sessions held on 24 April 1723 before Lord Chief Justice Sir John Pratt, Sir Gerald Conyers, Judge Robert Tracey and Sir William Thompson, despite frenzied pleas by Jack Finch 'and several noblemen' to be allowed to withdraw the charges, Sally was found guilty of assault and wounding, fined £1,000 and sentenced to a year in Newgate and to find two sureties for subsequent good behaviour. Finch tried hard to get her released on the grounds of ill-health but was unsuccessful. While in jail she received frequent visits from friends and lovers, but she contracted jail fever and was very ill.

On 8 February 1724 the *London Journal* reported that she was so ill that she would not live until her release in April, and a week later reported that '. . . the famous Sally Salisbury died on Tuesday last . . . of a Consumption . . . preceded by a fever so that she was almost reduced to a Skeleton.' In the next issue the newspaper reported: 'Last week the body of the famous Sally Salisbury was interred in the vault of St Andrews Holborn whither she was attended by four Mourning Coaches and had six Gentlemen to bear her Pall. Her death has provided a loss to the Sheriffs of last year she not having paid her fine. . . .'

Two purported *Memoirs* were published, both retaining a degree of respect for this dazzling darling of the gods by refraining from the customary snide remarks about sexual offenders and whores. Jack Finch mourned her for many years afterwards but by the time he died, on 12 February 1763, his beloved Sally had long been forgotten by the public.

Many young girls tried to follow in her footsteps but none except the equally charismatic Betsy Careless was worthy of the honour. Betsy's fame was bound up with the history of the Shakespeare's Head Tavern in the Piazza . . .

4. Tom and Moll King's Coffee-House

From about 1720 and for twenty years afterwards the focal point in Covent Garden was neither a theatre nor a brothel but the shacks in the market square in front of the church. They were known as Tom King's, and after his death as Moll King's. (As early as 1703 there was 'an humble shed, the precursor of all-night stalls'. There were in fact three long wooden sheds, each with an attic under the roof, running parallel to the row of houses erected about 1706 along the old wall of Bedford House. One was called the White House and another the Green Man.)

Thomas King was born at West Ashton in Wiltshire in 1694, the son of Thomas King, Squire of Thurlow in Essex, who had married in 1691 at St Paul's, Covent Garden, Elizabeth Cordell, daughter of Sir John Cordell Bt. Lady Elizabeth Cordell. Young Thomas was educated at Eton and admitted as a scholar to King's College, Cambridge, on 2 December 1713, but he was sent down 'under a cloud' in November 1716. He went to London, where he drifted about Covent Garden, earning the sobriquet of 'Smock-fac'd Tom' because of his smooth manners, but the only employment he could then get was as a handyman.

In contrast, Mary ('Moll') King was born in a slum garret in Vine Street in nearby St Giles-in-the-Fields in 1696, her father, Crispin (surname unknown), being a poor, feckless, drunken cobbler and her mother a hard-working, respectable woman with a fruit and greens stall in Covent Garden Market. From her earliest age the child kept close to her mother because of the father's constant drunkenness, but when she was about fourteen and 'tolerably handsome' she was given to service with a Mrs Attwood in nearby Charles Court. She did not stay very long because she found the surroundings 'too confin'd' and the work boring, so she hired a barrow, at first hawking fruit and later specializing in nuts, where-

Moll King late in life, after Tom's death. The conversation between Moll and Harry is in the special Covent Garden argot known as 'talking flash'

by she became well known and quite successful. By thrift she was able to save a useful sum of money – despite 'the depredations of her father' – and through her mother's influence 'remaining chaste and honest despite the surrounding atmosphere'. A gay and sparkling young creature with a gift for repartee, she was well regarded by all who knew her.

Sometime in 1717 Moll met *Smock-fac'd Tom*, and they were 'tack'd together' by one of the unfrocked priests in a Fleet Street marriage shop. She kept on with her stall and was befriended by many of the current 'women of ill-fame', including Sally Salisbury and the Drury Lane actress Nancy Cotton, both of whom 'showed much kindness and understanding to young Moll', who later claimed that she had made much money from the gentlemen and their 'misses' who patronized and recommended her nut stall.

The honeymoon was soon over. Tom began dallying with 'a lewd Wanton about the market', neglecting his bride, and when he started to beat her she left him and became an 'intimate friend' of William Murray, later the first Earl of Mansfield and Lord Chief Justice, who introduced her to various scions of the nobility and gentry as well as the world of fashion.

Meanwhile Tom had amassed some money while working as a waiter in a nearby bawdy-house, and he and Moll got together again, deciding to open a coffee-house. About 1720 they rented from the Duke of Bedford one of the row of 'little hovels' in front of the church at £12 per annum. By working very hard and selling coffee 'at a penny the Dish', they were enabled to rent a second and then the third of these shacks. The hours were very long – during the fruit season they often had to stay open all night, but Tom's aristocratic connections were a great asset so that by 1722 'Tom's' was much patronized 'by well-known Gentlemen to whom beds are unknown and who play at *picket* [piquet] all Night'.

On 30 August 1730 their union was blessed by a son, baptized Tom, who was reported to have been seen helping around in the shop when he was about six and who was sent, when fourteen, to Westminster School, leaving four years later to take up a career on the stage. He became in due course a famous actor-manager. At no time does he appear ever to have acknowledged his parentage, apart from once saying that his father 'had been a tradesman in Covent Garden' which was the description on his school docket at Westminster.

At Tom King's the young rakes and their 'misses' met to 'consult on their nocturnal intrigues'. Everyone from a Knight of the Garter to the meanest potboy 'could find a Nymph in waiting'. Gentlemen

Drunken rakes raise a riot in Covent Garden, c. 1735

The Women struggle, scream and scratch;
Loud swear the Rakes – in come ye Watch
Alarm'd by th'outrageous noise
And fall upon the Roaring Boys

of fashion and the gayest ladies of the town came every evening, seldom leaving before two in the morning, but at Moll's insistence there were no beds in any of the shacks. Customers could make assignations but had to effect consummation off her premises. In this way she frustrated the ambitions of that fanatical whore-hunter Sir John Gonson, who could arraign her for keeping a disorderly house (which merited a fine) and not a brothel (which could merit a carting and a whipping in addition). The only beds in the house were those of Tom and Moll, in the attic, and they drew up the ladder when they went to bed, to avoid being disturbed.

One of their most famous patrons was William Hogarth, who came frequently, drawing many of his characters in the shacks, usually waiting until they were relaxed by drink, to get them *au naturel*. He said that there was always some swaggering 'Rule-of-the-Roast' fellow guaranteed to make a noise and a bluster. Another was the painter Benjamin 'Philosopher' Wilson, but perhaps most notorious was Captain Marcellus Laroun (the Youn-

L. P. Boitard, The Covent Garden Morning Frolick, 1739

The famous courtesan Betsy Careless in her sedan-chair, accompanied by her protector Captain 'Mad Jack' Montague (later Earl of Sandwich) and her link-boy Laurence Casey, an evil dwarf known as 'Little Cazey'

ger), army officer, painter, actor, singer and swaggering man-about-town, of whom Henry Fielding remarked, 'I consider Captain Laroun and his friend Captain Montague and their constant companion *Little Cazey* the link-boy as the three most troublesome and difficult to manage of all my Bow Street visitors.' Laroun, who was born in Bow Street, painted scenes in the Garden; he also made a large drawing in red chalk of the interior of Tom King's for Horace Walpole's collection.

The coffee-house was also patronized by the players at the nearby theatres, who would go 'for a Dish at Moll's'; their beaux called the place 'King's College'. In addition to coffee, strong liquors were freely available, and customers were encouraged to stay until they were too drunk to go home or until they were escorted to a nearby bagnio. An added attraction was the comely and lovely black barmaid, Tawny Betty.

Moll's greatest virtue was that she remained sober when all around her, including her husband, got completely drunk. Moreover, when all about her were creating noise and disturbance, she always kept her temper. Nevertheless on 31 May 1736 'four men heated with liquor' left Tom King's and created a fracas during a Mass in the chapel of the Sardinian Ambassador, Cavaliero Giuseppe Osorio-Alarcon, in Lincoln's Inn Fields, 'abusing and striking several persons'. Moll and her nephew William King were censured for allowing the malefactors to get drunk on their premises.

In November 1737 Mary King and Isabella Tabor were charged at the General Sessions in Westminster 'with keeping a Disorderly House at which sexual offences were committed' whereby assaults had been made on James Donnithorne, Gent., his son Isaac and their friend John Arnold. The bouncers Edward and Noah Bethune were also charged with assault. All were discharged with fines.

Local bawds, famous in their day, were always to be found at Tom's, and very often their nymphs would also slip out for a breather, a drink or a gossip to vary the arduous round of their existence. *The Paphian Grove* (1738) relates:

> Each vacant *bagnio* is desert seen
> From Haddock's, Hayward's – down to *Mother* Green.

> Refrain from tears, ye *Haggs of Hell*, refrain
> Each girl will soon return and bring a Swain
> Loaded with Gold – who at a vast Expence
> For to support your curs'd Extravagance! . . .

All the 'Toasts of the Town' could be seen there 'all drest up fine and pritty and elegantly as if going to a box at the Opera', and after midnight they would be joined by beaux and bloods coming in from the taverns or the renowned brothel in nearby Charles Court, 'the Field of Blood'. By two in the morning the shacks would be crowded with '*Bucks, Bloods, Demi-Reps* and Choyce Spirits of all London . . . the *All-Night Lads*, otherwise the *Peep-o-Day Boys*'. One of the shacks was called the Long Room; of the smaller ones one was used only for drinking and the other for gambling.

George Alexander Steevens wrote of the Long Room: '. . . you might see grave-looking Men, half mizzy-ey'd, eyeing askance a poor supperless Strumpet asleep on a Bench, her ragg'd Handkerchief fallen exposing her bare Bosom on which these old Lechers were doating. . . .' It was common to see 'half-a-dozen of the Ladies of the Town fighting & scratching one another for the possession of a Man about whose person they cared for as much as a Sexton cares for a Corpse', while in the other room men and women '*Jolly Clarett-drinkers* were making a Jollity, joking and

Beadles evicting trouble-makers. The scene is outside a tavern at the corner of the Piazza and Russell Street. The hooligans have injured one beadle who is covered with blood, the women appear unconcerned

horsing around until the scene turned to shrieking, rioting, the breaking of bowls or even murder.'

Famous 'Mothers' could be seen there hunting for fresh goods, amongst them Mother Elizabeth Needham, recruiting for her establishment in far-off St James, Mother Burgess, famed for her expertise in flagellation, and Mothers, Catey, Lewis, Griffiths and Page, famous in their day.

Meanwhile the Kings had amassed enough to buy an estate on Haverstock Hill on the way to the attractive suburb of Hampstead and had built 'a genteel villa' and two houses thereon. Their patrons called the villa 'Moll King's Folly'. The investment was timely, for Tom King's health was rapidly declining because of his alcoholism; indeed, in early 1739 he died there. With her husband's death Moll's character underwent a great change. She took to drink and became very quarrelsome.

From this time the shacks became known as Moll King's, acquiring a reputation for turbulence and violence, becoming 'the Haunt of every kind of Intemperance, Idleness and the Eccentric & Notorious in every Walk of Life. . . . Noblemen would go in full Court Dress with Swords and Bags in rich brocaded Coats and walk and talk . . . with Chimney-sweeps, Gardeners and Market People. . . .' One of Moll's personal admirers was the very rich landowner Thomas Apreece, who always came in full fig, sitting quietly in a corner, drinking little, saying little and watching the scene avidly. Years later James Boswell was still admiring his dress and deportment.

On at least one occasion royalty was present. George II, accompanied by Viscount Gage, his equerry, sat at a table. When the King began to ogle a lovely lady at the next table, her escort objected violently, abused the King and drew his sword, whereupon Lord Gage began to draw his sword too. The King restrained him, saying, 'The gentleman perhaps does not know me', and they left the premises.

Moll was now described as 'The *Fat Priestess* . . . of portly Mien and Voice sonorous . . . inviting all to join the Bacchanalian rites'. With her particular crony, Mother Hayward, she 'would play a *finesse*' – a confidence trick, when the mood took her. A waiter would bring a tray of broken crockery to a completely drunk customer and present him with a bill for anything up to £20 'for the damage done . . . and extra for the broken china'. The customer

(Opposite) The constable arresting a gentleman, accompanied by a Toast of the Town, outside Tom King's

60

would usually be too drunk to know what he had done. It was an amusing and profitable way for the two ladies to pass the time. Between them they had developed an argot called 'Talking Flash' – 'a bawdy-house bottle' was short measure; 'member's mug', a chamberpot; 'a lady in mourning', a Negress, and 'a whore's curse', a gold quarter-guinea. The slang was devised to fox the police informers sent in by the hated Gonson or the equally detested Thomas de Veil or the odious Society for the Reformation of Manners. (One of these informers was Frank Rigg, who had once 'peached' on Sally Salisbury and had also been one of the informers leading to Mother Clap's arrest and the subsequent hangings of homosexuals.)

Moll was now drinking heavily, constantly ill-tempered and earning a reputation as a termagant. The premises began to be even more disorderly, and in June 1739 there was a terrible riot which brought her again to court, where she was fined £200, sentenced to three months in jail and required to find sureties for good behaviour for three years after her release. She refused to pay the fine, on the grounds that it was unwarranted and excessive, so she 'rested' in Newgate for the three months during which she 'negotiated' with the High Bailiff and got the fine reduced to £50. Her sojourn in Newgate was not onerous: '. . . she bribed liberally . . . and received many distinguished visitors.' On previous occasions, it was disclosed, she had bribed witnesses and been acquitted, but this time Sir John Gonson had his revenge – although the business did not suffer because her nephew William always stepped into the breach.

Sometime in 1745 Moll retired to her villa, living quietly and respectably, renting a pew in the nearby church on Haverstock Hill not far from the Load of Hay tavern (now renamed the Noble Art). The group of houses was known until 1888 as Moll King's Row – it is now called Dawson's Terrace in memory of her friend Nancy Dawson. She died peacefully in her bed on 17 September 1747, leaving a considerable fortune.

Several memorials were published posthumously, the most factual being *Covent Garden in Mourning*, certainly no encomium. Although generally she is remembered as a horrible, drunken, ill-tempered termagant as well as a vicious whoremonger, it is an exaggeration. In her latter years she was undoubtedly soured by

(Opposite) An elegy on the death of Tom King in 1737. Some famous bawds, here called his 'daughters', Jane Douglas, Molly Sturgis and Betsy Careless, are mentioned as well as the barmaid 'Black Betty'

When Monarchs die, ye World, in tears,
Thro' Force, or Fashion, mourning wears;
When Trade grows brisk, & in a Trice,
Sables are set at double price;
Unless some sure advice from C—rt,
(As lately chanc'd) stop the report:
But here no Empty, mimic Groan,

For thee all Bards all Pimps lament,
From every Bagnio sighs are sent:
No form no outward shew they seek,
Their very looks their Sorrows speak,
In ragged Shift, & tawdry Gown
See once ye Toast of all ye Town.
The batter'd Rake with breeches tore,

While poor Black Betty makes her face
More rueful than before it was,
Thy Genius rests & points aright,
To what was latly thy Delight!
While we these darling Trophies raise
And properly his shield imblaze
His Requiem drink ye Thirsty Souls

the loss of her husband, but she kept no brothel, nor was she a pimp for helpless girls. She always remembered the early days of her own struggle to remain respectable and honest, and while she grew to have no scruples about fleecing the rich and foolish, she would make loans to any woman in distress in and about the market – albeit the interest might be stiff by today's standards. She would lend money to any prostitute, making a distinction between those who had to sell their bodies for bread as against the 'town misses' who queened over their less fortunate sisters, on the principle that one was an industry while the other was a vice. In this she rebuked her neighbour Richard Haddock, whose treatment of his girls was harsh and vindictive; his story and those of the other bagnio-keepers must now be told.

5. The Bagnio-keepers

Many of Moll King's friends and cronies had been established in and about the Garden long before her time, and several were well known and esteemed. One of the most famous was Elizabeth Hayward (spelt variously as Heywood or Heyward according to the degree of literacy of the chronicler), ably partnered by her husband Richard, whose name appears as early as 1703. In John Gay's *Trivia* (1716) he called her 'Mother' Haywood.

In 1719 the Westminster magistrates complained to the King that there were so many '*Night-houses* and Houses of Ill-fame . . . in which liquor was served' that it was impossible for them to cope with the problems of detection and prosecution. Later that year, in another complaint, they added 'Gameing-houses' to the tally, explaining that many of these places were 'guarded by Souldiers . . . [and had] strong Hatches surmounted by Spikes on the street doors . . . [which obstructed] the entry of the Constables to the Inner Rooms'. Moreover, they could not get anyone to give evidence against these malefactors.

Finally, in February 1721, a strong force of constables and beadles raided 'the Hundreds of Drury' and Covent Garden. Amongst many others they arrested Richard and Elizabeth Hayward 'who kept *The King's Head* tavern in Russell Street'. Both were sentenced to three months imprisonment and a spell in the Covent Garden pillory, but within a few days their attorney 'Mr Kelletat of the King's Bench . . . swore an affidavit that the said Elizabeth was far gone with child . . . and her life would be endangered . . . by imprisonment and the hardship of the pillory.' The Sheriff was ordered to make an examination by a panel of matrons, but they found that there was no pregnancy. Both were therefore stood in the pillory on 11 March and were required to give sureties for good behaviour for seven years 'because of the length and extent of their evil activities'. Three months later they were back again in the same

Maurer's View of the Strand and Charing Cross about 1700 before the massive demolition and rebuilding starting in 1740

occupation, this time in Charles Street – a stone's throw from their old premises. With a couple of brief interruptions the Haywards carried on at this address until 1747; between 1733 and 1740 they also ran a 'house' in Rose Street.

The Rake of Taste (1736) equated the excellence of their establishment with the excellence of the food served by Le Becq, the famous cook at the Half-Moon Tavern.

In *The Paphian Grove* (1738) Elizabeth Hayward is linked with several other well-known 'Lenas' as one of the 'Haggs of Hell' to be found in Tom King's shack. In 1739 Paul Whitehead's savage satire against certain establishments with pretensions to respectability said bluntly 'Hayward's a brothel.' In December 1743 *The Gentleman's Magazine* announced: '*Mother* Hayward who for many years kept the *Bagnio* in Charles Street Covent Garden, a lady well-known to the Polite part of the World, is said to have died worth Ten Thousand Pounds.' Horace Walpole, in a letter to Henry Fox, one of her best clients, noted her death as a matter of some moment to the fashionable set, mentioning that the young Earl of Lincoln (also one of Mother Hayward's customers) fancied himself as a stallion to match Charles II. Richard Hayward continued in the business for several years, dying unsung and unmourned in his house in Russell Street in 1747. His wife's fame, however, was to last for at least another twenty years.

1721 was rather a bad year for local bawds. On 21 November the famous Mother Hopkins 'departed this life in her *seraglio* in Earls Court and left £600 to a Gentleman . . . by courtesy called *The Captain*, who was the prime Manager of her affairs'. Elizabeth Hopkins was operating in the Garden from about 1705 and in her latter years was one of Moll King's cronies. In the same month Mother Jolley of the King's Arms Tavern in Drury Lane was sentenced to hard labour and 'a whipping at the Tumbler's Arse . . . for keeping a Disorderly house'. (This is, in passing, evidence of a long folk memory since the ancient word 'tumbril' had long been superseded by the phrase 'the cart-tail' or 'the cart-arse'.) The year ended with the trial of Mother Elizabeth Hall who from 1715 had kept a brothel in Russell Street, but she was 'likely to be charged with murder, Bess having hit a client upon the forehead with her patten until he was past all hope of recovery'. She was later acquitted and continued in business at the same address until she died in 1733.

1721 also saw the birth of the Hell-Fire Club which then had forty members 'of which fifteen were Ladies of the Quality'. Others included such aristocratic hooligans as the Dukes of Argyle and

Dorset and the Earls of Bute, Lichfield, Kinnoull and Stafford, as well as a clutch of barons such as Lords Bathurst and Bingley. These were some of the successors to the brutal Mohocks, described in John Gay's *Trivia* (1716) when Rakes 'kept their Revells' and the 'flying *Nickers*' scattered pennies at casement windows, thus becoming enemies of sleep:

> Who has not heard the *Scourers* midnight Fame?
> Who has not trembled at the *Mohocks* name?

In March 1724 Lady Mary Wortley Montague wrote: 'Twenty very pritty Fellows – the Duke of Wharton being President . . . formed themselves into a Committee of Gallantry. They call themselves The *Schemers* . . . and meet three times a week to consult . . . on that branch of Happiness which the Vulgar call *Whoreing*. . . . Viscount Hillsborough [Trevor Hill, 'handsome and wanton and immodest'] . . . has turned his house . . . to this use . . . these Gallantries are to continue every Wednesday during Lent . . . and they have the Envy and Curses of the Old and Ugly of both sexes. . . .' These 'Schemers' were members of the Hell-Fire Club who raised hell where ever they went. The most famous were Sir Francis Dashwood (later Lord Despenser), John Montague (later Earl of Sandwich), 'completely depraved, as mischeivous as a Monky and as lecherous as a Goat', and Philip Dormer Stanhope (later Earl of Chesterfield). Their exploits were mainly round and about Covent Garden.

A lady who was catapulted into fame as a result of her association with the Club was Elizabeth Dennison, who as a young girl had been seduced by that black-hearted rake the Honourable John Spencer. She later became the mistress of Dashwood and Stanhope, and became known as 'Hell-fire Stanhope'. She married Richard Dennison, and they opened a brothel in Covent Garden sometime before 1730. Her close friendship with Dashwood and the others assured the venture of success – it was even rumoured that Dashwood had a share in the enterprise. Moreover, since Sir Francis was a close friend of 'Poor Fred' (Frederick Louis, Prince of Wales), who was known 'to be addicted to women', the quality of the Dennison's seraglio was never in doubt.

Whatever had helped her acquire her sobriquet of 'Hellfire' in her giddy youth, Elizabeth Dennison had certainly changed by the time she was running her establishment. She was then described as being a woman of pleasant manners, humour and wit, never descending to abuse or vulgarity or drinking to excess. In claiming to supply her guests with 'the very best Pieces' she never permitted

The York wagon arriving at the Bell in Wood Street, Cheapside and one of the country girls being importuned by Mother *Needham on behalf of Colonel Francis Charteris who can be seen in the doorway with his valet. Many of these simple penniless girls were cozened by waiting bawds and ended up as prostitutes in Covent Garden*

on her premises 'any Harlot whom she judged to be Improper for a Select Company'. Even so, she was not immune from the hazards which beset bawds.

At the Middlesex Quarter Sessions on 25 June 1731 a petition by 'a number of Neighbours and Shopkeepers' complained that, 'Several Persons of most notorious Character & Infamous Wicked lives . . . have taken up residence . . . in severall streets and little alleys and courts such as Russell Street, Drury Lane . . . mainly in the neighbourhood of Drury Lane which is Infected with such Vile People that there are frequent Outcries in the Night, Fighting, Robberies & all sorts of Debauchings. . . .' On 14 July forty-six warrants were issued, and amongst those taken into custody were 'Mother Sarah Osborne *alias* Vincent *alias* Roberts and Elizabeth Bird *alias* Trent *alias* Needham . . . [and next day] Richard and Elizabeth Dennison *alias* Stanhope'. All were committed to Newgate. However, the Dennisons were soon back in business, recovering their pre-eminence and reputation for supplying the best 'pieces' in the Garden; they also trained and launched upon society some of the most glamorous courtesans ever known. Elizabeth

Dennison retired in 1760, 'having acquired a very easy Fortune . . . on which she was able to live very Snugly enjoying her hard-earned Leisure'. She was still alive in 1779.

Elizabeth Needham was far and away the most notorious procuress of her time, but her opulent brothel was not in Covent Garden but in aristrocratic Park Place in St James, a small enclave in which her neighbours had included George Hamilton, Earl of Orkney, George Montague, Marquis of Halifax, Lady Tankerville, and Barbara Castlemaine, Duchess of Cleveland. Mother Needham's connection with Covent Garden was confined to seeking out likely young girls for the delectation of her very select seraglio and particularly for her close friend the infamous and evil Colonel Francis Charteris, known as 'the Rapemaster-General of the Kingdom' for his sexual activities. As the result of these proceedings she was sentenced by Sir John Gonson to stand in the pillory near Park Place and again in New Palace Yard. Despite the 'diligence of the Beadles and other persons paid to protect her . . . she was so severely pelted by the Mob that her Life was despaired of'. Indeed, a little boy was killed when he fell upon the iron spikes from a lamp-post' which he had climbed to see Mrs Needham stand in the pillory'. She died soon afterwards from her injuries. Her connection with Covent Garden is found in a mock-epitaph:

> Ye Ladies of Drury, now weep
> Your Voices in howling now raise
> For *Old Mother* Needham's laid deep
> And bitter will be all your Days.
> She who drest you in *Sattins* so fine
> Who trained you up for the Game
> Who Bail, on occasion would find
> And keep you from *Dolly* and Shame
> Now is laid low in her Grave. . . .

Mother Needham and other bawds haunted Covent Garden on the look-out for homeless young girls. Many could be found every night sleeping 'upon the Bulks' – the stalls which projected from shopfronts onto the footpath. Bawds also used the services of the Infant Office in St Giles parish nearby, which hired out children 'aged from four down to babies in arms . . . by the hour or by the day' to mendicants. (It is pertinent to recall that in 1706 there was 'An Act against the Discharge and Murder of Bastard Children', and full many of those thus saved were to be found eventually upon the bulks.)

The same Sessions then considered the case of a guardsman and three women 'being found in Bed all together'. The three women were sent to Bridewell, but the soldier pleaded 'that he had undergone enough punishment fornicating with three women at the same time' and was 'for once . . . let to go about his own business' by the Bench.

Another of Moll King's cronies was Margaret 'Nan' Griffiths, who had achieved notoriety in Edward Thompson's satirical poem *The Demi-Rep* (1766):

> When *Mother* Griffiths bawds and little Muse
> And makes the *Master Laureate* to the Stews;
> Oh! *Mother* Griffiths, bawdy Matron, Hail!
> With Langhorne's loose Effusions at thy Tail!

Mother Griffiths was an old-timer who had operated from King Street from 1710, one of a number of men and women of that name running 'houses' in the Garden. She is mentioned in Mother Needham's *Elegy* in 1731 and again in 1755 in the history of the Shakespeare's Head, but while the Poet Laureate, William Langhorne, undoubtedly frequented her establishment, no trace of a puff can be found in his extant poems.

Somewhat better known was Mother Burgess, likewise one of a clan of bagnio-owners. One, William Burgess, started in Russell Street in 1711 and graduated to Hart Street in 1719, where he died in 1753. Thomas Burgess occupied no fewer than five houses in Drury Lane 'for Tenants' from 1711 onwards at an annual rent of £60. James Burgess operated in James Street from 1720 to 1740, and John Burgess in Bow Street from 1727 to 1733. What singled out Margaret Burgess for attention was the fact that she specialized in flagellation, a *forte* exposed in *The Paphian Grove* (1738):

> BURGESS now does bemoan her absent fair
> And wishes their quick return:
> But let my MUSE advise, to ease your pain,
> Back to your *Flogging-house* will return again.
> With Breeches down, there let some lusty Ladd
> (To desp'rate *Sickness* desp'rate *Cures* are had!)
> With honest *Birch* excoriate your Hide
> And flog the *Cupid* from your scourged Backside!'

Another crony, Mother Cane first surfaces in 1730 as Mary Row *alias* Mother Cane *alias* Mother Dixon and was fined 'Two Marks and sentenced to six months in gaol . . . for keeping a Disorderly House'. In 1737 she was up before the Middlesex magistrates for keeping a disorderly house in Bedfordbury (a narrow, winding lane between Chandos Street and St Martin's Lane) but now her *aliases* are Shute and Monk. This time she was sent to the Bridewell at Tuttle Fields (Tothill Fields in Westminster) for three months but fined only one shilling 'on account of her extreme poverty'.

Mrs Cane is very probably connected with that Elizabeth Bridget Cane who was born in 1750, the daughter of a 'poor Methodist shoemaker', and who, as Elizabeth Armistead, was to become one of the most famous courtesans to grace the town and the Court. A really lovely woman, quietly witty and well educated at Mrs Goadby's exclusive 'nunnery' in Great Marlborough Street, she was courted by a great many rich and powerful noblemen and was briefly mistress to the Prince Regent. While pursuing her career she secretly married the politician Charles James Fox. The marriage was acknowledged publicly in 1795 and it was a very happy one. Her past conveniently forgotten, she was friendly with the royal family until she died highly esteemed at the age of ninety-five.

There were also Mothers Green, Haveman, Page, Lewis and Catey. Only Mother Green in Hart Street has some background, operating a house 'for tenants' in Henrietta Street from 1710 to 1720, and one Henry Green occupying a house in Hart Street between 1750 and 1752, in Bow Street until 1765 and finally in Rose Street in 1770. There is a reference to Mother Haveman at the Shakespeare's Head in 1755.

Richard Haddock, might have had the title of Whoremaster-General of Covent Garden. The extraordinary thing is that he has gained a spurious reputation as a decent sort of chap on the strength of having kept the Turk's Head bagnio in the Strand in 1721 which was regarded as 'respectable'. It was respectable only in the sense that its clientele was all male, thus avoiding the stigma attached to bagnios which had no sexual discrimination and were little better than brothels – as indeed were Richard's other establishment which masqueraded as coffee-shops, chocolate-houses and milliners' shops and were managed by a number of prostitutes. In this admirable public service he was assisted by his wife, Elizabeth.

The ploy was to rent small establishments run by nominees who were in fact employees. Occasionally he would rent a house in his own name and pay the rates 'for tenants' – a convenient euphemism for prostitutes. This he did in 1743 in Vincent Street and in 1733–45 in Russell Street and Little Piazza. He would put one girl in as manageress with two or three other 'nubile nymphs' as waitresses (or military hands as the case may be) who would offer 'refreshments and themselves to any who wished' in the back rooms. He charged them between 2 and 3 guineas a week rent and a large percentage of their earnings, besides hiring out such extras as decanters and glasses, a few rickety chairs and tables and old beds and linen 'not worth in all above Ten Pounds . . . against a *Note of Hand* [a promissory note] . . . for Forty Pounds'.

Haddock was a very hard taskmaster. If any woman failed to pay promptly or behave as he commanded or upset him or his wife, he would at once call in the debt and put the defaulter into one of the debtors' prisons, refusing to bail them out until they paid up and promised to behave themselves in the future. This tactic much displeased Moll King, who upon occasion would help out a hard-working girl but, as she put it, 'Not an expensive Courtezan', with a loan at lower-than-normal interest.

In a raid on Covent Garden in 1724 the constables caught Haddock's principal assistant, Sophia Lemoy, in his chocolate-house in King Street together with a handmaiden named Elizabeth 'Nancy' Cotton, who was a part-time actress at Drury Lane. They also caught another of his minions, Betsy Saunders, who with Nancy Dawson was running the Blue Posts chocolate-house in Exeter Street. On that occasion the magistrates described them as 'Women of Ill-fame'. From 1727 until 1733 Sophia Lemoy and Betsy Saunders ran the Corner chocolate-house in Brydges Street, a principal attraction being the sale 'to Gentlemen of two-penny glasses of *Usquebaugh* in the back room'. The Blue Posts was still going strong in 1740 when the *London Journal* remarked that it was 'one of those Houses . . . with a sign superimposed over the door . . . *Chocolate* or *Coffee* . . . a *Café* as they call it . . . constantly graced by three or four painted Harlots ready to serve you their Persons'. 'Usquebaugh' (whisky) here was, however, free.

Another accomplice of Richard Haddock was Mary Darking, who appeared as his nominee running two houses in Bow Street from 1729 to 1749 and from 1744 to 1747 in Brydges Street. When he took over his first premises in the Piazza in 1742, she and Anne Johnston are noted by the rate-collector as 'acting for Richard Haddock, Gent., of St Martin-in-the-Fields'. In 1745 Haddock was leasing it 'for tenants', among them being Elizabeth Cotton, Anne Johnston and Mary Darking. Anne Johnston's name appears in this period in several different locations in Covent Garden, un-doubtedly as one of his agents. In this house Haddock made contact with a notorious bagnio-keeper named Matthew Lovejoy as well as with another dubious character named John Bradley, a distiller, who was to become rich through selling 'Blue Ruin' (gin) and brothel-renting.

Then in 1745 the very commodious house at 8 the Piazza, next door to Callaghan's Coffee-House, became vacant and Richard Haddock took it over. He died in 1748 and his wife Elizabeth carried on until she too died in 1754, having appointed Sophie Lemoy as her executrix. Sophie promptly secured a licence for a coffee-house and carried on as usual until she died in 1762, being then described as 'Bagnio keeper of St Martin-in-the-Fields'. Lo and behold, Anne Johnston and Elizabeth 'Nancy' Cotton at once reappear, this time in the Little Piazza under the benevolent eye of the distiller John Bradley, until they make way for a Mrs Elizabeth Leese, who was to become very famous indeed under the name of Mrs Gould. (Nancy Cotton was to die early in 1769.)

The management of this establishment now fell upon Daniel Haveland until 1768 when a lease was granted to Bonnell Thornton Esq., Gent., MA and later MB. He was the clever son of a well-known local apothecary, John Thornton of Maiden Lane. After a brilliant school career and getting his MB he decided that neither medicine nor pharmaceuticals was his *forte*. He had already translated Plautus into English and he fancied to become a journalist and writer, his heart set on Covent Garden with its frivolities and politics and theatres. So he went to live in Bow Street to be nearer the theatres and to mix with wits and journalists. He founded about 1750 the *Drury Lane Journal* – otherwise known as 'Have at Ye!', a sort of Georgian *Private Eye* exposing the lives and loves and political misbehaviour of celebrities and containing theatrical reviews and criticisms. The journal was also a protagonist of female liberation. Writing under the pseudonym of 'Roxana Termagant', he once proposed the organization of a New Dispensation Society, a forum for the discussion of women's rights. Although sometimes written tongue-in-cheek, the *Journal* could occasionally be deadly serious. In one of the 1752 issues Thornton castigated the local constables who had needlessly harassed and struck some 'Doves of Venus' in Covent Garden. One of the women had then screamed 'Damn ye to Hell! Ye sons of Bitches! Ye live by us girls' misfortunes!' This was a rare exposure of the bribes extorted by the local keepers of the peace.

Haddock's *bagnio* was of course deeply involved in the lives of these doves. Sometimes the publicity was unwelcome. In October 1760 *The Gentleman's Magazine* reported the case of Anne Bellew, who with some friends, came 'at night to Haddock's *bagnio*, dined each of three days at *The Cardigan's Head*, in loose company and was found dead at Marybone the next night'. Nevertheless, Haddock's still attracted the richest and most aristocratic personages, the best-known actors and actresses and the most sought-after demi-*reps*. This was in part due to Thornton's fervent championship of the beautiful and tempestuous George Ann Bellamy, a most determined exponent of women's rights. Another was Lady Dorothy Seymour Fleming, who demonstrated her contempt of the shackles of law and sex imposed by men, by frequenting the Covent Garden bagnios for her many and public amorous encounters.

Barney Thornton was not long to enjoy the role of coffee-house proprietor and bawdy-house keeper for he died in 1768, leaving his widow, Elizabeth, to carry on, with his infant son, George. She was thereafter known as Mother Thornton although the coffee-house was still known as 'Haddock's'. In 1773 the Harris list eulogized a Miss Hill, who was to be found at Mrs Thornton's under the Piazza, as 'a pretty delicate girl, rather low in her behaviour – which might be because of the house in which she is living . . . her leaks have all been stopped-up and the carpenters have made her all tight and ready to cruise again'.

Haddock's other bagnio, the Turk's Head at Charing Cross, was also thriving in 1773 when Olivia Harrington was 'the Goddess of the Place'. She had achieved considerable notoriety because she had sued a Mr Hitchcock in the King's Bench for a debt of £300 'of which eighty pounds was for Jellies'. She lost the case. By 1794 she had changed the name to the Royal Bagnio.

The Widow Thornton ran her bagnio successfully during her son's minority, but he died at the age of twenty-five in 1790, when the lease reverted to her. The house still remained newsworthy. In a famous trial for adultery in 1780 one Samuel Hoskins claimed that his wife, Jane, had committed adultery there 'with other persons'.

When Elizabeth died, on 16 March 1798, she was described as 'the Widow Thornton, late Mistress of Haddock's *bagnio* under the Piazza'. She was always 'chagrin'd' when people were directed to her establishment as being 'next door to Jane Douglas' under the Piazza', which was the more extraordinary because Mother Douglas had been dead for very many years. She left a very considerable estate which included an annuity of £500 in Government bonds.

6. The Charming Betsy Careless and the Marvellous Fanny Murray

After the sad and much lamented death of Sally Salisbury in April 1724, the gap in high harlotry was filled by a bright and sprightly nymph well known in the Shakespeare's Head and Moll King's. She was known as Betsy Careless, a very clever adaptation of her maiden name, which was Carless. Careless by name and by nature was Betsy's hallmark throughout her career. She was born in London *c.*1704 of humble parentage and her earliest years are shrouded in mystery, but Henry Fielding recalled that in his youth he had happened

> . . . to sit behind two ladies in a side box at a Play, where in the Balcony on the opposite side was placed the inimitable Betsy Careless in company with a young fellow of no very formal, or indeed sober, appearance. One of the young ladies said to the other 'Did you ever see anything look so Modest and so Innocent as that girl over the way? What a pity it is that such a creature should be in the way to Ruin, as I am afraid she is by her being alone with such a fellow!' . . . it was impossible to conceive a greater appearance of Modesty Simplicity and Innocence than what Nature had displayed in the Countenance of that girl, and yet I myself (and remember it was in my youth) . . . had a few mornings before seen that very identical Picture of all those engaging Qualities in bed with a Rake at a *bagnio*, smoking Tobacco, drinking Punch, talking obscenity and swearing and cursing with all the Impudence and Impiety of the lowest and most abandoned Trull of a Soldier.

She was described as 'A peerless Beauty . . . the Gayest, most Charming, Wittiest of all the Courtezans around Covent Garden'. As a young girl she had been 'protected' by the riotous young barrister Robert Henley but had been cast off when her drinking

(Opposite) Hogarth's 4 Times of the Day: *the Morning shows Betsy Careless, attended by 'Little Cazey', her link boy, proceeding to Tom King's*

and licentious behaviour had threatened his career, although he was no paragon of virtue – indeed he was later known as the 'Great Buck' Henley for his amorous exploits. (In later years, when he had become the first Earl of Northington and Lord Chancellor of England, he was known as 'Surly Bob' and 'Sulky' because of his rough and uncouth behaviour in court.) He was still in contact with Betsy when she opened her own little bagnio in Tavistock Row about 1729, under the name of Mrs Elizabeth Biddulph, her constant companion then being Sir Charles Wyndham.

Wyndham was 'an unexampled instance of Debauchery who had more than once acquired instead of a Virgin, a *Vérole*'. (Lady Charlotte Wyndham, living in the Piazza between 1725 and 1727 had thrown him out and moved into Southampton Street.) Before homing-in on Betty he had been sponging off the actress Mrs Lattimore and the courtesan Nancy Featherstone. He asserted that he had left them to go and live with Betsy, with whom he was in love, but a more cynical contemporary said that his attachment was not so much to Betsy as to her house, in which he was living 'scot-free and elegantly'. It was probably a *quid pro quo* because having a lordling in the house encouraged other noblemen to come and spend their money. (Wyndham later succeeded to the earldom of Egremont, by which time he had plunged heavily into debt for jewellery given to several young ladies, one of whom, a Frenchwoman, was described as 'a Fireship who put him on fire'.)

Betsy's connections with the Shakespeare's Head were undoubtedly of great use to her in her career, and certainly by 1735 she was at her peak of notoriety and beauty. But she was recklessly extravagant and her hospitality was boundless, so that she was quite broke. She was highly successful as a courtesan and thought she could improve her position by becoming a bawd, as others had done before. In 1733 she took a house in the Little Piazza, but drink and debauchery compounded by a complete ignorance of management compelled her to vacate these premises by December 1734, and Jane Douglas took over.

In early 1735 an advertisement appeared in the *London Journal*: 'Mrs *Betty Careless* from the Piazza in Covent Garden NOT BEING ABLE to make an End of her Affairs as soon as expected intends on MONDAY NEXT to open a COFFEE HOUSE in Prujean's Court in the OLD BAILEY where she hopes that all her FRIENDS will favour her with their COMPANY notwithstanding the Ill-Situation & Remoteness of the Place, since her Misfortunes oblige her to remain there. NB. It is the Uppermost House in the court and Coaches and Chairs may come up to the Door.' It was a move of desperation. The Old Bailey was a long way from Covent Garden, on the border of the City of London, which, as regards her sort of entertainment, was very unfriendly. With youth and beauty gone and her body ravaged by drink and disease, her situation rapidly deteriorated. In October 1739 *The Gentleman's Magazine* announced: 'WAS BURIED from the Poorhouse of St Paul's Covent Garden the FAMED BETTY CARELESS who helped the gay Gentlemen of this Countrey to squander £50,000.'

Betsy's (or Betty's) charm, gaiety and beauty were not soon forgotten. In Boitard's engraving *Covent Garden Morning Frolick* she is shown in her sedan-chair with Lieutenant King and 'Little Cazey', an ugly, vicious linkboy who was a protégé of 'Mad' Captain Montague, in attendance. (In 1750) Lawrence Casey was transported to America.) With her death there was a gap in the top hierarchy of courtesans which was not to be filled until 1743, when the fledgling Fanny Murray burst upon the scene.

Fanny's story is the classic rags to riches saga of the poor country girl who became the premier 'Toast of the Town'. She was born in the city of Bath in 1729, the daughter of a poor musician named Rudman who played the fiddle in 'Beau' Nash's elegant establishment. When her father died in 1741, the little orphan 'with brown Eyes and rosy Cheeks and soft Features' tried to earn a living 'selling Flowres to the Ladies and Gentlemen in the Abbey Yard'.

Fanny then had the misfortune to meet and be seduced by 'Jack Spindle' – the Honourable John Spencer, favourite grandchild of Sarah, Duchess of Marlborough, and one of the most heartless and evil rakes of the time. He captured the heart of the innocent little virgin 'by a few tawdry Gifts and flattery' but after a few weeks deserted her, leaving her without a penny piece, so that she went back to selling flowers in the Abbey Yard. Her association with Spencer had, however, made her a mark for all the other rakes in Bath, one of whom, Captain Richard Harvey RN, then 'took her up and kissed her and ran away to the Wars', again leaving her penniless.

By this time Fanny's plight had been brought to the attention of Richard 'Beau' Nash, the reigning 'King of Bath', who literally ordered the child to come and live with him. He was then sixty-three. He grew greatly attached to this bright, merry and lovely child, already at the age of fourteen described as an extraordinarily beautiful girl, and despite the great disparity in age she was happy and comfortable, although there were many jealous scenes between the old rake and the child. After one particularly violent row, in 1743, she ran away to London, assuming the surname of Murray and taking lodgings in Covent Garden.

Like all the other hopeful little moths, young Frances was attracted to the flames of Tom King's 'fashionable Rendezvous for all Rakes, Spendthrifts and Strumpetts', but she was also to be found in Bob Derry's villainous Cyder Cellar in Maiden Lane, there meeting the young Ned Shuter and the writer George Alexander Steevens. She also began to visit the Rose Tavern 'because it served hot Suppers to the Nobility and Gentry'.

At times she was reduced to going to Lucy Earle's bagnio, the Turk's Head in Bow Street, but none of these places provided her with a living, and she was forced to go and live 'in a garret in Fleet Street', having to pawn her clothes to pay a doctor's bill to clear up a dose of the pox acquired from one of the rakes who frequented Tom King's shack. As a result (to quote her Memoirs), '. . . her Market was at a standstill, her Goods damaged, her small Stock of Money exhausted in Chirurgeon's fees, her Cloaths pledged on the same account (the surgeon took his last Fee produced by her last Gown) . . . in this strait her Landlady mentioned that Mother M . . . . in the Old Bailey had enquired whether she had any Clean Fresh Country Goods to replace her girls sent to Bridewell the night before.' Fanny had no option but to go on the streets under Mother Maddox's aegis.

In her memoirs, Fanny set out the details, of her first 'patrol' in Fleet Street:

1.	Board and Lodging	£1.15.– (in a garret, on small beer & sprats)
2.	Washing	7.– (2 smocks, 2 handkerchiefs, 2 pr stockings)
3.	Use of Brocade Gown	8.– (worth a Crown)
4.	Use of pr of Stays	3.– (not worth a shilling)
5.	Use of pr Silk Shoes	2.6 (not worth a shilling)
6.	Use of Smocks	7.– (old, coarse & patched)
7.	Use of Ruffles	2.– (darned; worth only 2/6 when new)
8.	Use of Petticotes	4.– (all of the lowest rank)
9.	Seeing Constables to prevent going to Bridewell	10.6 (Peace Officers' Fees – in Buckram)
10.	Use of a Hat	2.– (worthless)
11.	Use of Ribands	3.6 (unusable)
12.	A few Pins	6
13.	Use of a Capuchin Cloak	8.–
14.	Use of gauze Aprons	5.– (Rag-fair quality)
15.	Use of gauze Handkerchiefs	2.6 (the same)
16.	Use of Silk Stockings	2.6 (Yellow & pierced)
17.	Use of Stone Buckles	4.6 (most of the stones out)
18.	Carmine & Tooth powder and brushes	3.– (Brick-dust for the first two: Brushes unseen.)

Miss Fanny Murray, the greatest of the Great Impures and the nonpareil:

Here sportive Loves inviting seem to say,
Behold this Face, and gaze your Heart away.

For an expenditure of £5.10.0 she had earned just 6d, so she quitted after one week, during which her customers had been mainly 'poor apprentices'.

In lodgings in St James kept by a Mrs Softing Fanny recovered her health and managed to regain some of her clientele. Amongst these were John Montague, fourth Earl of Sandwich and Lieutenant-Colonel John Yorke; another 'protector' was the gentle barrister Henry Gould, later to become known as a humane justice at a time when severity was the rule. She was still hard up; the truth of the matter was that she was not a prostitute at heart and did not know how to extract maximum payment from her lovers. Then she was monopolized for a while by Sir Richard Atkins of Clapham (brother of the great beauty Penelope Pitt) who was known as 'Supple Dick' and 'the Waggoner's Whip' because he was so tall and slightly stooped.

Fanny had not escaped notice in the right quarters. In 1746 Horace Walpole had written a poem, *The Beauties*, extolling Lady Caroline Fitzroy, Lady Sophia Fermor, Mrs George Pitt (considered the most beautiful woman in all England) and the madcap Elizabeth Chudleigh, but his list was challenged by a well-known rake, 'Bloomsbury Dick' (Richard Rigby), who said that it was no good unless it included Fanny Murray, 'who was now followed by crowds of Gallants . . . it would be a Crime not to toast her at every Meal'.

One evening in 1747 at the Castle tavern in Henrietta Street, Fanny's temporary *inamorato*, having drunk her health in champagne from her shoe, ordered the cook, John Pearce, to dress the shoe and serve it up. This enterprising chef thereupon shredded the damask upper, minced the leather sole, and, mixing the whole ragout and frying it in butter, served it all up as a splendid dish garnished with thinly sliced wooden heels!

This exploit brought her to the attention of Jack Harris, the celebrated 'Negociator in Women', who approached her 'to be enroll'd on his Parchment List as a *New Face*' – although she had already been on the Town for four years! She paid his fees, signed his contract and joined his Whores' Club which met every Sunday evening to square accounts and exchange information about the 'cullies', as well as making a whip-round for any unfortunate sister who had fallen by the way or languished in jail. Other famous beauties who reached the top in this way included Annabella Parsons (Nancy Parsons who was eventually to marry Charles, Viscount Maynard), Nancy Dawson, 'who danc'd the Jigg at Sadlers Wells', and the aristocratic Charlotte Spencer.

From that time Fanny 'increased the Price of her Favours to Two Guineas'. In the autumn of 1748, at the pinnacle of her fame, she was telling 'Supple Dick' at breakfast about her poverty when he pulled out a £20 note. Contemptuously she clapped it between two slices of buttered toast and began to munch it, protesting that it was not even enough for a breakfast and shouting, 'Damn your £20! What does it signify?' He took it all in good part and thereafter supplied the greater part of her income, until he died suddenly in 1756. He was 'always on the point of marrying her' but he was catholic in his love affairs and never got around to it.

Fanny also became very intimate with Richard 'Beau' Tracey – also known as 'Handsome Tracey' (he married Susanna Owen, 'a poor harlot, daughter of a washerwoman' one day when he was drunk). Another lover was Captain Plaistow, who turned out to be not only a penniless adventurer but a bigamist into the bargain, but Fanny saved him from arrest because she was fond of him. She also had a narrow escape because of a chance association with the notorious James MacLean, 'the Gentleman Highwayman', who was hanged in 1750.

In May 1756 Sir Richard Atkins arranged a Mediterranean cruise in his yacht with his friends Sir Francis Blake Delavel and the comedian Sam Foote. Besides Fanny there was the glamorous Elizabeth de la Roche and other *demi-mondaines*. Soon after their return Sir Richard died, and Fanny, at the age of twenty-seven, heavily in debt without any rescuer in sight, was arrested and taken to a 'spunging-house'. The future looked bleak. She suddenly bethought herself of her early seducer, Jack Spencer, who had died of drink and debauchery in 1746. His son, John Spencer, recently married to the heiress Elizabeth Poyntz, was a decent, kind and generous man. When she told him of his father's part in her downfall, he was deeply shocked. When her account was verified, he sprang her from confinement, gave her an annual allowance of £200 and then persuaded the actor David Ross to marry her.

At first they were happy: she was a loving and faithful wife and no breath of scandal against her could be raised. Then in 1763 John Wilkes MP published his notorious *Essay on Woman*, dedicating it to 'Fanny' (It was more likely Frances Fielding, another *demi-rep* of 'the Quality'), and Lord Sandwich, a former paramour raised the matter in the House of Lords to embarrass Wilkes, although another ex-lover, Lord Northington, was loth to do anything to hurt her.

Fanny's name was dragged into the limelight, much to her anger and distress: she and David were not allowed to forget that she had once been a most famous courtesan. Ross, fearing for his career, began to play around with other actresses, and by 1767 he quitted Covent Garden. Fanny carried on her household affairs with dignity, and many noble friends rallied round her. On 16 October 1768 the King of Denmark invited her to be his guest at the famous *bal masqué* at the Pantheon, and Fanny, at the age of forty, was hailed as 'the Belle of the Ball'. Following this *succès d'estime* David came back home, and they lived peaceably together until Fanny died on 1 April 1778.

Between 1746 and 1754 no one could challenge Fanny Murray's supremacy but there were three young ladies girding up for her title.

7. The Places of Resort

Carpenter's Coffee-House – 'The Finish'

When Moll King retired from active life, the shacks reverted to the lessee of the market, George Carpenter, who about 1762 had succeeded a brewer named William Gifford. For a premium of £500 he secured rentals of about £700 annually by an agreement with the Duke of Bedford.

George had started life as a strong man who had become a registered Covent Garden porter, renowned for his knack of balancing upon his head fifteen half-cherry sieves (as the baskets were then known) and being able to shed them singly or in other quantities to the stallholders. By the time of Moll's departure he was a market salesman, buying his fruit from a well-known woman named Ivy Bride at the sign of the Fox-under-the-Hill (a tavern on the riverside wharf near today's Adelphi, from which fruit and vegetables were unloaded), and selling the produce to the stall-holders. He did very well and amassed a considerable fortune but was then struck by a protracted illness which brought him to the verge of ruin, so that (according to old Twigg) 'he was reduced to pawn his Silver Watch, but with the proceeds got better and by honest endeavour and savings became lessee of the Market and flourished. He often referred to his watch as "his Saviour" and had it put into a gold case.'

He took over two shacks facing the hummums, retaining the business of a coffee-house, which was henceforth known as Carpenter's and putting his parents in as managers. He lived in Tavistock Court, a dreary little alley running between Tavistock Row and Tavistock Street. In 1773 he is described in the Rate Book as 'the lessee to the Duke for the Market', and also had properties in Bow Street and Southampton Streets 'for tenants'. (His father, John Carpenter, was listed as the ratepayer of a house in Hart

Street between 1733 and 1739, also sub-letting 'for tenants'.)

Carpenter's was certainly not a very respectable coffee-house. In 1766 William Hickey described it as 'a dirty dissipated shed in Covent Garden dignified by the name of Carpenter's Coffee-House . . . where they dole out a spartan mixture difficult to ascertain the ingredients but which was served as coffee'. Since most of the customers were already the worse for liquor before they got there, it is unlikely that George Carpenter saw any need to bother about the mixture. For a penny the dish the customer could not expect much, and in any case he had come more for the doxies of a wide range of prices.

George Carpenter died about 1785, wealthy and well respected, and the management was taken over by Anne Crosdell, who was at the time living with John Gibson, a cook at Richard Stacey's Bedford Arms in the Little Piazza. Gibson committed suicide one evening by cutting his throat at his lodgings in James Street, and his paramour then took up with Jack Gould, a well-known market salesman and a man of some substance, greatly interested in the new sport of boxing, being a close friend of Daniel Mendoza, the famous Jewish pugilist.

By 1768 Carpenter's had also become known as 'The Finish', and Hickey described it as 'the last of those nocturnal Resorts for which Covent Garden was famous . . . it bore the same horrid reputation as the *Soup Shop Ale House* in nearby Brydges Street', being the last place for a man to go to when kicked out of all the other coffee-houses and taverns. The famous comedian Sam Foote had been the potboy there and had become well known for feeding the rats in the cellar on the beer dregs, reputedly able to call them by name. There was also a tavern in James Street known as The Finish, and another in Charles Street. It seems to have been a sobriquet attached to any low dive open all night and not particular about its customers.

By the time of George III's first bout of 'madness' in 1788, Carpenter's was also known as the Queen's Head being run by Mother Elizabeth Butler who had been a successful procuress in King Street. It was still 'a dirty disreputable place . . . where . . . if you were shut out of your Lodging you might find shelter till Morning often in the very best of Company'. Mrs Butler, described as 'a witty generous-hearted, always cheerful and extraordinary woman', must have been tough too because this 'best of Company' included thieves and robbers as well as 'Gentlemen Depredators of the Night'. Their *modus operandi* was to follow and rob travellers of their money and watches (colloquially known as 'blunts and

George Carpenter's coffee-house is the shack on the right. Later, under Mrs Elizabeth Butler, it became notorious as 'The Finish'

tatlers') assaulting the victims and often murdering them. It is said that the famous actor John Kemble once started to spout some lines from Shakespeare's *Coriolanus* there but was forced to leave hurriedly by a completely drunken and unappreciative audience.

By the end of the century Carpenter's was being patronized by all the boxers of the day, among them George the Brewer and Cribb, Belcher, Dan Mendoza (known as 'the Light of Israel') and other young Jewish boxers known as the 'Fighting Israelites', Dutch Sam and Big Ben. Here too would be found Jack Gould and his friend Sir Thomas Hussey Apreece Bart., son and heir of Moll King's old admirer.

Elizabeth Butler carried on until about 1812; in 1815 the place was being managed by Ann Butler but her licence was suspended for some years. Elizabeth Butler was, however, still alive in 1825, when a licence was granted to the new lessee, Jack Rowbottom. Pierce Egan, in his book *Tom and Jerry*, called the Finish 'a notorious Night-House . . . [to which] Swells, bundled out of Offley's in Henrietta Street at four in the morning would bundle-in at Jack's till nine and ten a.m.'. It was a drinking-den of unexampled roughness and coarseness and Jack Rowbottom had several brushes with the law – so much so that in 1832 it was remarked that, '. . . his Residence alternated between the Fleet and the King's Bench prisons'. The Finish was demolished in 1866.

Henrietta Street seems to have been one of the most respectable of Covent Garden's areas. The historian Strype noted that between 1712 and 1716 a whole range of new houses had been built on the south side, 'predominantly Tradesmen', with few persons of title until about 1750. In 1763 the residents were a surgeon, a baker, a linen-draper, a mercer, two stockbrokers, three apothecaries and three artists. At the corner with Bedford Street, in 1774, the tavern formerly known as the Cross Keys became the Bedford Head, which was later converted into warehouses for William Duesbury, the manufacturer of the famous 'Derby' china.

William Offley had established his house at No. 23 on the north side of Henrietta Street in 1807, specializing in 'Burton Ale and Shredded Shallots . . . free from vulgar Coffee-rooms' finery to distract one's relish of the good things provided . . .' In 1843 he moved into the much larger premises next door at No. 24. Despite all his care and attention, his customers were just as rowdy as those in any other similar establishment. In Henrietta Street, too, at No. 24, Edward Braxton had founded his own refreshment business which in 1715 was taken over by John Rawthnell who made it into a coffee-house and a resort of painters and others connected with the arts. He rebuilt the premises in 1730 and included No. 25 where, in 1754, the Royal Society of Arts was founded. No. 37 was the Unicorn Tavern.

The Rose Tavern

The glitter and attraction of Moll King's shacks were matched in obloquy by the neighbouring tavern in Russell Street known as the Rose. This, however, had the advantage of length of years since it had been in existence before King Charles II was restored to his throne in 1660, when it shared a bad reputation with very good food. It had the added good fortune to be 'by the Playhouse in Drury Lane'. That well-known entrepreneur 'Orange Moll', who had the monopoly for the sale of oranges, lemons and 'other sweetmeats' in the theatre, frequented the Rose from 1663 until the theatre was burnt down in 1674. She also dispensed another form of 'sweetmeat' by introducing her maidens to amorous gentlemen.

Samuel Pepys, whose chief, Lord Brouncker, lived in the Piazza, was often in Covent Garden in pursuit of amorous adventure. He mentions the Rose as early as 1663. Two years later he drove in his coach round the Covent Garden alleys, especially Dog and Bitch Yard by Drury Lane, where he saw 'an abundance of women standing about the doors' and took fright, driving hurriedly away, but in the next month, June 1665, he took from the Rose Tavern in Drury Lane 'one of their fairest flowers' with whom he frolicked pleasantly in Tothill Fields. In July he tried the alleys around Long Acre and found 'loathsome people and loathsome houses'.

Pepys returned in January 1667 to the Rose Tavern 'frigging with Doll Lane' and complaining that he had nits in his wig, and rendezvoused there with her several times more or less satisfactorily. He notes that in December 1667 the Rose was being run by Mr (William) Long (whose son Robert was running it in 1706) and that he had eaten well, drunk some burnt wine at the door and at two in the morning had seen the constables and bellmen rounding up pedestrians. He had just come from the Court where he had seen Lady Castlemaine 'in her Nightdress looking pretty'. On 18 May 1668 he dined alone at the Rose on half a breast of mutton off the spit: this he compared with 'a base dinner at Chatelin's in Covent Garden' which had cost 8s. 6d. apiece.

By the turn of the century the Rose was already described as 'the Resort of the worst Characters in the Town, male and female, who make it the Headquarters of Midnight Orgies and drunken Broils where Murders and Assaults frequently occur'. Frequent visitors at this time were the sisters Anne and Beth Marshall, daughters of a royal chaplain, both actresses with whom Nell Gwyn was at bitter odds. Thomas Brown of Shifnal in his *Midnight spy* (1701) called the Rose 'that black School of SODOM . . . [where men] who by proficiency in the Science of Debauchery were called *Flogging Cullies* . . . these unnatural Beasts pay an excellent Price for being scourged on their Posteriors . . . by *Posture Molls*' a group of women who would perform either function, flogging or being flogged. They were not prostitutes; indeed, they resented being asked for carnal copulation, although there was no limit to the indecencies they would otherwise perform so long as they were handsomely paid.

G. Gent in his *The Rake Reform'd* (1718) said that the Rose had a pendant sign as a tavern:

> Where to the Travellers sight the full-blown *Rose*
> In dazzling *Beauties* doth in Gold disclose;
> And painted *Faces* flock in tally'd Cloath.
> Thither conducted, I embrace an *Whore*
> And when enjoy'd, I kick'd her out of Door.

This particular reveller 'with giddy Brains and uncertain Feet' left the Rose at dead of night, was chased by and arrested by the Watch and had to buy his freedom from the Round-house with gold, 'which made them *Slaves* who were my *Foes* before'.

Another and much more innocent attraction was the beautiful and charming Mary Mogg, universally known as 'Molly Mogg of the Rose.' She was the waitress-cum-barmaid who never succumbed to any of the men swarming around her but nevertheless was considered one of the 'Toasts of the Town'. John Gay wrote a love-ditty to her charms, while the Welsh bard Gwynfrid Shone (*anglice* Winfred Jones) warbled:

> Some sing Molly Mogg of *The Rose*
> And call her the Oakingham *pelle* [the *Belle* of Wokingham]
> While others does Farces compose
> for peautiful Molly Lepell!

(who later became Countess of Orford). Mary Mogg died on 9 March 1766, advanced in years and possessed of a good fortune as Mistress of the Rose, a tavern in Wokingham.

Another, quite different, attraction was the porter and bouncer Richard Lethercote, an immensely strong hulk of a man who for a pint of beer would lie down in the street outside the Rose and let a

Hogarth's The Rake's Progress, *1735. A* Posture Moll *is undressing in the Rose Tavern in Covent Garden amidst a scene of drunken disorder. There is a fiddler and a harpist as well as a trumpeter to add to the orgy*

carriage pass over him. A much greater attraction, however, was the 'Posture Girls' who specialized in striptease and flagellation. *The Midnight Spy* spoke of 'girls who stripped naked and mounted upon the middle of the table to show their beauties'. Others stretched upon the floor offering just those parts of her body that, were she not without all shame, she would most zealously seek to hide. She is given to drink, arrives usually half-drunk and after a few glasses of Madeira exposes herself in this unseemly manner. Look, she is on all fours like an animal . . . men gloat over such prostitution of incomparable beauty!' In 1762 a woman known as 'Posture Nan' was the greatest mistress of this art.

In *The Adventures of a Young Gentleman* (*c*.1745) such lascivious movements so inflamed 'these sons of debauchery' that they proposed each to choose a girl to perform what they had just seen mimed. At this point the Posture Girls jibbed because 'They had a great Aversion to Whoreing . . . their function was to flagellate or be flagellated to arouse sexual desire in the Gentlemen', leaving carnal copulation to prostitutes. On this particular occasion they were so outraged that they attacked the customers and created a riot. However, Hogarth's picture shows a number of condoms amongst the detritus on the floor of the Rose, so obviously someone in the sisterhood was breaking the rules.

All of the most famous 'Toasts' in their generations passed through the tavern's doors during the hundred years of its existence: the marvellous Sally Salisbury and her successor Betsy Careless, Lucy Cooper and Nancy Dawson, and the lovely Fanny Murray, who was to start at the bottom and use the Rose as one step in her ladder to become the most famous courtesan of them all. Despite its dreadful reputation, it was a venue to which all sections of society had to come at some time in their careers. The most famous of the 'Mothers' were to be found there, sometimes with their *mignons*, looking for fresh goods. 'Blue Ribbons' and 'Stars of the Nobility' entertained their constantly changing loves of the day: scions of the royal House were to be found there in the time of George II – one was his unfortunate son the Prince of Wales, better known as 'Poor Fred'. There they were served by pretty barmaids and *dames de comptoir* in frilly caps, darting amorous glances.

The most riotous behaviour occurred regularly. Drunken bullies would beat up starving but drunken whores; men and women would be rolling on the sanded floor fighting and scratching; women, often drunk and bared to the waist, would be wrestling together. None was barred: homosexuals and lesbians (the latter's activity called 'the Game of Flats') were as welcome as prize-fighters or justices' clerks. Class distinctions vanished in the welter of drunkenness. *The Convent Garden Eclogue* (1735) describes part of the scene:

> The Watch had cry'd 'Past One', with hollow strain
> And to their Stands return'd to sleep again.
> Grave Cits and Bullies, Rakes and squeamish Beaux
> Came reeling with their Doxies from *The Rose* . . .

They would wend their way to Tom King's shanties until the dawn or until they had chosen their favourite brothel. Upon occasion they would be picked up by the watchmen and put in the Roundhouse to come before the magistrates next morning. Or they could go into one of the hummums 'good lodgings for Persons who shall desire to lodge all Night . . . to sweat and bathe . . . and be cupped after the newest manner . . . price as always . . . for two in one Room eight shillings but who lodges there all night, ten shillings . . .', so that sensible beaux and doxies could sweat it out together.

Another nymph of the Rose was Kitty Fordyce, 'a young girl who spends her evenings in *The Rose* or *Bedford Arms* . . . running from Room to Room where she can meet with a Man or a Present'. Her preference was always for a silk gown but if she had 'a real passion for a Man . . . then her passion is unbounded'. The *Meretriciad* (1765) said:

> Of all the daughters *Venus* ever had
> So fair as Fordyce, none, nor half so mad!
> The greatest Pleasure that she ever chose
> As, to set Friends together by the Nose
> Or Riot at *The Rose* and *Bedford Arms*
> And fire the Bob-Wigs to dispute her charms . . .

but the vignette ended with the wry information that although Kitty had been 'in keeping' with a noble lord, a rich mercer and even a 'Scarlet Coat', she was 'ever receiving but still without a Groat'.

Another beauty, in her time called 'the Queen of the Garden', was the captivating Elizabeth Thomas, who lived round the corner in Bow Street and who was 'looked upon by several Gentlemen as alone Equivalent to all the other Women of Pleasure in the purlieus'. She was very often in the Rose and Mrs Weatherby's Ben Jonson tavern. Harris thought she was 'rather too lusty and fat' but she was 'sweetness in Face and sprightly in Manner' and now in full bloom. Her price was one guinea, 'with half-a-Crown to the servant'. She frequently 'pops into Baptiste's *Jelly House* in Russell Street.' (Alexandre Baptiste, a Frenchman, kept a house between *c.*1740 and 1765.) Jellies had become a popular delicacy, and in 1776 there was a reference:

> The Jelly-Houses are now become the resort
> Of abandon'd Rakes and shameless Prostitutes.

Then in the sixties the Rose was honoured with the presence of the most famous 'Toasts' of all, the 'wall-ey'd' Betsy Weems, Nancy Dawson, the dancer, and Lucy Cooper, all of whom could be guaranteed to bring vivacity and hilarity, as well as riotous behaviour coupled with extravagant wining and dining (at their 'keepers' expense).

Before the Rose was demolished in 1775 to make way for the rebuilding of the theatre next door, it was to be host to a galaxy of actors and actresses whose names still adorn the annals of the stage: Peg Woffington, Sarah Siddons, George Anne Bellamy and Sophia Baddeley, 'that pritty ideot', together with David Garrick,

93

Richard Brinsley Sheridan and Jack Kemble, to mention only a few. For a century it had blazed with evil glory: it was to die without a whimper.

The Shakespeare's Head Tavern

Indissolubly linked with every activity in Covent Garden from its very earliest days was the infamous tavern under the Piazza known as the Shakespeare's Head. As early as 1640 the map made by Wenceslas Hollar shows a tavern in the north-east corner; it was probably a concession, because up till 1720 none of the grand houses was allowed to be converted into 'public Ordinaries or Victualling-Houses or for the sale of Coffee, Chocolate or any Liquor'. This tavern was called the Lyon's Head and it occupied the ground floor. The original residents were Sir Edmund and Lady Pye, until 1693, and after them Admiral Matthew Aylmer (later Lord Aylmer) occupied the house until he died in 1720. By then the majority of the original aristocratic residents in the Piazza had moved out, the opening of the market in 1705 having brought undesirable neighbours.

The first mention of the premises as a commercial enterprise comes in an agreement dated 10 September, 1717, when the house was divided into two parts, Harry Heasman (who owned property elsewhere in the Garden) being given 'the east and south parts' and Admiral Aylmer 'the Portico Walk on the west, backing on to Hart Street on the north'. Two years later it was let to John Rich for two years at £120 per annum with permission for 'a Coffee House, Liquors and a Victualling-house'. In 1726 Aylmer's portion 'in the north' section was leased to Sarah Gardiner as the Bedford Head Coffee-House, Henry Heasman still holding the other half, seemingly still the Lyon's Head.

In March 1730 it was recorded that John Rich had torn down the back parts and rebuilt 'the messuage formerly divided into two parts with the Coffee-house built backwards'. Both parts of the house were, however, 'demised to John Rich for the Theatre for the profit to the theatre'. Rich let part of the premises, then known as the Shakespeare, to a hairdresser named Low, who (according to old Twigg) had been at one time in the workhouse whence he had been expelled for trying to stab the workhouse-master; he had kept a lodging-house in Henrietta Street and had eventually become a barber in Southampton Street but was in a constant state of penury because he was such a reckless gambler. When he had ruined

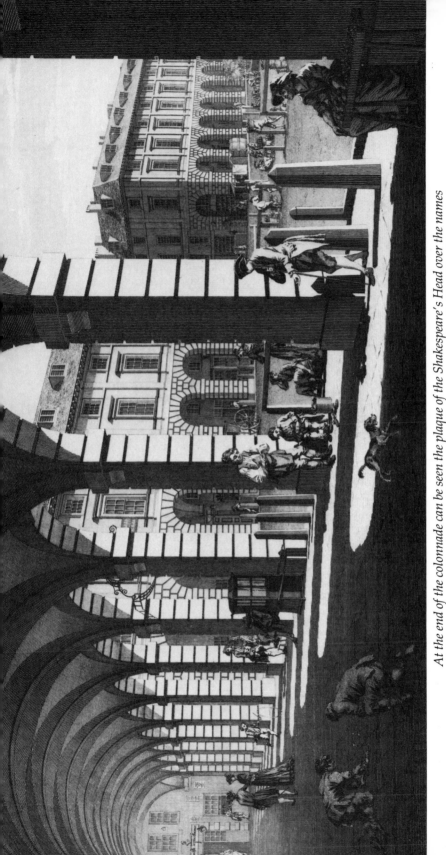

At the end of the colonnade can be seen the plaque of the Shakespeare's Head over the names of the proprietors, Tomkyns and Richardson. The entrance to the Bedford Head is masked by the end column. (1768)

himself in 1736, Rich leased the premises to Richard Croft, from which time it became known as the Shakespeare's Head Tavern – although the old-timers still called it the Lyon. Possession of the old effigy seems to have conferred a *cachet* upon both owner and premises.

Under Croft's management the tavern became the meeting-place for men of wit and culture, a serious rival to Tom King's because amongst other advantages it boasted a renowned cook, John Twigg. Twigg was a poor boy, born and bred in the Garden. As a child (he reminisced), he played marbles in the alley between the Piazza and Hart Street when it was common for thieves to dress up as journeymen bakers and carry a small boy in their baskets. As they went round the market selling the fresh hot bread and rolls, the child would steal the best hats, which were quickly offloaded onto a man who kept a small stall at the corner of Russell Street and the Piazza. It is very likely that one of these small boys was Twigg himself, for he was a small man.

By 1742 he was famed for his marvellous cooking, his speciality being turtle soup. He was to stay at the Shakespeare's Head for many many years, and was still alive in 1816, gossiping about the people he had met as well as their behaviour to anyone who would listen; he was affectionately known as *Old Twigg*.

The tavern was not immune from uncivilized behaviour. On 15 May 1736 the Honourable John Stanhope, MP for Derby (a younger brother of the Earl of Chesterfield), had a fight there with Lord Thomas Southwell and 'much blood was spilt' before the men could be separated. The presence of many 'ladies of the town' likewise caused quarrels and arguments with fighting exacerbated by the normal drunkenness to be expected in a tavern.

The cooking, however, still drew the *haut ton*. An advertisement in the *London Journal* in December 1737 stated: 'The Gentlemen educated at Eton School are desired to meet at *The Shakespeare's Head* tavern on Tuesday January 31st. 1738 being the first Meeting of this Season.' This represented a triumph over the Old Etonian Tom King, in whose premises these gentlemen were formerly wont to meet.

Richard Croft died in 1742 and was succeeded by Richard Mytton (sometimes miscalled Milton), who undertook a number of repairs and improvements, including the manufacture and ornate painting of a new sign, for which he reputedly paid £200. The pride and joy of the establishment was still Twigg's 'magnificent cooking' which was especially appreciated by the members of the clubs which now met in private rooms – the Shakespeare's Head is reputed to have been the first tavern in Covent Garden to have special private rooms for such purposes. There were, of course, other purposes for which these private rooms could be used, but these were not then trumpeted about.

There were three clubs, each with its own room, which met permanently for the convenience and entertainment of the directors and officers of the East India Company. These were the Madras, the Bengal and the Bombay. After indulging in good food and drink and the swapping of information about their voyages and experiences, these convivial nabobs would round off their pleasures with a visit to Mother Douglas's equally famous 'House of Civilitie' next door, where they were always very welcome as big spenders and lavishers of exotic gifts.

The tavern employed seven waiters, who with wages and tips earned large sums of money – they thought it a bad week if they had not earned at least £77. Small wonder therefore that some of them amassed enough capital to start their own businesses. One such was the headwaiter, Richardson, known as 'a smart character about the Garden', whose home had once been in the cellar under Low's lodging-house. By about 1766 he was taken into partnership by Tomkyns, when the sign above the entrance read 'Tomkyns and Richardson', under the effigy of Shakespeare's head.

There was a gambling-room known as the Hazard Club. Old Twigg reminisced that he had often seen winners there with their hats full of guineas. One of the most reckless gamblers was Dick Mytton himself, who when he was winning 'was up in the air' but his losses brought him eventually to ruin, and in 1747 the tavern was taken over by a City vintner named Packington Tomkyns. His father, of the same name, was a wealthy Herefordshire landowner, a Justice of the Peace, with large business interests in the City of London. The young Tomkyns had already lived in various addresses in the Garden since 1740. Taking over the Shakespeare's Head was a golden chance to fortune as well as fame. Mr Tomkyns senior died in April 1754, a ruined man but still with assets enough to leave his son a house in the country and a fine coach and horses. Tomkyns junior was often to use both when his own problems became overwhelming. With his advent the Shakespeare's Head became the Mecca of anyone who was anybody. Twigg's food became even more famous, as did the turtle soup – indeed, Tomkyns was to boast that he bought fifty turtles at a time to make enough soup also to supply a large number of customers in the country.

Another boost to the business was the activity of the head waiter, the notorious Jack Harris, known popularly as 'the Pimpmaster-General' for his organization of the Whores' Club which met every Sunday evening in a private room to discuss their business. Amongst the ladies who were eulogized in Harris' *List of Covent Garden Cyprians* was the youngster who later became the most famous courtesan in London, Fanny Murray; others in the first echelon were Betsy Careless, Lucy Cooper and Nancy Dawson.

Although a famous rendezvous for wits and literati, the tavern was by no means decorous. In 1755 a visitor observed, 'drunken Men and Women, starving Harlots . . . the wanton embracing of girls rolling upon the sanded floor . . . who complained that it soiled their Cloaths'.

On 16 May 1763, three days after he had first met Dr Johnson in Thomas Davies' bookshop in Russell Street, James Boswell staggered into the Shakespeare's Head with two pretty harlots he had picked up in the Piazza. After telling them that he had no money, he offered them 'a Glass of Wine and his Company . . . to be gay and obliging to each other without money'. He then called out: "Waiter! I have a couple of Human beings here" . . . We were then shown into a good Room and had a Bottle of Sherry . . . I surveyed my *Seraglio* and found them good for amorous play. I toy'd with them . . . and solac'd my Existence with them one after the other . . . enjoying High Debauchery with genteel Ceremonial . . .'

That precocious young wencher Willian Hickey was sitting in the tavern in November 1766 when Packington Tomkyns told them that, 'He had that day received a letter from Lucy Cooper, long in the King's Bench prison [for debt] almost naked and starving, without a Penny to buy Food or Raiment or Coal to warm herself. I put down Ten Guineas and altogether the Gentlemen raised Fifty Pounds which I gave to Tomkyns. This seasonable aid had probably saved the Life of a deserving Woman who in her prosperity had done a thousand generous actions . . .' In passing, Tomkyns mentioned that the Sisterhood used to raise money to help those who had fallen into distress, whence it can be deduced that by this time Harris's Whores' Club was no longer functioning. Harris was, in fact, dead by the time of this anecdote. *The Meretriciad* (1765) remarked

> The *Shakespeare's Head*, the *Rose* and *Bedford Arms*
> Each alike profits from my Lucy's charms . . .

which will explain Tomkyns' interest in her welfare. She was to survive this setback and resume her patronage, but she was but

Thomas Davies, ex-actor, opened this bookshop at No. 8 Russell Street. It was frequented by all literary lions. Here in 1763 James Boswell was introduced to Samuel Johnson

one of the lovelies to contribute to Tomkyns' profits. Another was the 'Wall-ey'd Beauty' Betsy Weems who is said on one occasion to have dropped her artificial eye on the floor, causing chaos until it was found.

Then there was the bizarre affair concerning the luscious Italian opera singer Caterina Ruini Galli who had briefly been the *inamorata* of the rich Moses Mendez, that 'Paragon of Foppery'. He had spent so much time chasing young ladies that he was regarded as 'The *Toast* of every Fine Woman'. His attachment to Signora Galli, whose extravagances were outrageous, led him to neglect his business – he was a Stock Exchange broker – almost to ruin by the time he died on his Norfolk estate in 1758.

La Galli was then taken up by Count Sergei Musin-Pushkin, the Russian Ambassador, but even he was unable to meet her demands, and cast her off.

In 1770 her husband had the bright idea of 'auctioning her off' at the Shakespeare's Head, and she was 'bought in' by Julian Howard for £300, but even he could not stand the pace, and the last heard of her was that she was gracing Mrs Courage's well-known place of assignation in Suffolk Street off the Haymarket.

Tomkyns seems also to have had some regard for the welfare of young William Hickey because he warned him that some of his boon companions were taking advantage of his extreme youth and fleecing him, so that if he went on in this way he would be ruined. Young Hickey did not heed this good advice and continued his debauchery until his father woke up to what was going on and packed him off to India, where in the course of time he reached high estate and respectability.

These junketings apart, there was still the serious business of eating, at which Twigg still excelled, as evidenced by the invitations sent out on 1 August 1772 by the Bow Street Magistrate: 'SIR JOHN FIELDING presents his Compliments to Mr Richard Palmer and acquaints him that the announced TURTLE FEAST of the GOOD-NATURED SOCIETY will be held at Thursday next the 6th instant at 3 o'clock precisely in The SHAKESPEARE'S HEAD TAVERN in Covent Garden. YOUR COMPANY EARNESTLY REQUIRED.'

About this time too the old Beefsteak Society, originally founded by John Rich and the artist George Lambert, had forsaken its original home in the Bedford Head and now enjoyed Twigg's efforts. The membership included such luminaries as David Garrick, Richard Brinsley Sheridan, John Wilkes, the painters Hogarth and Thornhill, the Dukes of Argyll and Leinster and later on the Prince of Wales who was to become Prince Regent and King George IV. Once a week '. . . they ate the choicest Beefsteaks with great Ceremony.' Twigg later said that when the cook at the Bedford Arms was sick, he used to cook the club's meals; it was perhaps because of this that the Shakespeare's Head was chosen when the time came to move.

All accounts, however, maintain a certain reticence when describing what usually followed such occasions. As soon as the meal ended, any ladies present were asked to retire, and the chamberpots were brought out of the cupboard in the dining-room, to allow the bloated gentlemen to relieve themselves while still sitting round the table, still drinking and 'settling the affairs of the Nation . . .', as a French visitor remarked in 1765. Lord Chesterfield solved the other problem by tearing pages out of any book he was then reading. As for the ladies, Samuel Rolleston in an essay *Concerning Decency* contrasted the 'over delicacy of English ladies' with the use in Holland of a mussel-shell which 'had the advantage of being usable again and again and could be offered to a guest in need'.

In February 1778 Packington Tomkyns died, leaving a fortune of between £20,000 and £40,000 (accounts differ) to his daughter, a Mrs Longman. The management of the tavern was left to James Campbell, although Richardson was still a partner. Richardson eventually took over the Great Room in W. C. Evans' Grand Hotel,

(Opposite) Cash in advance: The earliest depiction of soliciting in the Piazza

which he ran as a café. When in 1809 the lion came up for auction, he bought it, and when he died in 1824 this heirloom came into possession of the Bedford estate; it is now quietly resting at Woburn Abbey.

In 1779 James Campbell was to be involved in one of the greatest newsworthy events of the century, when the lovely young Martha Rae, mistress of 'Jemmy Twitcher' (the Earl of Sandwich) was murdered in the tavern's vestibule by the Reverend James Hackman.

Twigg's superb skills were fully tested in 1782, when he catered for the huge banquet given by Admiral Augustus Keppel to celebrate his appointment as First Lord of the Admiralty. The charge was 7 guineas a head – since the usual charge was but a guinea a head, even Twigg thought this too expensive.

On 25 March 1785 James Campbell was able to get the lease of the premises assigned to him and promptly changed the name to 'The Star', which name it bore until the premises burnt down in 1808. Whether Twigg was still working there is not known but he was still alive in 1815 and referred to this incident as 'poor Campbell's misfortune'. By this time, however, the fame of the Shakespeare's Head had passed into history, soon to be forgotten.

The Covent Garden Cyprians

Contributing in great measure to the fame and prosperity of the Shakespeare's Head was the booklet published by the waiter John Harris giving the names, addresses and intimate accomplishments of a number of local harlots. Such lists were nothing new: in Jacobean times the famous astrologer Simon Forman had circulated his *Register of the Ladies of Love,* and between 1660 and 1663 John Garfield had published *The Wand'ring Whore,* whose first editions contained lists of bawds, prostitutes and pimps in a format derived from Pietro Aretino's *La Puttana Errante* more than half a century earlier.

There was a crude broadsheet published in 1691 entitled *The Catalogue of Jilts* which listed a number of poor ambulant whores roaming the City's streets. Doubtless there were many others circulating about the ancient red-light districts of Clerkenwell and Moorfields, as well as Lewkenor's Lane, one end of which reached the perimeter of Covent Garden, which was then regarded as the very sink of iniquity. (In 1722 it was renamed Charles Street to erase its infamous reputation, and when that in turn also stank it was renamed Macklin Street to commemorate the old actor-manager.)

Both Tomkyns and Harris were on to a very good thing. The first lists appeared about 1746, for on 19 July of that year Horace Walpole noted that there was circulating a list entitled 'An Exact Description of the Person, Temper and Accomplishments of the several Ladies of Pleasure who frequent Covent Garden and other Parts of the Metropolis'. Harris' first lists were hand-written and distributed amongst the tavern's customers, but the demand was so great that by 1758 a printed edition was published, entitled *The New Atalantis*. It sold for half-a-crown 'sewed', i.e. in a hard cover. At first it was sold only about Covent Garden, extolling local 'Cyprians', but the demand escalated all over the town and eventually some eight thousand copies were subscribed for annually.

A copy of the 1761 edition in a private collection was described in 1920 by Horace Bleackley; it was a small book in hard covers, six inches by four, and the title page read: 'HARRIS LIST OF COVENT GARDEN LADIES OR NEW ATALANTIS for the Year 1761 to which is annexed *The Ghost of Moll King* or a Night at Derry's. London. Printed for H. Ranger, near Temple Bar. MDCCLXI.' There follows a list of about a hundred names in alphabetical order (with the vowels omitted, but the names are quite easy to decipher), and then a series of vignettes giving the address and a brief description of the lady's charms – not always flattering, so as to give an air of verisimilitude and truthfulness. Most vignettes run to half a page, but some few are of greater length and even include eulogizing verses, depending perhaps upon the amount paid to Harris for the advertisement. It soon became a *cachet* to have one's name thus published, and many top-ranking courtesans utilized the service while they were climbing the ladder to fame and fortune.

Jack Harris claimed to be the younger son of a 'good Somersetshire family'. His father, 'being antagonistic to Robert Walpole's regime', had landed in the King's Bench prison for three years and been fined £500. He also claimed to have been educated at Westminster School. In 1751 he was living in Russell Street and working at the tavern, although alleging that he had 'no particular occupation'.

The earliest account of his operations is to be found in Fanny Murray's *Memoirs*. When her fortunes were at a very low ebb in 1746, she encountered Harris, who sized her up and offered to put her on his list. She had to give him an undertaking in writing that she would forfeit £20 if she had given him any false information

The title page of the 1764 edition of Jack Harris's popular publication with names, addresses and physical details of his Covent Garden Cyprians. Eight thousand copies were annually distributed to subscribers

HARRIS's LIST

OF

Covent-Garden Ladies:

OR,

NEW ATALANTIS

For the YEAR 1764.

CONTAINING,

An exact Defcription of the Perfons, Tempers, and Accomplifhments of the feveral Ladies of Pleafure who frequent COVENT-GARDEN, and other Parts of this Metropolis.

LONDON:

Printed for H. RANGER, near Temple-Bar.
MDCCLXIV.

about her health, and after she had agreed to pay him a poundage of a mere twenty-five per cent of her earnings 'her name was enrolled on his parchment' and she was eligible for membership of his Whores' Club. In 1747 he published a vignette to extol her charms – as if he was selling a horse: 'Perfectly sound in Wind and Limb. A fine Brown girl rising nineteen years next Season. A good *Side-box* Piece, she will show well in the Flesh Market and wear well. May be put off for a Virgin at any time these twelve months. Never common this side of Temple Bar but for six months. Fit for High Keeping with a Jew Merchant. NB. A good *Praemium* from the same . . . if she keeps out of the *Lock* she may make her Fortune and Ruin half the Men in Town.'

Harris claimed that he had emissaries all over the Town 'seeking always new Faces among Serving Maids and apprentice Milliners' as well as in the 'Petty Register Offices' (the employment agencies for domestic staff) and that in furtherance of his services to gentlemen he had made a trip to Dublin 'to raise some Irish recruits'. He would, moreover, 'himself teach the girls to become perfect adepts' and boasted that, 'It is entirely up to me that there is such a fine Nursery of Whores, particularly Fresh, in the Town.'

In the Harris issue of 1764 is a page advertising previous issues back to 1761 which could still be obtained from H. Ranger 'near Temple-Bar' as well as some other offerings such as *Frank Hammond's Songs for the Present Year: with the Bucks Toasts & Sentiments.* 'Price Two shillings, Bound in Red.' He offers 'The Atalantis for the years 1758 to 1763' separately from 'Harris's Lists' which is priced at 2s.6d., and also *Cupid in High Life* being a 'Select Portion of Secret History', price 1s.6d., and finally *Memoirs of Nancy Dawson to Which is Added her Jests etc.,* price one shilling. None seems to have survived.

A few samples of Harris's method and style will give an idea of his presentation.

Polly Gold. Spring Gardens. Short pretty and very agreeable as to her Person and sings a good song. Has been on the Town about ten years . . . she is like a *Kite,* sometimes high and sometimes low. She and Miss Metham are constant customers at *The Yellow Cat* near Exeter Exchange.

Poll Talbot. Bow Street, Covent Garden. A fair comely Dame who by long intercourse . . . has learnt that the profession of a Purveyor is more profitable than that of a Private Trader, and for that reason has opened a House for the amusement of genteel Company where Gentlemen and Ladies will meet with a Civil Reception. She loves the smack of the Whip sometimes . . .

Poll Davis. Manchester Square. A delicate genteel Lady of the First Fashion and Price . . . seldom to be seen in the street unless in a Sedan-chair . . . her connections are mostly with Gentlemen of Rank and Fortune . . . never less than Ten Guineas and half-a-crown for her servant.

Poll Johnson. Russell St, Covent Garden. A delicate plump girl who has various prices from ten shillings to Five Guineas according to the pocket of the *Cull.* Her principal Trade is with Petty Officers, some of whom have paid handsomely for their frolics.

Miss Bird *alias* Johnson. Brydges St, Covent Garden. A tall thin genteel girl agreeable in her manners . . . seen every night at the *Ben Jonsons Head.* She has a northern brogue and is too often in a state of intoxication.

Mrs Paterson *alias* Jackson. Haymarket. This Piece of Affectation is the daughter of a strolling Player and was for some time an actress but not having the good fortune to please . . . is entirely in her present Profession . . . returning to England was taken into keeping by a Jew whom she soon left not on account of his Religion but because the Israelite, who was not one of the richest, paid her but poorly. . . .

In addition Harris had private arrangements with local madams to 'place into High Keeping' any of the women whom he had procured; he also had similar arrangements with many of the nobility and gentry 'to find them fresh young tits straight up from the country'. One such client was Charles Wyndham, later Earl of Egremont.

In 1759 Harris ran into trouble with the law, and arising therefrom there was published a purported *Remonstrance*, setting forth 'his many Schemes in Town and Country for the Service of the Publick' in which he averred that '. . . the whole amount of the Charge against me is that I am a Pimp. I grant it. That I have executed it with uncommon Talent is also true . . . I need not be ashamed of the Profession because of its Antiquity. . . .'

This 'honourable profession' was eagerly utilized by many ladies who were to reach eminence through such advertising. One was Annabella Parsons, known to history as Nancy Parsons, adored mistress of the Duke of Grafton, who was prevented from marrying her only because of royal pressure. Another was the famous actress and dancer 'of the Jigg' Nancy Dawson, and yet another was Isabella Wilkinson, the celebrated wire-rope dancer (but only while she was 'resting' after having broken a leg), the much esteemed but capricious lover of Count Giovanni-Battista Pizzoni, the Venetian Ambassador, whose *sobriquet* was 'Wilkinson's Pizzle'.

In a two-page spread Harris extolled Betsy Davis, first mentioned in his 1764 edition and already known as 'Little-Infamy Davis', in verse:

DAVIS, a second *Circe* in her wiles
Who, Syren-like enchants ye and beguiles;
Sings, swears and riots o'er the sparkling Wine
Until she makes ye, like Ulysses – a Swine.

The Rose and *Shakespere* owe a debt to Thee
Begot by *Lewdness* upon *Infamy* . . .
Who would imagine from so mean a Thing
So fair a Face, so sweet a strum could spring?

On 18 May 1766 John Harris was buried in St Paul's, Covent Garden. The publisher H. Ranger then engaged the impecunious hack Sam Derrick to continue this valuable work. Shortly afterwards Derrick was appointed to succeed 'Beau' Nash as Master of Ceremonies at Bath, but his so-called Will implies that he was editing these lists till his death in 1769.

Harris was remembered long after his death. In the 1770 edition of his satire *The Courtesan*, Edward Thompson wrote:

> Tho' Harris out-pimps *HERMES* with the Gods
> I'll bet they beat him – and I'll lay the odds!

These Harris lists shed valuable light upon the real manners and morals of Covent Garden during his lifetime, as well as identifying men and women who would in many cases not now be known. The very use of his name in the many future publications ensured their success long after he was dead, and until almost the end of the century such directories were in great demand.

The Bedford Head Coffee-House

The Bedford Head – more often just called 'the Bedford' – had a slight edge over the other establishments in the sin-stakes because it was first licensed in 1726 to Sarah Anne Gardiner, who had been committed the previous year to the Gatehouse Prison in Westminster 'for keeping a disorderly house in the Parish of St Paul's Covent Garden'.

Because the Russell family owned almost all the property thereabouts, quite a number of inns, taverns and coffee-houses included their title in their signs – houses were not to be numbered until almost the end of the century. As early as 1702 there was the Bedford bagnio in Tavistock Street. There was a Bedford Head Tavern in Southampton Street which was leased to a brewer named Wildman in 1759 – it became known as Wildman's because it was a gambling-joint. The Bedford Head Tavern in Maiden Lane was originally an ancient inn, the Olde Welsh Ale House. (The dramatist Andrew Marvell lived next door, and two doors further down, on or near the site of present-day Rule's restaurant, was the White Wig, or White Peruke, in which Voltaire once lived.) There was the Bedford Arms in the Little Piazza, and there were other hostelries in and about the Strand using the Bedford name.

Mrs Gardiner's 'Bedford Head under the Piazza' attracted all sections of society, particularly those known as 'the Toasts' whose services were greatly in demand. Since it stood next the entrance to the Covent Garden Theatre, it became the haunt of actors and actresses, actor-managers and dramatists as well as of hordes of beaux, Fopps, Mohocks, 'persons of the quality' and anyone who pretended to wit or literature. Voltaire visited it in 1730, and when Button's closed down many of the *cognoscenti* transferred their allegiance to the Bedford, since it was said that '. . . for those so inclined there was always a Whore to be found there . . .'

The splendid *cuisine* contributed to Mrs Gardiner's popularity, receiving the accolade in 1730 when the actor-manager John Rich and the well-known painter George Lambert founded the Beefsteak Society wherein only the very finest cuts of beef were prepared. 'It was crowded every Night with Men of Parts . . . Politicos, Scholars and Wits . . . [and] every branch of Literature.' Every courtesan of note could be found there at some stage in her career, but the magnets were Betsy Careless, Sarah King and a most beautiful creature known only as 'the Kitten'.

The Kitten had first met Richard Edgecumbe at Moll King's in about 1734. He was a notorious gambler and wencher with a particular interest in music and the playhouses. When later he became Lord Mount Edgecumbe, he was regarded as a musical connoisseur. For several years the Kitten resisted all his efforts to make her his mistress but suddenly, in the middle of an *affaire* with Lord Belfield, she switched her favours to Edgecumbe. In April 1745, while spending the night with Belfield, she was taken ill and died soon afterwards. Edgecumbe's heart – so says Horace Walpole – was broken, but by July he was chasing after a friend's chambermaid and complaining bitterly about having to pay the expenses of the Kitten's funeral.

Stars like Lucy Cooper and Kitty Fredericks both made their début at the Bedford, and another *habituée* was Elizabeth 'Little Infamy' Davis, who was equally welcome at the Shakespeare's Head and was to be savagely attacked in the vicious, scandalmongering *Town and Country Magazine* in 1771 when she was a house-guest of the Duke of Rutland whose bastard son Captain John Manners was her recognized lover. The magazine charged that the Duke was 'surrounded by Bastards Whores and Parasites . . . a *fille de grace* in the character of Miss Davis joins the honourable Board'.

An even more interesting visitor was a vivacious prostitute, Peggy Lee, who (*vide* Horace Walpole) had been inscribed in Harris' List of 1746 and was *inter alia* 'Lord Lincoln's Whore'. Henry Fiennes Clinton, Earl of Lincoln, had been infatuated with Peggy for several years and she had borne him several children, the latest a lovely little girl, which inspired Walpole to compose an eclogue promising a bright and happy future for 'Little Peggy', intimating that with such a noble father she would be able successfully to follow her mother's profession.

Walpole had once driven to Peggy Lee's house in Covent Garden, asking her what was the best 'receipt' (recipe) for keeping a man. She replied that she knew 'no other way than being kept by some very rich man'. Lincoln became Duke of Newcastle in 1768 and a prominent politician but the fate of his lovely little bastard daughter is not chronicled.

Sarah Gardiner died suddenly on 12 June 1739. The premises were empty until on 1 January 1740 William Colborn became the lessee, paying rates also 'for tenants', which indicates that the rooms above were rented out to prostitutes. In 1743 the premises were leased to Richard Mitchell. Under him the coffee-house revived but he was not to enjoy his success for long because he died in 1746, whereupon his widow Mary took charge.

Mary Mitchell was no newcomer to the bagnio business: in 1734 she had been fined for keeping a disorderly house in Southampton Street and she was still carrying on there while running the Bedford after 1746. Her period of management encompassed the most brilliant and gay events ever known in Covent Garden, the Bedford became the resort of the stars from the theatres, often appearing still in their flamboyant costumes, flaunting their charms, the women displaying enticing breasts, the men 'strutting male vigour', making assignations which could be fulfilled upstairs or arranged for later, after the show. Edward Thompson's *The Demi-Rep* (1766) mentions in connection with the Bedford:

> The Town's infested with a Pack of Dames
> Burnt with the hottest meretricious Flames!

One of the most popular demi-reps was the lovely, gently bred and well-educated young Jewess Hannah Norsa, who was making her name as a singer and actress at Drury Lane. She was the daughter of Isaac Norsa who kept the Punch Bowl tavern in Drury Lane. Another frequent visitor was Moses Mendez, who was then living in Bow Street, assiduously seeking the favours of large and beautiful ladies of the chorus or from the opera. Apart from being an immensely rich bill-broker on the Exchange, he had composed several songs and even an opera. He was one of a number of English-born Jews who were often to be found on pleasure bent in the purlieus of Covent Garden, and Drury Lane in particular.

Mary Mitchell gave up the Bedford in 1757 and went back to her house in Southampton Street, where she enjoyed a reputation as a procuress of note until she died in 1787.

Her successor in 1757 was Stokes Hobster, under whose reign the house became extremely popular. In 1763 the *Memoirs of the Bedford Coffee-house* were published, the author being 'A Genius'.

(This was most likely Sam Derrick, who was often found there being treated to drinks. By such writings he could earn a little money to ease his chronic impecuniosity.) Although designed as a puff for the establishment, the work unwittingly exposes the emptiness and banality of the conversations of the so-called wits and scholars, and their crude behaviour, which (he especially remarks) including much spitting on the floor. Apart from the excessive drinking, there would be sentimental songs to start with, usually ballads extolling the joys of drink and tobacco, soon leading to bawdy ballads bordering upon the obscene, and a great deal of lavatorial humour. Despite the presence of bouncers there would always be some kind of fighting – even a stabbing – until the revellers could be persuaded to leave or be ejected.

One sample of 'scholarly conversation' is, however, of some historical interest. In a purported House of Commons debate on the merits of contraceptives, it is disclosed that Theresa Phillips in Half Moon Street was advertising them for export, her wares being of a texture superior to those of a competitor, one Solomon Moses d'Acosta 'born 1686'. Mr d'Acosta was advising the Government to regard them as a 'staple commodity'; by keeping the manufacture in their own hands, they could, he said, in a short time pay off the National Debt.

Amongst the regular visitors the 'Genius' lists Jenny Poitier, a well-known singer and comedy actress of French descent then appearing at Drury Lane. Derrick thought that the only impediment to her being a truly great actress was her accent. At the age of fifteen she had married another artiste, Joseph Vernon at the Savoy Chapel, but the marriage was annulled when it was discovered that the priest was not licensed to perform marriages. In the squabble that ensued, Vernon had to 'go into temporary exile' to Dublin but Jenny now decided upon other partners, one of whom was Lord Rochford. She appeared often on the stage under the name of Mrs Vernon and enjoyed a long professional career.

Most revealing was the confirmation that the Bedford was also a bawdy-house, 'settling the Price of the Ladies according to their different Classes as well as the Rates of their *Bagnio* Bills'. A sample expense sheet read:

Bread and Beer	2.6d
Soals and Dressing	£1.6.–
Scotch Collops	9.–
Tarts	3.–
Wine	£1.4.–

Fire	3.–	
Wax Lights	2.6d	
Ribbons for Nightcaps	5.–	
House	10.–	
Breakfast	4.6d	
Chair-hire	6.–	
Bar (repaid to Lady)	£1.1.–	Total £5.14.–

Besides the present to Madam.

This was deemed to be excessive, although Mother Douglas or Mrs Gould would have added in similar circumstances a number of 'necessary Articles' such as fees for birching instruments, luxurious foodstuffs, extra cosmetics for the ladies and anything else they could have thought of that an amorous guest might be rooked for.

Hobster's success is confirmed by an anonymous contemporary rhymster:

> Here buskin'd *Beaus* in rich lac'd Cloathes
> Like Lords and Squires do bluster;
> Bards Quacks and Cits, Knaves Fools and Wits
> An odd surprising Cluster.

These 'clusters' included such characters as the poets Alexander Pope and Charles Churchill, writers Oliver Goldsmith and Henry Fielding and actors Richard Brinsley Sheridan and David Garrick as well as such diverse wits as Dr Samuel Johnson and the permanently poverty-stricken Sam Derrick. Despite his vicissitudes, Derrick always maintained his sense of humour. One night, when the young actor Floyd was wandering about the Garden looking for somewhere to sleep, he came across Derrick fast asleep on a bulk (a wooden stall in front of a shop). When he was awakened, he murmured, 'My Dear Floyd, I'm sorry to see you in this destitute state. Will you go home with me to my lodgings?'

Of his occasional visits to the Bedford Dr Johnson was to remark that, 'When we talk of pleasure we mean sensual pleasure: when a man says that he had pleasure of a woman he does not mean conversation but something of a very different nature!', but he was careful to say that pleasure of itself was not a vice.

Some further idea of the sort of witty and serious conversation and repartee can be adduced from Adam Smith's account of his first meeting with Dr Johnson. In the ensuing argument Johnson thundered, 'You lie!' to which Smith retorted, 'And you're the son of a whore!' Johnson of course could be devastatingly witty upon occasion. When Maurice Morgan asked him whether he reckoned

Christopher Smart or Sam Derrick the better poet, Johnson replied 'Sir! There is no settling the point of precedency between a louse and a flea!' Even so, when Derrick died, in 1769, Johnson said that 'He had a kindness for Derrick and I am sorry that he is dead.'

It was in the Bedford Head that Hogarth quarrelled with the poet Charles Churchill and where in 1766 the precocious young rake, William Hickey, then only fourteen years old, went with his sexual teacher Nanny Harris, who was living in a nearby little alley off Bow Street.

Stokes Hobster died in 1775 and his widow Mary managed the business until 1778, when Stephen Kinsey became leaseholder. A great tragedy occurred in the following year when the lovely Martha Rae, long-time mistress of Lord Sandwich (and the mother of his nine children), was shot dead by young James Hackman when she was coming out of the next-door theatre. Hackman had been hanging about in the lobby of the Bedford Head for some hours previously. Weeping, and overcome with remorse, Hackman was arrested by the constables there.

The coffee-house was still operating in 1785, when considerable repairs had to be done 'to that part of the messuage called The Bedford Coffee House', and the last record is in 1790 when it was leased to John Wallis, who in 1804 assigned his lease to one Robert Toy, a licensed victualler, with the curious stipulation that Toy 'may have so much of the late *Shakespeare Head Tavern* as now laid to the said *Bedford* coffee-house, without payment'.

The Bedford Arms

At the far end of the Little Piazza, adjoining the hummums, lay the Bedford Arms, often confused with the Bedford Head and enjoying an equally poor reputation. The Bedford Arms was a tavern with a number of rooms overhead, ostensibly for the use of travellers, but it was generally conceded that these rooms were used by light ladies and their friends. It abutted on Tavistock Row, and indeed in after years when it became a hotel it was often referred to as 1 Tavistock Row. It was conveniently adjacent to Matthew Lovejoy's infamous bagnio and to Elizabeth Gould's rather more up-market bordel.

From 1710 until 1727 it was leased to William Luffingham, who was in some way connected with the stage. He was 'assisted by Mary Furness'; the exact nature of the assistance is unclear but may

One of the several small kiosks about the Piazza which remained open long
after neighbouring shops had closed. They sold not only souvenirs but also a
wide variety of items including quack medicines and contraceptives, as well
as obscene prints

be inferred from the fact that some years previously she had been convicted and sent to jail for disorderly conduct.

The tavern's real history began when Richard and Mary Mitchell took it over in 1729 and re-named it the Bedford Arms. Mary Mitchell had been one of Moll King's particular cronies. The Mitchells ran 'a House of Civilitie' in Southampton Street and maintained it all through their long careers. In 1743 they also took over the Bedford Head in the Piazza.

Subsequently a man named Charles Sommer leased the premises 'for tenants' until in 1751 John Venables – who had other properties in the Garden – took over and the hostelry again came into the news. It would seem, however, that the Mitchells still maintained an interest in the establishment because in 1756 the poet Thomas Legg in his *Covent Garden Satyre* wrote:

> . . . paint the charms
> Of Mitchell of *The Bedford Arms*:
>
> Behold – a Room both long and neat
> Where Men of mix'd conditions meet,
> Each degree from Lords to Cits,
> From authors down to puny Wits.

John Venables gave way in 1761 to John Streating, whose manager was a local celebrity named Hartley, but in 1765 Richard Stacie became the lessee, and the Bedford Arms became famous as one of Covent Garden's sin-shops. *The Meretriciad* (1765) said that it owed much to the greater charms of Lucy Cooper but it was not only Lucy's appeal that brought in the customers. A whole bevy of fashionable pulchritude gathered there, including the up-and-coming beauty Charlotte Hayes, who was later to be dubbed 'Santa Carlotta' when she became 'abbess' of the most prestigious 'nunnery' in King's Place, St James.

In his youth Dick Stacie had been a successful jockey and was reputed to have won about £8000 on the turf which enabled him to take over the tavern. The famous comedian Henry Woodward, who was a racing enthusiast, spent most of his leisure hours there, as did such celebrities as Oliver Goldsmith, the brothers Fielding, Charles Churchill and Hogarth. Stacie also ran a Gossipers' Shilling Club for whist players, which was probably a cover for off-course betting, besides being a *bona-fide* cards club.

Another welcome client was the immensely rich playboy Robert Coates, known as 'Cock-a-doodle-doo Coates' for his crowing when winning and as 'Romeo Coates' for his amorous adventures. The son of an Antiguan planter, he spent his whole life in London as a dilettante actor and poet. His extravagances were legendary, as also were his contributions to charity, and in the end he was saved from bankruptcy only by making a composition with his creditors. His end was as dramatic as his life – he was knocked over and killed outside the Bedford Arms (by then known as the Imperial Hotel) in 1848 by a hansom-cab.

One extraordinary person who divided his time between both the Bedford hostelries and who was usually unwelcome in both of them was the unsavoury Captain David Roche of the Madras Regiment. A small, dark, scowling, Irish swashbuckling bully, he lived by his wits after he had been 'broken for cowardice' while on service in India. *En route* to India in 1773 he killed a fellow officer in a duel in Cape Town, for which, on return to Britain, he was tried and acquitted of murder. Thereafter he wore a black patch over one cheek. He attached himself to John Wilkes, especially during Wilke's quarrel with Colonel Luttrell, and organized a band of roughnecks to disrupt Luttrell's meetings, during one of which he fired on some demonstrators. After this he was known as 'Tiger' Roche (or Roach). He was also nicknamed 'Captain of the Lumber-troopers' (hooligans). In April 1769, the Bedford Arms having been just burnt down, he patronized the Bedford Head Coffee-House where, having drunkenly tried to bully one of the bystanders, (who happened to be a boxer), he was 'completely discomfited and shown to be a coward'. Wilkes' friends, who had actually egged him on, were greatly pleased thus to have got rid of him. He died in prison in September 1779, aged only thirty-nine and universally execrated.

There were other hazards. In June 1768 William Hickey was in the Shakespeare's Head when Tomkyns warned him that he was in danger. He finished his tea and with his two female companions, Elizabeth 'Priscilla' Vincent and Mary Newton, and a casual acquaintance named Jennings went 'on his way back to Stacie's' but he was knocked down in the street and robbed, receiving considerable head injuries, waking up in the notorious Cross Keys Tavern in Little Russell Street.

Disaster struck the hostelry in March 1769 when the hummums caught fire and the whole row of properties in the little Piazza was totally destroyed, the façade, falling down with a mighty crash. After the houses had been rebuilt by John Henry Rigg, Richard Stacie handed over the lease to his son John.

Fire was one of the greatest hazards: a few years previously Fielding had remarked from the Bench that, 'There was a great scarcity of water; an evil generally met with at fires as well as the absence of turn-cocks.' He recommended that more pipes should be laid on from the main with turn-cocks in cases affixed to the wall of each house marked 'TURN COCK . . . wrote in large characters. . . . If householders would paint their names on their fire buckets they might be more willing to bring them out . . .' Moreover, the plugs on the fire-engines often did not fit the turn-cocks, because each fire insurance company had its own engines and its own turn-cocks. After this great fire, new 'universal' fire plugs were fitted in Covent Garden in 1769. The maximum cover for a brick-built house was then £2,000 at a deposit of 12s. plus 4s. premium per cent per annum, but it was double that rate for timber houses, with the maximum still remaining at £2,000.

Drama too was not lacking. One evening in August 1776 the Honourable John Damer, eldest son and heir to the miserly Lord Milton, 'supped at *The Bedford Arms* with four common Whores and a blind Fiddler and no other man. At three in the Morning he dismissed his *Seraglio*, bidding each to receive her Guinea at the bar and told the Fiddler to come back in half-an-hour. When he came back he found Mr Damer on his chair, dead, with a Pistol in his hand.' He left a note: 'The people of this House are not to blame.' A contemporary observed that John Damer 'had passed his life as he had died, with troops of Women and blind Fiddlers'. He was only thirty-two years old and seemingly happily married to the charming Lady Jane Seymour.

Suicide was not uncommon at that time among the nobility. Hard drinking, endless debauch and mindless gambling resulted in complete *ennui*; in some cases a severe venereal disease and the ghastly 'cures' were enough to drive a man to suicide. Doctors such as Jean Misaubin MD with his constant cry of 'Prenez les pillules' and quacks like 'Doctor' Richard Rock made themselves rich on the sufferings of both rich and poor. Misaubin was a Huguenot, a son of a pastor at the Spitalfields church. He had a genuine MD degree but a thirst for money. After his son was murdered, Misaubin's great fortune was eventually dissipated by his grandson, who died in St Martin's workhouse – not very far from his grandfather's original residence. Constant blood-letting by leeches, advocated by most doctors as a cure-all, weakened the constitution and the will to live.

John Stacie enjoyed very good repute, being generally known as 'Honest Jack' and he carried on until about 1789. In 1800 the premises were rebuilt and converted and became the Imperial Hotel – and even later the New Hummums Hotel and the Bedford Arms was by then long forgotten. 'Honest Jack' died at the age of seventy-six on 14 March 1815.

The Ben Jonson's Head

Three pretty *gamines* emerged from the slums of Covent Garden to make their fortunes as high-class harlots, aiming to occupy the places left vacant by the death of Betsy Careless and the withdrawal from public life of Fanny Murray.

One of them, Nancy Jones, struck misfortune before she was nineteen by catching smallpox, which ruined her pretty face and her health and reduced her to abject poverty. When, at the age of twenty-five, she caught syphilis from one of her noble customers, she died within a few weeks in the Lock Hospital and was buried in a pauper's grave.

Charlotte Hayes was not only pretty and witty but also a clever organizer, and after she married Captain Denis O'Kelly, owner of the unbeatable racehorse 'Eclipse' and mixed in high society – while continuing her 'nunnery' – she died at a very great age in the palatial mansion of the Duke of Chandos.

The third of the trio, Lucy Cooper was to enjoy the greatest success and acclaim as 'Perfection' in the annals of the 'Great Impures' of Covent Garden. She was born in the Garden about 1733 to poor parents, probably criminals. The Westminster Sessions Register for May 1737 records the widow Mrs Elizabeth Cooper living in Tavistock Street, being sent for correction for keeping a disorderly house, being drunk and disorderly and misbehaving. In addition she was charged with assault. Lucy's earliest years are unchronicled and were certainly hard, but she was not only pretty, with a sharp faculty for witty repartee, but also had that indefinable quality of charisma which made men her abject slaves. She was an irrepressible madcap: wherever she was, there was always much noise and merriment and overmuch drink.

By the time she was fourteen, Lucy was carrying a basket of fruit about the market, blossoming into a great beauty. It was about this time that Moll King was giving up and an energetic woman named Elizabeth Weatherby (or Wetherby) was beginning to operate a low-class dive called the Ben Jonson's Head in Little Russell Street, which was generally known as Weatherby's. She befriended the young girl, who thereafter seems to have regarded her as a surrogate mother. Weatherby's aspired to attract as much of Moll King's former clientele as possible and was quickly to be crowded with 'all the Rakes, Gamesters, Swindlers, Highwaymen, Pickpockets and Whores'. It also drew many of the 'Gentlemen of the Quality' and amongst them was the well-known rakehell Sir Orlando Bridgeman, a rich baronet and member of the Hell-Fire set. Sir Orlando was much smitten with young Lucy: by him, said *The Meretriciad*, she was 'exalted from a Basket to a Coach'. Nevertheless, Weatherby's was her background and despite all vicissitudes her name was to be indissolubly linked with it.

Because the entrance fee to the Ben Jonson's Head was just the price of a cup of Capuchin coffee, 'a great number of Venus's Votaries attended . . . to serve all Ranks and Conditions, from the Chariot-kept Mistress down to the *Two-penny Bunters* who ply under the Piazza . . . the unfortunate Strumpet who had been starving in a Garrett all day long while washing her only and last *Shift*, upon making her appearance at *Wheatherby's* might probably meet up with a green-horn Apprentice boy . . . if his Finances were in a proper plight he might be induced to tip her Eighteen-pence worth of *Punch* . . . and then be deluded to go to a *Horse-pond bagnio* . . . for the remainder of the Night . . .'

Orlando Bridgeman's generosity to his protégée was unbounded and Lucy's extravagances included unlimited food and drink for all who might be in Weatherby's at the time. Even so, she did not claim, or, indeed, intend to be faithful to him; among her conquests were the actor John Palmer, the poet Charles Churchill and John Calcraft, and she often accommodated such penniless friends as Sam Derrick. Her sexual appetite elicited from the *Meretriciad* a eulogy that she was

> Lewder than all the Whores in Charles' reign;
> But that and more, in thee, Lucy, she's excused . . .
> At fam'd Bob Derry's where the Harlots throng
> My MUSE has listen'd to thy luscious Song
> And heard thee swear like worser Drury's *Punk* . . .
> Cit, Soldier, Sailor or some bearded Jew
> In triumph, reeling, bore thee to some *Stew*.

When relations between Mrs Weatherby and Lucy were a little strained, she would hold court in the Shakespeare's Head or the Bedford Arms, being the life and soul of the party, but before long she would always be back in Mrs Weatherby's affectionate embrace.

Then in 1764 disaster struck: Orlando Bridgeman died, and according to *The Meretriciad* (1765);

> When Bridgeman made his last dear WILL and groan,
> A good Annuity was then thy own –
> With this Proviso – that you'd rake no more
> Nor play the vagrant mercenary Whore . . .

Whether this is true or not, Lucy still continued her way of life, so that any such proviso was ignored and any such benefit became void. But then disaster struck again. Mrs Weatherby died in 1765, and without her ever-protective embrace Lucy was lost. She was also deep in debt, because she had ignored the cardinal principle that harlots spend only their customers' money. She began to drift downwards, firstly to the Golden Cat at Charing Cross and then to Bob Derry's infamous Cyder Cellar in Maiden Lane. A contemporary visitor said he had gone to be entertained but 'found a scene of Confusion, drunkenness and stupidity . . . the many prostitutes . . . were like so many dressed-up Carcasses in the Shambles [the public slaughterhouse in Newgate Street] . . . drinking away to keep up their spirits'.

The Cyder Cellar contributed to Lucy's undoing, for one evening in 1765 there was a dreadful fracas there in which two Jews, 'a Bobwig and Beau', were murdered. The constables threw all the rioters into the Roundhouse, taking Lucy, 'the captive Queen', into custody to await the Bow Street magistrate next morning. Because she was deemed partly responsible for the fracas, she was sent to prison, which occasioned the following elegy:

> Fat Weatherby's sunk now in eternal sleep;
> Weep, weep, my Lucy, Wheatherby's no more . . .

Indeed, she now had cause to weep. Her drunkenness and intemperate speech had alienated many who otherwise might have come to her rescue. In prison she was in dire plight, and it was in this situation that Tomkyns inspired Hickey and his friends to make their whip-round in 1766.

One source says that when Lucy was released she opened up a bagnio in Bond Street but could not make it pay, and it was clear that by now drink and dissipation had destroyed her beauty and her charm. Her debtors pursued her and put her into a debtors' prison. Here, once more, the *Meretriciad* (1770) fills in a gap:

> Usher, Orlando, Weatherby, are gone,
> In dismal Sackcloth . . .
> But O! my luscious dissipated Wench
> How come ye lately to the close *Kings Bench*?
>
> Was it the *Mercer* for a load of Silks?
> Or a desire to live with *Honest Wilkes*?
> But now thou're out I cannot call the Fool
> To put so great a value on thy *Tool*.

119

Thou art the *Tennis-ball* of Drury Lane,
For ev'ry stroke you get, you rise again;
Yet don't rebound so very strong, to rise
Next to that Parlour nearest to the skies . . .'

John Taylor's *Records of my Life* recalled that in his youth William Donaldson had two houses in Turnham Green 'one of which was let to a lady more celebrated in the regions of promiscuous Gallantry when Fanny Murray and Kitty Fisher were her chief rivals . . . this Fair and Faded tenant . . . retained traces of a Face not strikingly handsome but of interesting Languour . . . her Figure of middle size . . . at this time retired for many years from public life with an annuity which enabled her to live comfortably at Turnham Green'. She had 'a good-looking young man in the house with her . . . who looked like a clergyman', and he confirmed that she was an ailing woman. In fact, Donaldson's was a 'spunging-house'.

Lucy certainly had no annuity and was living from hand to mouth, hoping that some good friend would spring her from this prison-adjunct. In the event, in 1769, 'after a long confinement, being left without friends or money and now destitute of beauty and past the time when youth supplied the place a charm', she was released, and no more is heard of her until the notification of her death on 10 October 1772, in dire poverty and buried in a pauper's grave.

Weatherby's other scintillating star was Betsy Weems, Lucy's friend and rival and an offshoot of the noble Scots family of that name. (The chroniclers had difficulty in spelling her name – she is Weems, Wheemes, even Wymes.) She had only one eye, having lost the other in some fracas early in life, and had an artificial eye, which did not detract from her beauty – indeed she was known as 'the Wall-ey'd Beauty' or 'Wall-Ey'd Betty' and she would make great play with this artificial optic by dropping it sometimes to create a diversion or compelling her *inamorato* to go on hands and knees scrabbling in the sand or sawdust on the floor. She and Lucy were of similar temperament, sharp-tongued and quick witted, fond of practical jokes. They frequented the same haunts and shared the same clients.

A ballad about 1760, sung to the tune of *Kitty, Beautiful and Young*, goes:

Bet Wymes, of WEDDERBY'S the Pride
By bailiffs yet untam'd
Bespoke *Moll* Fulgame by her side
With Lust and Rage inflam'd!

The rage was supposedly directed against her stablemate, Lucy at a time when trade was poor, and there is a revealing stanza in a lewd ballad published in *The Gentleman's Bottle Companion*:

> Must Lucy Cooper bear the *Bell*
> And give herself such airs?
> Must that damnation *Bitch of Hell*
> Be haugh'd by Knights and Squires? . . .
> That all Mankind with her do lye
> While I have scarce a *Cull*?

That rivalry was soon over, for Betsy Weems died before the end of 1765 and Lucy's paramountcy was unchallenged, although there were some others in the Ben Jonson's Head being advertised by Harris in the 1764 list. The tavern was in reality a place of last resort comparable in infamy to the Rose.

One young 'tit' making a name was Polly Talbot, 'always lively and on call' and picked out in *The Meretriciad* (1765):

> See TALBOT now, who drank with pomp of Sin
> Thro' wretched want, a sad, sad Magdalene,

but in 1773 the Harris List describes her as a 'smart lascivious Lass, altho' too fond of strong waters which occasions her to riotous behaviour'. She lived in Martlet Court off Bow Street, whence she was later picked up by Old Q – Britain's most famous lecher, William Douglas, Marquess of Queensberry – who after a while 'dismissed her for this frailty'.

Best known of all frequenters was the glamorous young beauty Elizabeth Thomas, dubbed 'the Queen of the Garden', who quickly disappeared from sight 'into high keeping' and was not further mentioned.

On Mrs Weatherby's death John Roberts took over the management. He had earlier been in the Covent Garden pillory 'for keeping a Bad House'. Small wonder then that in March 1768 Hickey could describe it as 'an absolute Hell on Earth'. He gave a rare first-hand account of the place, saying that the front door was secured with iron bars and knobs as also was the small wicket.

Upon ringing at the door . . . a cut-throat looking Rascal
asked in a hoarse voice 'Who's there?'. Being answered
'Friends!' we were admitted one at a time, when the door
was instantly closed and secured by an immense lock and
key . . . the room was in an uproar . . . men and women promiscuously
mounted on chairs tables and benches . . . (the better to see)
a sort of conflict on the floor. Two she-devils engaged in
a scratching boxing match, their faces entirely covered

with blood, bosoms bare and their clothes nearly all
torn from their bodies. . . . Nobody cared a straw what mischief
they might do to each other, and the contest went on with
unabated fury till both were exhausted . . . in another corner
three Amazonian tigresses were pummelling a young man
with all their might. . . .

The tavern was much patronized by Ned Shuter, the comedian,
'who had been the lover of the dancer Nancy Dawson'. This takes
the story right back to Moll King's.

Nancy Dawson and Friends

The extraordinary thing about Nancy Dawson is that this little,
vulgar, comic actress is even after more than two centuries unwittingly remembered every day when children sing 'Here we go
round the Mulberry Bush'.

She was born about 1730 'within a Musket-shot of Clare Market'
a sleazy, dismal enclave off the Strand near St Clement's Church,
notorious for being a nest of homosexuals and their Mollies houses
as well as of a diverse collection of criminals. Her father, described
as 'a pimp and porter', was a shiftless rogue named Emanuel
Dawson. Her mother sold greengrocery from a stall in Covent
Garden. She is most probably that Anne Dawson who was working in 1717 in one of Richard Haddock's bagnios and who, in 1724,
was taken in a raid on another of his bagnios masquerading as a
coffee- and chocolate-house in Exeter Street together with Haddock's manageress (and successor) Sophia Lemoy and the well-
known courtesan Betsy Saunders.

Nancy's parents died when she was very young and she was
adopted by a staymaker in Martlet Court, Covent Garden, named
William Newton and his wife, Eleanor, but she was a pretty,
vivacious child who before she was sixteen, says a contemporary,
was going about in every tavern and coffee-house, picking up a
good deal of pence by 'showing her tricks'. For a while she was
employed by an itinerant puppet-master, William Griffin but deserted him to set up skittles in a Covent Garden tavern, where she
met 'a Figure-dancer from Sadlers Wells' and herself took to the
stage. 'She gave convincing proofs of prodigious and amazing
abilities – she danced, she tumbled, she sang, she played the tabor
and the pipe.' By these exertions she charmed the audiences, who
used to throw handfuls of silver to her. In this way she earned
between 10 and 12 shillings a night. She set herself up in a garret in

Nancy Dawson: a famous dancer and singer at Drury Lane who 'danced the jigg to smutty songs' and reached immortal fame for 'Here we go round the Mulberry bush'

Drury Lane, for which she paid the exorbitant sum of 7 shillings a week, but this was no problem because,

> Now Nan was a Free Port of Trade
> For every Vessel to unlade
> And whoever came to her
> French, Dutch, Italians, pimps or Peice
> 'twas, Si Signor, 'twas Ja Mynheer,
> 'twas S'il vous plait, Monsieur.

She used to frequent Mrs Weatherby's bordello, playing the tabor and the drum but because she was so saucy and precocious the whores resented her. She would go to Bob Derry's Cyder Cellar where the men would ply her with drink until she often got 'tearing drunk'. By many she was considered to be 'next to Miss Lucy Cooper as the first lady of the house'. The old termagant Moll King took a fancy to her and remained friendly to her all her life. At 'Tom's' she met all the principal actors and actresses from the nearby theatres. The 'Figure-dancer from Sadlers Wells' arranged for her to dance there occasionally, although it was remarked that she was still 'little known beyond the neighbouring Bawdy-houses, Taverns and Whores' lodgings'. At Sadler's Wells she was liked for her jovial sprightliness and good nature.

In February 1758 Nancy was lucky enough to attract the attention of the actor-manager Ned Shuter and began to dance 'Jiggs' at Covent Garden Theatre and sing the accompaniments. 'Jiggs' were specially scripted ballads for two or more actors singing a cross-dialogue of a lewd nature with lascivious gestures and dancing. Ben Jonson described Jiggs as concupiscent, and Thomas Dekker called them 'nastie and bawdy Jigges' but they were immensely popular with the audiences, being performed after the end of the play as a sort of *bonne bouche* to send them home happy. They often brought a measure of fame to the performers. In 1612 King James I – himself no prude – was compelled to promulgate an 'Order for Suppressing Jigges' because of their lewdness, and also because of the presence of cut-purses and pickpockets and hooligans causing 'tumultes and outrages'. Nonetheless, they continued and never lost their popularity.

By now, Nancy, being regarded as a heartless mercenary and shrewish whore was living in fashionable Manchester Square with a popular young courtesan named Polly Kennedy, 'well-known for fleecing her customers'. She too was an actress at Drury Lane from 1745 and occasionally thereafter; her last appearances were between 1773 and 1774.

In 1759 Nancy was dancing the hornpipe in John Gay's *The Beggars' Opera* at Sadler's Wells, and her performance was acclaimed by all for its lascivious and provocative dancing: she became famous overnight.

Ned Shuter then enticed her away to Drury Lane, and in September 1760 she began to dance there. However, she was still to be found regularly 'playing the whore' at the Rose, the Bedford Head and Maltby's Coffee-House in the Piazza. Then, it is said, Ned Shuter wrote: 'Dear Nancy, thou has been long enough a hackney-jade; come out and shelter in the warm stable of my arms . . . as housekeeper', and she took up her abode with him in Manchester Square together with Polly. She was then 'enroll'd amongst the stage Nymphs' and in 1760 again danced the hornpipe, this time at Covent Garden. Her success was assured, and by 1761 *The Ballad of Nancy Dawson* was all the rage. The tune was 'Here we go round the Mulberry Bush' and the words went as follows:

> Of all the girls in Town
> The Black, the Fair, the Red and Brown
> That dance and prance it up and down
> There's none like NANCY DAWSON.
>
> Yet vainly she each heart alarms
> With all Love's hoard of heavenly charms;
> She's only for NED SHUTER'S arms
> The smiling Nancy Dawson.

In April and May 1761 Nancy had benefit performances at Drury Lane 'at the request and desire of His Excellency the Aga Hamid, the Tripolitanian Ambassador'. (His Excellency was simul-taneously negotiating the terms of concubinage with the delectable opera-singer Elizabeth Gambarini, who was much in demand else-where.) The Aga ensured that adequate numbers of tickets would be sold to guarantee Nancy's financial success.

Meanwhile the house in Manchester Square was burned down, and between 1763 and 1765 Nancy and Polly shared a house in Bedford Street, Covent Garden, in which favoured visitors were welcomed. Amongst these was Prince Henry Frederick, Duke of Cumberland, a vulgar, noisy, indelicate but intrepid and gay little man, the most foolish of 'Poor Fred's' sons. (His indiscriminate *amours* involved him in 1769 in an unsavoury case of 'criminal conversation' with Lady Henrietta Grosvenor.) Nonetheless, despite Nancy's very considerable revenues from such rich and influential gentlemen, she sought more money in the Harris List for 1764, when she and Polly were also flaunting their wares in Matthew Lovejoy's bagnio in the Little Piazza.

Although the Manchester Square house had been rebuilt, Nancy had moved over to the more salubrious heights of Hampstead, leaving Polly as Ned Shuter's mistress and still sharing his bed occasionally while appearing on the stage. The *Meretriciad* (1765) remarked that she was 'still tripping it merrily . . . despite her obesity'. By this time she was in failing health. Shortly afterwards she left the stage (later claiming that she had retired prematurely) and she died on 27 May 1767.

In her Will, as Anne Dawson, 'living at Averstock Hill', she left a very considerable estate: £50 each to her brother William and his daughter Elizabeth, to the latter only 'if she behave herself in a prudent manner and marries a man of Good Character', and to her old chum Polly Kennedy 'a furnish'd house in King Street, Covent Garden'.

Nancy's memory was kept alive by the publication the following year of *Nancy Dawson's Choyce Ditties*, the sub-title declaring that these were her 'famous Smutty Songs'. The smut was mainly lavatorial, only a few ditties being sexually suggestive. They were songs designed to be sung to male audiences who could join in the choruses. The book ran into several editions. *The Ballad of Nancy Dawson* was played at the funeral of the famous General Sir Eyre Coote in Madras in 1783

The 'buxsome and very handsome' Polly Kennedy (whose maiden name was the prosaic one of Jones) stayed on in Manchester Square and, although by now Ned Shuter's acknowledged mistress, continued her career as a highly successful courtesan, one of her most assiduous clients being Frederick, Viscount Bolingbroke, 'a profligate tawdry fellow . . . who boasted that he could seduce any innocent girl whatever'. She also satisfied the sexual needs of that 'young comely and dissolute Divine' the Reverend William Dodd DD, LLD, who was for a time the King's chaplain. He was known as 'the Macaroni Preacher' because of his ultra-foppish dress and behaviour. Polly took his death, by hanging at Tyburn in 1777, like all the other hazards of her trade, with 'equanimity and fortitude'.

Like her old friend Nancy, Polly was avid for money. In 1773 her name appears in the Harris List, in which she is described as 'Our Modern *Thaïs*', still in business and well considered, living in Great Russell Street and having another residence on Shooters Hill. The advertisement gives a real description of her person and character: 'Has a very snug annuity besides a number of very pretty things called Diamonds and Plate, etc., etc., . . . she never knew what

Love is – she has no heart susceptible to that Passion. When she holds you in her arms she thinks she beholds a Diamond Ring, a Necklace, an *Aigrette* or other Bauble. In person she is a fine woman, rather too lusty and going downhill, brown hair, middling teeth, tolerable complexion – but she has made her Market and cares not what we or anyone else can say – it has served her turn.' As to her relationship with Ned Shuter, Harris retails an occasion when Polly invited him to dinner and he then stayed overnight. Early in the morning her maid came into the bedroom, all breathless, saying that, 'A Mantua-maker has called, for an immediate fitting', whereupon Polly nipped downstairs and accommodated the gentleman on the sofa in the dining-room, in this way making up 'for the loss of her night with Ned.'

In June 1781 it was announced that 'Miss Polly Kennedy, *alias* Jones, Courtesan' had died. She was only about fifty years old.

8. Mother Jane Douglas, 'The Empress'

By far the most famous of all madams in the kingdom after the demise of Elizabeth Needham in 1732 was the woman known as Jane Douglas, operating from a high-class establishment in the north-east corner of the Piazza.

She was born about 1700 to a respectable Edinburgh family, her maiden name being Marinet. She had three sisters and at least one brother, but Jane was the only one to go to London to seek her fortune. When and why she adopted the name of Douglas cannot be ascertained but she was known by that name when she arrived. She was already a professional harlot by the time she was about seventeen, operating from a house in St James, Piccadilly. She was then 'a tall straight genteel woman with a clear complexion and a dignified comportment'. John Gay, who knew her, eulogized her as 'that inimitable Courtesan'.

In the St James house '. . . she entertained Princes, Peers and Men of the highest Rank . . . and also Women of the highest Rank . . . who came *incognito* . . . the utmost secrecy being preserv'd. . . .' She was already a procuress, her young ladies 'all chosen for their elegance, sweetness of disposition and sexual expertise'. The house was very well furnished, and fine meals were served by liveried flunkeys. The informant, one of her ex-employees, also remarked that the clients 'were all fleec'd in proportion to their Wealth and Dignity'. Some part of her success must be attributed to her intimate friendship with the young John Williams (later Viscount Milton and first Earl of Fitzwilliam), although she had other equally important paramours.

For some as yet unexplained reason Jane moved in 1735 to a house in the Little Piazza, previously occupied by one of the Du Bois painter brothers, under the sign of the Three Chairs, on the corner with Russell Street. She likewise furnished it with the

Hogarth's March to Finchley *(1750, detail). Mother Douglas and her 'Cattery' at the King's Head, Tottenham Court Road, are cheering the troops who are leaving for an encounter with supporters of Bonnie Prince Charlie. Mother Douglas (bottom window on the right) is praying for the safe return of 'her Babes of Grace'*

utmost elegance. One great advantage was the presence of lovely but ill-paid young actresses from the nearby theatres who had to supplement their meagre earnings with part-time whoring. One such was Peg Woffington, who often 'sacrificed there at the altar of Venus' when she was hard up.

Covent Garden was excellent for business but there were some drawbacks, one being the rowdiness and drunkenness of the crowds milling about by day and half the night, and the riotous behaviour of the bucks and beaux who used her establishment. Amongst them were Lord George Graham (the Duke of Montrose' brother), the Honourable John Spencer (grandson of the Duchess of Marlborough) and the Honourable James Stewart, who one evening when leaving her premises beat up a number of girls, creating such havoc that the constables arrested everyone in sight. The 'poor women' who were their companions were thrown into the cage; the gentlemen were, naturally, not further troubled.

This incident caused some trouble for Mrs Douglas, who managed to bribe her way out of actual imprisonment. By good chance other and more desirable premises became available when poor Betsy Careless had to move out of her house under the Piazza. In 1741 Mrs Douglas moved into the King's Head and went on to her greatest triumphs. It was a very large and commodious house with a large garden abutting on the rear of the theatre; it had piped water into the basement as well as a room which could be used as a closet or privy. (Up to that time it was amongst the whore's duties to proffer a chamberpot to her guest; the chambermaid would then empty it elsewhere.) The honoured guest could now perform his natural functions in privacy, if he so wished. Later, in 1746, she made great improvements by renewing the roof and chimneypots and the fine staircases and had the piped water extended 'from the side of the house through lead pipes into the garden and a newly constructed drain' to the privy and cesspool. This was a great step forward. (Incidentally, in the document detailing this event occurs for the first and last time the shadowy Mr Douglas – the bill was made out to him!)

Jane Douglas then furnished the house with the best furniture and *objets d'art* available, Old Masters in heavy gold frames, fine carpets, fine china and glass – everything deemed necessary for a seraglio of the highest class and greatest luxury. There was an excellent restaurant with first-class food and wines and liveried lackeys to serve the exigent guests – and of course the finest choice of lovely ladies to accommodate every whim. A regular client was HRH Prince William, Duke of Cumberland, whom she always addressed as 'Great Sir'. He showed his appreciation of her services by giving her some massive silver plate, thereafter displayed on her sideboard and referred to as 'Billy's Bread Baskets'.

Moreover the house was extensively patronized by army officers home-based or on leave from foreign services, and even more important by the captains of the East Indiamen who were wont to reward Jane Douglas and her young ladies with expensive silks, 'chintzes and damasks and glittering China' as well as jewels and money. This occasioned a spiteful remark from Mother Haywood who declared that, 'If a Dogg was to come into [Mrs Douglas' house] from India, she would give it a fine dinner in acknowledgement of the many handsome presents she had received, and the many Long Bills paid to her by Christians who come from those Parts!'

Amongst her customers were the famous wits and writers of the day. Hogarth frequently sat in a corner quietly drawing his characters from life around him. He immortalized her in *The March to Finchley* (she can be seen on the right of the picture), and Thomas Burke's engraving *A Constable's Ramble* (1762) depicts her finely apparelled, with rings on all her fingers, in company with the up-and-coming young Scottish courtesan Betsy Weems and six men.

Mrs Douglas claimed that the great physician Dr Richard Meade visited her house 'once a year and always spent a hundred Guineas . . . his great Delight was to have a number of wretched women dance naked before him'. (By this time it would seem that the aged doctor had been reduced to voyeurism instead of the action he had enjoyed in Mrs Whyburn's many years before!)

She was mindful of the good health of her distinguished guests and supplied them with prophylactics. She bought 'at Wholesale . . . *cundums*' from J. Jacobs, 'Salvator & Cundum-maker' in Oliver's Alley in the Strand. These she sold 'at a very high profit' at retail to her clients, all nicely decked out in a silken bag tied with ribbons. She also sold such aphrodisiac nostrums as Doctor Jean Misaubin's *pillules* prepared by this famous quack at the Green Hatch & One Lamp in Holborn.

Mrs Douglas tried hard to keep an honest household: when the actor Robert Winter complained that his watch had been stolen, she quickly apprehended the thief and dismissed her. In contrast, some of her wealthiest clients must have bilked her. When in 1749 her famous namesake Lady Jane Douglas (with whom she was often confused) sued in the King's Bench Division to have her name cleared, Lord Chief Justice Mansfield, doubting the veracity of some witnesses, observed '. . . that the noted Mrs Douglas had brought an Action against several Gentlemen of Distinction for non-payment of Tavern Bills contracted in her house . . . we are not to imagine that they have come off without discharging their Reckonings with her. . . .'

From time to time 'her honest peaceful trading' was interrupted by Sir John Gonson's anti-vice squads, but she usually managed to get away with a fine; although on one or two occasions she had to spend a short time in prison, by judicious bribery none of these spells was long or too unpleasant. In 1759, however, she was involved with Jack Harris in a nasty affair when both came before Mr Justice Saunders Welch charged with 'procuring a young girl for a Gentleman . . . and taking poundage from her'. The chronicler went on to say that 'the Veteran Abbess of the Piazza, by finding Bail, preserv'd her liberty' although Harris was sent to jail. At this time the poet Thomas Legg in his ballad *Covent Garden* put in a stanza:

> Dear DOUGLAS still maintains her Ground
> EMPRESS of all the Bawds around.
> (Where *Innocence* is often sold
> For *Hard Cash* – for shining sordid *Gold*.)
> By *Craft* she draws th' unwary in
> And keeps a *Publick House* of Sin!

Further advantages to her honest trading were the alley alongside her house, which was the entrance to John Rich's Opera House in Bow Street, and the proximity of the Shakespeare's Head right next door, which was a rich source of constant customers.

There were, of course, some traumas. About 1746 it was complained that, although her house was patronized by the highest in the land, '. . . the *Demi-reps* of an inferior class now resorted thither', and Sir Charles Hanbury Williams – admittedly no friend of Mrs Douglas, described it as 'a *Cattery* of which the Principal Figure is a noted fat Covent Garden lady, *Mother* Douglas . . . a great flabby stinking swearing hollowing ranting Billingsgate Bawd, very well known to most Men of Quality and Distinction in these Kingdoms, *Bawd* to all the World in general and *Whore* to Lord Fitzwilliam in particular . . .', although he had to confess that she was a very good-looking woman. Clearly drink and debauchery had taken toll of the erstwhile slender, genteel beauty of St James.

There was, however, another trauma: Hanbury Williams and Horace Walpole were engaged in an anxious and protracted corres-

pondence as to whether Mrs Douglas' expected child by Fitzwilliam should be named Charles – or indeed whether he should
even recognize the bastard at all. Hanbury Williams' witty *Eclogue*
speculated upon all the possibilities, forgetting that Mother Douglas was quite able to look after any child of her own, since she was a
rich woman too.

By 1759 she was a sick woman. In that year the lessee was Amelia
Douglas, who was a relation, possibly because of the need to
protect the premises in case of further trouble with the law. When
the playwright Charles Johnson was introduced to Jane in 1760, he
observed that, '. . . her Face presents the remains of a most
pleasing sweetness and beauty . . . her Body much bloated by
Drink and Debauch . . . her Legs swelled out of shape . . . a nice
cheerful old woman although suffering great discomfort.' Bonnell
Thornton at this time wrote that, 'The King's Head is a *Cattery* run
by a fat Covent Garden lady . . . Arch-Bawd of Covent Garden.'

Jane Douglas died in her house on 10 June 1761, 'thanking God
for a successful life and [*vide* Thornton] for the continuing succes-
ses of the Army and the safe return of her many *Babes of Grace* in the
Forces'. She left a very considerable estate. The contents of her
house were sold off by her old friend and neighbour the auctioneer
Abraham Langford, who 'made many witty remarks . . . as he
auctioned . . . fine Old Masters and rich furniture and costlie
properties'.

Her funeral was an impressive one, if the *Meretriciad* is to be
believed: it purports 'to mourn Great Douglas, Wheatherby and
Weems':

> Then big in Flesh see Mother Eastsmith stride
> With Gould and Goadby by her side:
> To bear their Trains, behind, three Pages creep . . .
> High on a Wand the WILL of DOUGLAS hung
> And *Bet*, the praises of the Donor sung. . . .
>
> How can an honest MUSE expect to live
> When Rogues Thieves Pimps and Buggers thrive?

When Amelia Douglas died a few years later, her Will disclosed
a codicil dated October 1760, referring to a young girl named
Elizabeth Holmes 'who had spent her whole life in my house'.
She was to get £500 at the age of twenty-one, a pair of diamond
earrings, a silver kettle and teapot, a silver lamp, half a dozen
silver spoons and a silver 'Mugg'. This was Jane Douglas' child
about whom Williams and Walpole had agonized: it was a girl, and

the father was not, after all, Lord Fitzwilliam but Admiral Charles Holmes, another of Jane's lovers.

It is often stated that Mother Cole in John Cleland's *Fanny Hill* and in Sam Foote's comedy *The Mirror* is based upon Mrs Douglas. There was, however, a real live Mother Cole, 'a sanctimonious Bawd, an infamous *Governante* . . . originally a fruit-seller in the Playhouse gallery' who ran a so-called milliner's shop in Russell Street in which (*vide* Twigg) '. . . three lovely young Harlots served the Gentlemen in a spacious Drawing-room at the back . . . in which a select Band of young Fops were wont to gather.' She had, he said, latterly grown big in her person like Nancy Dawson.

There was a sort of Cole *mafia* operating in the Garden. William Cole was in Maiden Lane from 1710 to 1737, when his son Christopher took over and continued until 1752. Christopher had other establishments, one in Southampton Street from 1740 to 1764 and the other thereafter in the Bedford Ground. James Cole was in King Street from 1710 to 1715, Henry Cole in Tavistock Street North in 1763, and Hester Cole in Bedford Street at much the same time. Hester is most probably the Mother Cole seen in Rowlandson's *Mother Cole and Loaders* (10 April 1784), complaining to Charles James Fox that she had been living for the last sixteen years in St Stephen's Chapel 'comfortably and creditably . . . no knock-on-the-door doings in *my* house . . . having a Set of Regular Sedate Sober Customers and no Riots . . . paying both *Scott and Lott*, twice threatened with Impeachment and three times with the Halter', yet she is now being harassed by the constabulary. She seeks Fox's help and protection as a customer and as a man of influence. Her name was still being bandied about as the archetype of the evil old bawd until well into the next century.

9. Pharaoh's Daughters

Gambling was another attraction of the Garden. As early as 1698 the Royal Oak Lottery was created by an Act of Parliament. As popular as it was, it was superseded the following year by the quite illegal Wheel of Fortune at a penny-a-share ticket. In Covent Garden the lottery office was at the Lord Blakeney's Head in Bow Street (popularly known as the Blakeney's Head), right next door to the magistrates' court. It was run by Catherine O'Neill, who was married to Peter Dillon, the lottery officer. As Mother Dillon she conducted a brothel on the same premises.

Dicing games were often played in the streets of Covent Garden, although earlier in the century the suburb of Fulham was best known for this activity. Indeed, crooked dice were known as 'Fullams'. In obscure rooms in sleazy alleys the game known as 'E & O' ('evens and odds') was played, using an eight-sided spinning-wheel. It was such an out-and-out fraudulent device that it was outlawed later in the century.

Above all, there were the card games, particularly faro, which was a mania amongst the moneyed classes. Covent Garden had its fair share of faro tables – popularly known as Greek shops – and there were many gaming-houses and gaming clubs. Rooms were set aside at Will's and Tom's for card games. None was highly regarded: even the most famous, Arthur's and White's, which were exclusive resorts of the high and mighty, were stigmatized by John Gay as 'Dens of Thieves'.

The earliest gaming-house in Covent Garden was that kept by William Vandernan in 1710 in Playhouse Yard, next to Drury Lane theatre. As early as 1704 Queen Anne had promulgated an Act for the Reform of Indecencies which included gambling and bad behaviour in the theatres, but William Vandernan's activities were not disturbed by the good Queen's enactment nor by the subsequent one of January 1712 with its stirring words, '. . . for encouraging Piety and Virtue and suppressing Vice Profanation and

Immorality', requiring that 'All Persons who keep Bawdy-houses, Musick-houses, Gameing-houses . . . be effectually prosecuted and punished'. Although rewards of up to £100 were offered, the magistrates complained that nobody would come forward to give evidence, even when people had been taken in their own bawdy-houses and Gaming-houses.

In a violent affray on 11 March 1713 five Mohocks actually killed a bawdy-house keeper in her own house in the Strand, and the High Constable was dismissed for having released the arrogant Mohocks before they had been charged.

The advent of the first randy Hanoverian in 1714 would have caused Vandernan no trouble, but the situation had been getting so far out of hand that in April 1721 even George I was compelled to make an Order in Council 'Against Prophaneness and Immorality and Debauchery . . . from the *Mascorades* and Gameing-houses, the encrease in Play-houses and Publick-houses where Vice and Immodesty are encouraged'. The Order charged that every tenth house sold liquor and, because those who frequented these places never informed about them, '. . . it is difficult to get legal evidence.'

That these were not hole-and-corner affairs can be seen from the details given in the London Mercury of 13 January 1721, which stated that there were twenty-two gambling-houses in Covent Garden, 'some of which cleared a Hundred Pounds and seldom less than Forty Pounds a Night. They have proper Officers, both Civil and Military, with salaries proportional to their degrees. They have a *Commissioner* (who is always the Proprietor): he looks in once a Night to audit the weekly accounts.' The newspaper then sets out the details of the staff employed:

A Director	to superintend the Rooms
An Operator	the Dealer at Faro
Two *Croupees*	to watch the cards and the money for the Bank
a *Puff*	who was given money to decoy punters into playing
a *Squib*	his understudy 'a person of lower Rank than the *Puff*'.
a Clerk	who checks on the *Puffs*
A *Flasher*	who sits at the Tables and swears that he has often seen the Bank stript.
Dunners	Waiters
An Attorney	a solicitor
A Captain	to fight and eject angry or dissatisfied persons or losers out of humour at losing money
Ushers	Guardians at the door
Porters	Recruited from the ranks of ex-soldiers

Runners	used to get intelligence of all meetings of Justices of the Peace or Constables preparing for searches

In addition, a half-guinea was to be given to any linkboy or sedan-chairman or coachman who gave warning of a search.

The mounting dissatisfaction spurred on the magistrates to take some action. Accordingly, on 1 July 1721 they reported that they had suppressed several Covent Garden faro houses, some 'catering for a better sort of Customer and a more Polite Company', some of the people fleeing through back doors, trapdoors and secret doors.

William Vandernan's turn was soon to come. In 1722 his gaming-house in Playhouse Yard was raided. When the constables burst in, informing him that he was in breach of the Proclamation, he waxed very indignant, shouting, 'A Turd on your Proclamation! I don't take a Fart for it!' Several gentlemen there present drew their swords, whereupon the constables – unarmed – sent for a platoon of the King's Life Guards. When the soldiers appeared, one gentleman shouted, 'Damn Ye! We are taken! Put out the Candles and draw your Swords!' The Head Constable, recognizing Sir Edward Galloway and not wanting to be involved with persons of quality and influence, quietly said to him, 'Friend! Go about your Business!' to which the choleric baronet replied, 'God Damn Ye! There's not a Man among ye; you're a Pack of Informing Doggs and ought to have your Brains bashed out!' They were overcome, and charged, and all were fined £50 each and given a year in prison suspended for four years.

After the raid William moved to Brydges Street nearby, where he and his son Joseph carried on until 1750. In June 1751 William, whose temper had not improved with the years, was again charged with 'keeping a Disorderly House' and was, together with Mary Durand,' whipped in the Gatehouse [Prison]'. It is probable that as a result of this experience he died shortly afterwards. Sarah, the Widow Vandernan, carried on until she died on 3 April, 1753. Other members of the family operated elsewhere in the Garden: another Sarah in Brydges Street East from 1751 to 1754; Joseph from 1733 to 1750 with a break in residence between 1741 and 1747, and Mary held the fort for a year in 1755. William had another branch in Charles Street around 1739.

All were buried in St Paul's Covent Garden despite their unorthodox means of making a living.

The most famous of these gambling-joints was that run by George Douglas, fourth Earl of Mordington, a dissolute and unstable character, a heavy drinker and a compulsive gambler, who had come to England with no other qualification than a Scottish title of nobility to seek a fortune. His personal life was in a mess. He arrived in Covent Garden about 1700 and in November 1704 married a local girl, Mary Dillon – probably connected with the lottery officer in nearby Bow Street. In April 1706 he was lying in 'the worst part of Newgate prison . . . for a debt of fifty pounds'. In December 1707 he was in the Fleet debtors' prison, and his only chance for a speedy release was to petition the King on the grounds that he was a peer of the realm. He was released on 27 December and shortly afterwards deserted his wife, bigamously marrying a respectable girl named Catherine Launder, daughter of a clergyman, and fathering two children upon her.

Mary Dillon was left in parlous plight. As a peeress she secured a pension of £40 a year in 1708 but by 1715 this had been reduced to £20, supplemented only in 1713 by 'a Gift of Ten Pounds'. When in 1721 she petitioned for an augmentation, 'for relief in view of her husband's way of life', the document was marked 'To stand as she do's.'

Lord Mordington was running a 'Gameing House' in Bow Street about 1730 and in Charles Street in 1734, and later in that year he took a ten-year lease on a house in the Piazza. Thereafter 'Lord Mordington's' became one of the most esteemed gambling-dens, much favoured by his peers and every *nouveau riche* anxious to be seen hobnobbing with the aristocracy.

Then, suddenly, on 15 May 1741, Lord Mordington dropped down dead in his house in the Piazza and within a month his bigamous wife Catherine likewise died. Mary, Lady Mordington, immediately occupied the house and managed it successfully until May 1744, when she ran into trouble as a result of a complaint by some disgruntled employee and the incidence of another anti-vice campaign. A Grand Jury for the County of Middlesex was convened and started off by roundly rebuking the constables for being remiss in their duties because they had reported that all was well in their districts '. . . whereas the contrary was the case, as the Jury could read in the Daily Papers . . . advertisements inviting everyone to attend . . . the severall Places kept apart for the Encouragement of Luxury Extravagance and Idleness . . . and other Wicked and Illegal Purposes.' Moreover, the jury thought it was quite disgraceful '. . . especially because it was a Time when we were engaged in Expensive Wars & so much overburthened with Taxes of all sorts . . . it was difficult even . . . for Prudent Men to live according to their Standards.' They continued:

The country squire gets a rapturous reception at the Old Calf's Head where he will be sure of 'kind and tender usage'

WE Accordingly do hereby PRESENT as Places of Great Extravagance Luxury Idleness and Ill-Fame the severall Houses, to wit:-
1. The Lady Mordington's and her Gameing House in or near Covent Garden.
2. The Lady Castle and her Gameing House in or near Covent Garden.
3. The Proprietors of the Avenues leading to and from the severall *Play-Houses* in Covent Garden and Drury Lane . . . for not preventing Wicked Loose and Disorderly Persons from loitering at the Front of their severall Houses at Play Nights. . . .

The Lady Castle was Susan, Countess of Cassilis, a daughter of the Earl of Selkirk and sister of the Duke of Hamilton. She had married her cousin John Kennedy, eighth Earl of Cassilis in 1738, bringing him a dowry of £8,000. (By some Freudian slip, she was often called 'Lady Castleless' so difficult was it to recall her proper name and title.) She was an unlucky woman. Her husband not only dissipated her fortune and shamefully neglected her but when he died in 1759 it was discovered that he had secretly entailed all his estates to a distant cousin.

Lady Cassilis had opened her gaming-house in the Piazza at about the same time as Lady Mordington opened hers, and next door to Mother Jane Douglas. Both ladies, conscious of their exalted station, protested that the judgement could not apply to them, but nonetheless on 1 January 1745 the Middlesex Bench ordered the closure of both houses, prudently adding a proviso: 'without incurring any Breach of the Privileges of Peers and Peeresses to which they may lay claim'. No justices wanted to tangle with the tremendous privileges of the nobility.

On 8 January 1745 an advertisement appeared in several journals: 'I, Dame Mary, Baroness of MORDINGTON do hold a House in the Great Piazza in Covent Garden . . . for an Assembly where all Persons of Credit are at Liberty to frequent and play at such Diversions (as they may wish) . . . and I have hired Joseph Dewberry William Horseley Ham Cropper and George Saunders as my Servants and Managers under Me: and demand all those Privileges which belong to Me as a Peeress of Great Britain.' The House of Lords, disallowed her claims on 29 April 1745.

Lady Cassilis, a born peeress, vacated her premises shortly afterwards, but Lady Mordington, being Covent Garden born, was made of sterner stuff: she turned over the house to William Horseley 'acting for Tenants' and carried on. But the Law had kept a beady eye on her activities. In October 1746 the *London Journal* reported that '. . . a Common Gambling House under the Piazza lately known as *Lord Mordington's* had the audacity to say that they have made their Peace with the very Men who had caused the Disturbance.' (The premises were known indifferently as Lord or Lady Mordington's.) In the following year the ownership passed to Calvin Hawksbee and Abraham Carter, who were to run the premises thereafter as Sam's Coffee-House. Lady Mordington was still alive in 1756.

Her choice of servants and managers likewise would not inspire confidence in the minds of the Justices. Joseph Dewberry was running a brothel in Charles Street between 1747 and 1753; in 1762 he took over Mother Douglas' premises and when he died his son James ran it as the Piazza Coffee-House. The whole family were involved in one or other aspect of prostitution, the most famous being Sarah Dubery with her splendid 'Nunnery' in King's Place in St James, towards the end of the century.

William Horseley was much better known: he was running a house 'for tenants' in Bow Street, and he and Alexander Fry from 1742 were running Callaghan's Coffee-House under the Piazza. Callaghan's had been established at No. 7 the Piazza since 1733 by Timothy O'Connor. In 1743 Horseley secured a licence to run it as a bagnio, but it was still known as Callaghan's as late as 1786. One William Horseley, 'a garotteer' of Covent Garden, was hanged in 1776, and it is tempting to believe that Lady Mordington's servant paid for his sins in this way.

The last nobleman to leave the Piazza was Thomas, Lord Archer of Humberslade, who moved to Portman Square about 1755, but his son Andrew kept the link with the Garden by marrying a local beauty, Sarah West, and setting up a faro table in Charles Street. When he succeeded to the title, Lady Archer was criticized as 'a young Peeress remarkable for her tawdry dress and prodigious quantities of Rouge'. Lord Townshend called her 'Lacker-fac'd Archer', and Horace Walpole composed a mock-alphabet starting with 'A is for ARCHER, painted her Face'. Their gambling-house prospered although their reputation was far from spotless – indeed after her husband died in April 1788 Lady Archer was criticized for 'fleecing young Ensigns . . . because her stakes were ruinously high'. As a result her business suffered but by February 1790 *The Rambler* reported that, 'Lady Archer's Pall Mall *Faro-Bank* again has a flood-tide . . . she is sanguine again.' She was then one of the select clique of ladies of the quality known as 'Pharaoh's Daughters'. In 1801 she married William Pitt, Lord Amherst, and her financial troubles were over.

The other two 'Daughters' were Sophia, Viscountess Mount

Lord Andrew Archer's fine mansion at 43 King Street; for many years a noted gambling house. Lady Sarah Archer was one of the first of the 'Pharaoh's Daughters'. The house is the last surviving monument to the glory that was the Piazza

Edgecumbe (whose activities did not impinge on Covent Garden), and Albinia, Countess of Buckinghamshire. Albinia was a daughter of Lord Vere Bertie and when she married George Hobart he was penniless, earning a living as a stage manager at the Haymarket Theatre. She supported him by running 'House-parties for Routs' and for gambling, being slightingly known as 'Mrs Hobart'. When George became the third Earl of Buckinghamshire, an irate peer commented: 'The title of Buckinghamshire brought an accession of Dignity without an accession of Fortune, and to supply a Deficiency of the latter she is liberal in prostituting the former. Twice a week a *Publick Faro Bank* is kept at her house and the unfledged Ensigns of the *Guards* . . . are invited to contribute in a Polite way to the Establishment of this needy Countess. . . .'

In her middle years Lady Buckinghamshire grew enormously fat and was nicknamed 'Madame Blubber' and 'Mrs Roundabout' and her activities cruelly lampooned. At one time Lord Chief Justice Kenyon threatened 'without fear or favour' to have all runners of 'faro banks' flogged at the cart-arse, but he flinched from inflicting

Lord Chief Justice Kenyon had publicly vowed that he would pillory any person, no matter what their rank or station, found guilty of gambling offences. The noble ladies, including the Countess of Buckinghamshire, collectively known as Pharaoh's Daughters, *who were charged at Marlborough Street were nonetheless only rebuked and fined. Two other 'Daughters' complete with feather head-dresses can be seen in the pillory while Lady Buckinghamshire is flogged at the cart-arse. (James Gillray, 1797)*

this on these noble ladies – hence Gillray's savage prints in March 1797 satirizing the LCJ's empty threats.

All three 'Daughters' outlived their detractors. Sarah died in 1801, Sophia in 1806 and Albinia in 1816, and none of them died in poverty.

10. Mrs Phillips' Sex Shop

About the beginning of the eighteenth century there emerged in the vicinity of the Strand and Covent Garden a class of tradesmen who called themselves 'Salvators'. Their principal product was a certain type of 'machine' or 'engine' devised to be worn by concupiscent gentlemen about to indulge in carnal copulation to help them avoid some of the dangers arising from such sexual exertions. Today these are known as contraceptives and are in common use but in those days they were a great novelty, and their purveyors were few and unadvertised.

The original inventor was the Italian Gabriele Fallopio, who about 1550 (using part of a sheep's intestine) manufactured a sheath to be worn as a protection against the ravages of the epidemic of syphilis then sweeping over Europe. He also recommended it as a contraceptive against pregnancy. In 1597 Hercules Saxonia described a similar device made of fine linen soaked in brine or a saline solution as being just as efficacious but much cheaper to produce. The noted English doctor Daniel Turner thought both claims were made 'with greater Vivacity than Veracity'.

The earliest contraceptives were imported from France. Indeed, Mother Whyburn recalled that, 'His Grace the Duke of York had secured from Sir John Birkenhead a gross of Dutch *condoms* imported by the Jew Mendes' (Dr Fernando Mendes, Court Physician to Catherine of Braganza in 1669).

In England they were brought into prominence by John Wilmot, the rakish Earl of Rochester, who claimed they had been invented by a certain Colonel Condon. Rochester extolled them in his 1674

(Opposite) Constantia Theresa Phillips in her prime when mistress to the Earl of Chesterfield. She is thought to have established the famous sex-shop in Half-Moon Alley

Panegyrick vpon Cundums, particularly useful against 'unwanted Brats'. Soon afterwards they began to be manufactured in England of treated linen. John Gay in his satire *The Petticoat* (1716) called them 'masterpieces of Art', rhapsodizing them as

> The new *Machine*, a sure Defence shall prove
> And guard the Sex against the Harm of Love!

They were usually sold in packets of eight in three sizes, tastefully bound in a silken sachet with silk ribbons. (According to *Almonds for Parrotts* (1708), they were being sold at several places including the Playhouse.) This occasioned another eulogy in *The Potent Ally* (1741):

> Happy is the Man who in his Pocket keeps
> Whether with Green or Scarlet ribbons bound
> A well-made *cundum* . . .

although in 1680 the Marquise de Sevigny described a sheath made of goldbeaters' skin as 'an Armour against Enjoyment and a Spider's Web against Danger'.

About the time when Mother Douglas was starting her successful career, an enterprising young lady, Constantia Theresa Phillips, was establishing a useful ancillary business in a small shop, the Green Canister, in Half-Moon Alley (now Bedford Street). She was born in Chester, her father being Captain Thomas Phillips of the 5th Dragoon Guards, who left the army in 1717 and arrived in an impecunious state in London. His daughter, under the patronage of the Duchess of Bolton, went to a prestigious finishing-school in Westminster, but by 1721, when she was only thirteen, she was mistress to the Earl of Chesterfield. Being soon involved 'in a little embezzlement' in order to avoid arrest, she went through a form of marriage on 11 November. 1722 with a Mr de Vall 'with whom she never exchanged a word'. Luckily for her, he was a bigamist so it was a non-marriage. Then, although her *amours* were as public as Charing Cross', she married on 9 February 1723 a wealthy Dutch merchant, Henry Muilman, at one time a director of the South Seas Company. Discovering too late that he had married a promiscuous whore, he secured a nullity of marriage from the Court of Arches, agreeing to pay her an annuity of £200, which he stopped when soon afterwards she ran off to Paris with an admirer. This was the start of a series of *amours* in France, Britain and the West Indies – with hindsight it is clear that she was a nymphomaniac.

She returned to Britain about 1730 determined to blackmail as many of her former lovers as possible, starting with the Earl of

Chesterfield, who adopted the attitude of 'publish and be damned'.

Sometime about 1738 she opened the shop in Half-Moon Alley – although judging from events it is more probable that she let her name be used as a front, her relationship with the Earl and other scions of the nobility guaranteeing publicity. Her name does not appear in the Rate Books at any time.

She was still calling herself Mrs Muilman and despite her many lovers was always in debt and several times in the debtors' prisons. Henry Muilman, deeply embarrassed by her activities, eventually sprang her out of the Marshalsea Prison and in 1754 sent her off to Jamaica, where she married several times and amassed a fortune and such massive unpopularity that when she died in 1765 not a soul attended her funeral.

The business must have been carried on in her absence and in her name since the fourth edition of her so-called *Apology* to Chesterfield was published in 1761; probably occasioning the debate in 1763 detailed in *The Memoirs of the Bedford Coffee-house*. This took the form of a spoof Parliamentary debate on a petition from Mrs Phillips complaining about unfair competition. After describing her *modus operandi*, she claims that, '. . . she had made it her sole Imployment to study the construction of a competitor, Moses Solomon d'Acosta, born 1686 . . . her *Engines* were made of the most lasting texture well calculated for the foreign trade for wear and tear . . . while d'Acosta's were . . . more suitable for home consumption . . . her *Machine* had been tested . . . blown up . . . for a full month while the others . . . collapsed (after a fortnight) and therefore could not be used with safety by any uncircumcized Person. . . .' It was decided that Mrs Phillips' goods could best be exported and those of Mr d'Acosta were good enough for home consumption.

The secret of her success was that her 'Engines' were made in the original manner, using sheep-gut which ensured elasticity and imperviousness; they were justifiably more expensive. Cheaper ones were made of treated linen – the French specialist Dr Edouard Bourru stated that these *capotes anglaises* were riddled with pores and easily torn. James Boswell, using this 'armour' in 1763 found it cumbersome and uncomfortable, although he was careful to wash it out carefully after use as directed.

In 1743 Mother Douglas was buying '*cundums* at Wholesale from J. Jacobs, *Salvator* in Oliver's Alley' and selling them to her grateful clients at an enormous mark-up. There was another manufacturer, named Lewis, whose whereabouts are unknown. Oliver's Alley, a

A sale of English Beauties in the East Indies

On the right is a 'warehouse for Unsaleable Goods from Europe'. These were English prostitutes, mainly from Covent Garden, transported as minor criminals and auctioned on arrival at Madras like cattle. The auctioneer is using as his rostrum a bale of goods marked 'Mrs Phillips, the Original Inventor, in Leicester Field, London' and additionally 'For the use of the Supreme Council'. One bidder has in his pocket a paper headed 'Instructions from the Governor-General'. (James Gillray, 1786)

narrow alley between the Strand and Maiden Lane (almost opposite the Savoy Hotel), now closed and overbuilt, contained only four tenements – and there is no mention of Mr Jacobs at any time. From 1746 to 1757 all were empty, and in 1767 the alley was closed. He probably rented a couple of rooms as a workshop.

The Phillips saga would have long since faded in public memory had not a bitter quarrel erupted arising from an advertisement in the *St James Chronicle* of 9 October 1776 which read: 'Mrs PHILLIPS who about ten years ago left off Business and having been prevailed upon by her Friends to reassume the same again . . . since her declining they cannot procure any Goods comparable to those she used to vend BEGS LEAVE to acquaint her Friends & Customers that she has taken a House No. 5 Orange Court near Leicester Fields . . . at the sign of *The Golden Fan & Rising Sun*, a Lamp

148

adjoining the sign and a Fan in the window . . . [she will] carry on her Business as usual.'

However, the sex-shop in Half-Moon Alley was now being run by Mary Perkins (who claimed to be Mrs Phillips' niece and her legitimate successor), who purveyed 'all sorts of fine *Machines* called *cundums*' as well as a range of 'Perfumes, Wash-balls, Soaps, Waters, Powders, Oils, Essences, Snuffs, Pomatums, Cold-creams, Lip-salves and Sealing-wax . . . [and] Ladies' Black Sticking-plaisters'.

The claim to have wide export markets is upheld as late as 1786 in James Gillray's cartoon 'A Sale of English Beauties in Madras' from a 'Warehouse for Unsaleable Goods from Europe'. By the auctioneer's rostrum there is a bale of goods from 'Mrs Phillips, original inventor, in Leicester Field, London . . . for the use of the Supreme Council'. Amongst the pile of books also to be auctioned are *Crazy tales, Mrs Birchini's Dance* and *The Female Flagellants*. The other unsaleable goods were the 'English Beauties', mostly Covent Garden prostitutes who had been transported as minor criminals and were auctioned like cattle upon arrival. They were bought by the personnel of the East India Company.

This same Mrs Phillips was mentioned in a cartoon by E. Topham in 1773 when she brought to the Pantheon Ball on 12 May 'a parcel of advertisements for her modest commodities'. The auctioneer was Mr Langford from Covent Garden. It would seem that this was a real Mrs Phillips, although clearly not the woman who had died in Jamaica, and it would also seem that she had the edge over Mary Perkins, who again stressed that the Green Canister 'seven doors up from the Strand on the left-hand side . . . is Mrs Phillips' shop and [Mary] is the same person behind the counter as has been for many years'.

There are some unanswered questions. In the rates register for Half-Moon Street there is no mention of any Mrs Phillips: from 1755 Israel Colson was the lessee and took over the next-door shop in 1756. On 1 January 1765 Mary Perkins became the lessee (the huge Civil Service Store now covers the site) so clearly both of them were trading under the name of Phillips.

The trade of 'Salvator' still flourished: a Mrs Muilman died on 21 February 1789 in Salvator House in the Strand – she was perhaps Henry Muilman's widow since he died in May 1772; but the best 'engines' were still being imported from France and Holland because of their superior quality.

11. The Heyday

While Covent Garden was rejoicing in its scandalous reputation as London's 'sin city' and the Mecca of all pleasure-seekers, the plight of its ordinary inhabitants was decidedly unglamorous.

From about 1725 to 1760 there was a deterioration in working and housing conditions unprecedented in the capital's history. In that same period the gulf between rich and poor had also widened enormously. Formerly fashionable streets and elegant houses had now become noisome slums. St Clement's Lane, which during the seventeenth century and the early years of the eighteenth had been the resort of the noble and rich and of wits and beauties, had become by 1730 'a disgraceful Rookery, filthy and squalid and disreputable to the last degree . . . a narrow stale-looking crooked little street . . . with an atmosphere redolent of the exhalations . . . of a grimy grovelling class . . . who lived hand-to-mouth by uncertain daily labour . . .'.

Wych Street, by 1708, had merged with Drury Lane, and Drury Lane likewise had lost its greatness. Addison then reported: 'Where noble Dames once moved with costly flowing Robes . . . women in Rags rocked to sleep the children of misery . . . upon those once polished floors . . . human beings now lay stretched . . . the once elegant *boudoir* of some long-dead Duchess was inhabited by seven or eight wretched human beings . . . where once flaxen-haired children of Wealth disported neglected children in filth and rags doze out their existence. . . .' John Gay had then written of 'the soft and low doors where old Lechers tapped their Canes for the *Fair Recluses* that lived in Drury Lane'. To be poor was to be regarded *ipso facto* as a criminal; nor did they share in the increasing prosperity of the middle classes.

In 1724 the High Constable of Holborn mustered a large posse 'to get rid of the Vermin that infested the Hundreds of Drury'. They made a huge catch from thieves' kitchens, Mollies houses and

J. Maurer's view of Covent Garden about 1730–40, looking west. There are now two sets of shacks, the inner ones being stalls. The three outer ones are Tom King's

J. *Maurer's* A View of Covent Garden from the Church Portico looking east, *1749*

counterfeiters' workshops and brothels. A specially convened Bench of Justices then determined to deal 'with these *Nurseries of Debauchery* at least once in a month'. There were, however, many vested interests to ensure that this threat was not carried out.

Moreover, for every upright magistrate there were two venal ones. At this period a magistracy was usually a means of making a livelihood; they were appointees of sheriffs or high officials of a county – a relic of feudal times. Tobias Smollett described them as 'Tradeing Justices' 'of profligate lives, needy, mean, ignorant and rapacious . . . who had bribed their way into appointments . . . to make a living out of the Publick by extortion and corrupt use of their powers . . .'. They were allowed to accept 'fees' or even outright bribes within their discretion. Sir Samuel Gower in Westminster admitted to taking bribes to protect bawdy-houses and unlicensed ale-houses. When his misdeeds were uncovered, he was merely rebuked, because he promised not to offend again – and promptly resumed his malpractices.

Another instance of the power and venality of these guardians of the law appears in the report of the Westminster Sessions of 13 November 1728. An order of the Court was made against Robert Jennison, who kept 'a very disorderly house' at the Three Tuns Tavern in Drury Lane. When the bailiff came to remove two of his women, he threatened to run him through with his sword and was taken into custody. Next day, his brother 'Francis Jennison, a Justice of the Peace in Surrey . . . officiously demanded . . . an absolute discharge . . . desiring the Bailiff to scratch out or erase the Certificate of Commitment . . .'. The bailiff could not refuse such a demand from a Justice of the Peace, and the full Bench of Justices later decided that they could not interfere in the matter.

There was the old soldier Captain Thomas de Veil, generally considered a man of integrity but who masked his venality by great 'uprightness' on the Bench. When appointed a Justice of the Peace in 1729, he moved to a house in Bow Street whence he dispensed justice. This house became the later famous Bow Street Magistrates' Court. In 1744 he put down with great severity a demonstration by a 'union' of Covent Garden footmen, who had banded together to complain about low pay, bad conditions and unfair competition. Subsequently he levied such harsh sentences that he aroused great hatred amongst 'the people at large'. For these services he was knighted in 1744, but when he died in 1748 his body had to be carried out of the house at three o'clock in the morning to ensure 'a quiet interment'. He was succeeded by Henry

Hogarth's Harlot's Progress *Bridewell as it really was. The jailer watches the women beating hemp until their hands are flayed. One woman is pinned into the wall pillory. A bawd, with her nose slit, enjoys the discomfiture of the newcomer who is being threatened with leg irons, while another prisoner begins to strip her of her finery and good clothes*

Fielding, who was considered an honest, fair and humane judge, but he too was not averse to accepting fees upon occasion.

The result of magisterial venality led to an immense increase in crime and, *vide* Fielding himself, to a great increase in bawdy-houses 'of an inferior quality'. His own court had a brothel on either side, and it was remarked that the magistrate must have been deaf as well as blind not to have known what was going on there. Not until 1792 were stipendiary magistrates appointed to remedy the situation and bring honesty to the benches.

These problems were to be aggravated by the opening of a new theatre which drew in a great mass of new visitors. John Rich, who had made a fortune by staging John Gay's play *The Beggar's Opera* in his Lincoln's Inn Fields theatre, spent it on a site in Bow Street. This splendid edifice, designed by James Shepherd with pillared porticos, could hold up to two thousand people. It was called the Theatre Royal in Covent Garden – later called the Covent Garden Theatre to distinguish it from the other royal theatre in Drury Lane.

It was opened with great *éclat* on 7 December 1732 with a performance of William Congreve's *The Way of the World*. Hogarth's painting *Rich's Glory* shows his coach being dragged by admirers along the Piazza to the entrance under the portico. (The Bow Street entrance was through a narrow alley between two houses.)

Rich put in train a series of spectacular shows, with himself as 'Harlequin', alternating the entertainments with ballets and operas, and when later Handel came over from the Italian Opera House in the Haymarket he put on the first performance of the *Messiah* in 1743. Peg Woffington came over from Drury Lane when she was experiencing serious competition from George Ann Bellamy.

According to custom, the doors opened at five o'clock, the play starting at six o'clock, the intervening tedium being relieved by three selections played by an orchestra. These were known as the First, Second and Third Music. There were no reserved seats, so that the playgoer had to sit it out or pay somebody to occupy the seat until he arrived. One poster advised ladies to send their valets beforehand in good time. There was usually a prologue spoken by the manager or some other person in authority, and an epilogue. It was remarked that these had three main topics: abuse of the town, criticism or condemnation of contemporary – usually rival – authors, and the extolling of the high merit of the play to be presented.

The audiences were often unruly as well as noisy. At both theatres iron spikes ran along the front of the stage and a couple of strong men stood on either side to try to restrain people from going behind the stage to talk to or harass the players.

In 1737 an Act was passed to regulate the conduct of the theatres, giving the Crown control under the Lord Chamberlain. The number of theatres was to be limited and new ones to be permitted only under Royal letters patent.

There were only three 'Winter' theatres, the King's Theatre or Italian Opera House in the Haymarket, the Drury Lane Theatre and the Covent Garden Theatre. In 1738, after a riot in the Haymarket Theatre in protest at the appearance of some French players, it was enacted that the public had a legal right to manifest their dislike of a play or the actors. This was the playgoers' Magna

(Opposite) The magistrate Thomas de Veil in his house in Bow Street in 1742. There was then no real court. He dealt only with petty matters and serious crimes were committed for trial at the Middlesex Sessions or the Old Bailey. On his death in 1744 Henry Fielding became the tenant making the house ipso facto into a court-room or Public Office

Carta. In 1744 there was a riot at Drury Lane Theatre over contemplated rises for admission: the damage came to more than £2,000. In another fracas in 1755 there was a free fight with gallants jumping from their boxes into the pit, their swords being drawn and blood being shed while the women screamed when the mob tore up the scenery and smashed up the seats. It cost £4,000 to put the damage to rights. Nor was there much consideration for the female sex: even Peg Woffington was pelted with orange peel on one occasion.

The audiences at the Haymarket and at Covent Garden were perhaps a little more restrained because these two theatres were still patronized by what Henry Fielding called 'The People of Fascination'. *A Trip Through the Town* (1735) remarked that the ladies and gentlemen came just to be seen and exchange gossip: 'They talk continually no matter of what, for they talk only to be taken notice of, for which reason they raise their voices to be taken notice of by those who pass by.' The mothers of all maidens were warned not to allow them to go for rides 'with strange young *Bucks* . . . in a little bawdy vehicle . . . for every jolt gave a sexual titillation', and there was a further warning about making too frequent visits to Lady Mordington's 'Gameing Table' and becoming 'a Cully to Jilts and Sharpers . . . who will send him home with his pockets empty'.

The Tricks of the Town Laid Open (1743) remarked that the 'theatre procuress' chief Place of Rendezvous is at The Playhouse . . . in the Pit she keeps her Office by the Concourse of *Whores* and *Gallants* perpetually crowding about her for Advice or Assistance . . . having a little more Business among the Quality and Gentry . . . [for as low as] a Shilling and a Glass of Raspberry . . . at all Sorts and Prices from a Guinea to Five, and from Five to Five Hundred . . .'. The author then described the seraglios which had over their doors the superscription 'Coffee or Chocolate', constantly guarded by 'three or four painted Harlots . . . who invite you into their *Café* (as they call it)'. Once lured inside, the cull is properly rooked and if he tries to escape will be met at the bottom of the stairs 'by Bullies and Ruffians . . . and will be lucky to escape away with his life, let alone his money and clothes'.

Huge fortunes were being made on the Stock Exchange, by bankers and by merchants. The gentry were entering commerce and manning the Civil Service. The ranks of doctors, dentists and apothecaries were being swelled from the ranks of ex-leeches, quacks and barbers. The poor, however, were completely excluded from such benefits: there was tremendous unemployment with concomitant starvation and misery, while all workmen's associations were completely forbidden and, if uncovered, very harshly dealt with.

In 1744 Saunders Welch, High Constable of Middlesex (and a close friend of Henry Fielding and Sam Johnson), who had just helped Fielding to suppress a riot in Covent Garden in which three bawdy-houses had been destroyed, reported: 'Of the poor . . . above a thousand in a year . . . died . . . of wasting and other diseases in consequence of hunger . . . you meet a man begging: you charge him with idleness. He says to you "I am willing to labour . . . will you give me work?" You answer "I cannot". "Why then you have no right to charge me with idleness!"' The same magistrate reported that he had found in Covent Garden 'One woman who owned seven houses filled from cellar to garret for twopenny lodgers; several beds in the same room, men and women, strangers to one another occupied beds promiscuously. The price of a double-bed was threepence, thus there was encouragement to save a penny and share a bed . . . these places are adapted to whoredom . . . open for the receipt of all comers at the latest hours. . . .'

The Lock Hospitals were built to attend to sufferers from syphilis and gonorrhoea 'which has been spread by the spread of Empire', but those hospitals, like St George's, kept the wards reserved for VD patients with the windows closed 'so that the infection should not escape outside'. In consequence the wards were absolutely foul!

Meanwhile the stalls and booths in the market were causing a great deal of anxiety to all worthy citizens who valued their amenities and resented the noise and traffic jams as well as the hooliganism engendered by the assemblies of great crowds, which had grown even greater by the influx of sightseers and parasites coming from John Rich's theatre. This led a number of aggrieved citizens to petition the Duke of Bedford in 1748 referring to the first Duke's regulations when the market was established. They protested against the current situation and the presence of 'sundry Trades and Occupations . . . which could never have been intended to be permitted . . . bakers, haberdashers, cookshops, retailers of *Genever* [gin] and other spirituous Liquors . . . to the great annoyance and prejudice of Tradesmen . . . who pay large Rents and great Taxes for their Houses . . . these Stands . . . cause greate Inconveniences to the Parishioners . . . whose movements are totally obstructed [because of] . . . the Stench and offensive Smells and Smoake of the Market . . .'. They asked therefore that

The opening of the new King's Theatre in Bow Street in 1732. The main entrance was under the north-east corner of the Piazza, the other entrance was then through an alley between Nos. 5 and 6 Bow Street

the rents should be reduced in proportion to 'the encrease in these Nuisances'.

One of the nuisances from about 1720 was James Street's Sunday market in birds, the favourites being linnets, jackdaws and magpies. The noise and disturbance were enhanced by games of football by rowdy crowds in this narrow street. Another diversion was Alice Neil's Turk's Head bagnio in which for a reasonable price you could get 'a Bath and Shampoo'. From about 1710 you could also look into the workshop of Francis Clay's house in which two French women could be seen chewing paper 'all day long' for his papier mâché trays, which he had introduced into Britain and which he sold from his bookshop at 16–17 King Street, at the corner with Bedford Street. In his advertisements he was careful to point out that he was selling 'Fancy Japanned-paper goods . . . popularly but erroneously called papier-mâché'. He died in May 1738 in his house 'at Bedford Street' having amassed a fortune of some £60,000. In 1742 there was a report about 'the late famous Mr Clay, maker of a famous Musical-clock sold by Mr Auctioneer Cock'.

King Street too was full of interest. In April 1710 the 'Four Indian Kings' were lodged in Mr Arne's house there. They were in fact Red Indian chiefs of the Maqua and Sachem tribes who had been invited to meet Queen Anne. Two years afterwards the house was burnt down, but curiously enough when another group of Indian Kings came in September 1730 they stayed in the rebuilt house. It was then reported that: '. . . the Indian Chiefs were carried from their Lodgings in King Street Covent Garden to . . . Whitehall . . . before the Lords Commissioners they sang four or five songs in their Countrey's language . . . after which they were sent for to join in Peace with King George . . . upon which the King stood up and gave a large Feather he had in his hand to the Prince. . . .' They had come to solicit aid against French settlers who were over-running their lands. During their stay they were followed by great crowds of sightseers as 'natural curiosities'.

In 1742 at the Three Stags' Heads Mrs Leadbetter advertised 'the Sale of her entire Stock of China-ware, she being obliged to clear out before next Lady Day . . . some great Curiosities, particularly Images of an extra-ordinary stature representing Chinese *Brogdanones*, *Lillipushes* Etc.'. Nearby, at the Golden Cup, a snuff-dealer would supply 'Special Havanah' at 3s.6d. the pound. At No. 6 was the Essex Serpent Tavern, formerly known as the Cockatrice after an apparition which had appeared many years earlier near Braintree – the tavern was still in existence in 1906. In King Street too it was claimed that mahogany furniture was first made, the origin being a door made of that wood supplied to a house in Ludgate Hill. In 1756 at the Spinning Wheel 'a Choyce Parcel of Irish Linnens' was on offer at from 7d. to 9s.6d. the yard.

The market was a favourite shopping centre for ladies of the quality accompanied by their little black pages, who would carry the smaller purchases while the larger packets were carried by porters chosen at random from the hundreds of unemployed men only too anxious to earn a few pence. The coming of the hackney-carriages had put hundreds of sedan-chairmen out of work. A further nuisance was the hucksters who importuned all passers-by, the vendors of leeches, then much recommended by doctors and quacks, and snail-sellers – snail soup was guaranteed to cure consumption. There were also many harpers – considered just a cut above fiddlers – who tried to make themselves heard above the cacophony, and the importunings of shoeblacks, some of whom, with regular pitches, earned a good livelihood – one outside Lord Archer's house at 43 King Street was reputed to have saved more than £80 in a short while.

A report to Henry Fielding in 1744 stated that the great number of brothels and irregular taverns in Covent Garden were the cause of robberies and burglaries, but a contributory cause was 'neglect by the Watchmen and Constables of the Night . . . these taverns and houses are kept by Persons of the most abandoned Character such as Bawds, Thieves, Receivers of stolen goods and also the Marshalsea and Sheriff's officers who keep Lock-up Houses . . . the principal of these houses are situate in Covent Garden'.

These lock-ups, or spunging-houses, were lodgings in which malefactors – usually debtors – could stay to keep them out of the prison proper. They were usually run by ex-jailers or ex-constables in connivance with the head jailer of the prison (prisons were still let out as franchises at this time), and later even thief-takers and Bow Street Runners. (One such was William Donaldson.) When the malefactor could no longer pay their charges, he would be unceremoniously thrust into the adjacent prison.

To try to control the crime wave there were also 'voluntary' groups of ratepayers expected to do guard duties when great crowds were expected, as at fairs and executions at Tyburn – there were exemptions known as 'Tyburn tickets' which could be bought from venal officials by citizens wishing to avoid this unpleasant chore.

The great increase in all sorts of crime was in great part aggravated by the consumption of immense quantities of 'Blue Ruin' (gin) and other spirituous liquors. Benjamin Franklin, when work-

Bow Street Court about 1800. On the right two Bow Street Runners holding a criminal. They had no distinctive uniform but often wore a red waistcoat: their truncheons had a metal crest to show their authority. (Rowlandson, 1808, detail)

ing in a Weld Court printshop in 1725, remarked upon the drinking habits of his British companions. Henry Fielding said that every fourth house in Covent Garden was a gin shop and complained of 'the dreadful effects I have to see . . . and to smell too . . . every day' in his court.

Crimes of violence were frequent and vicious. One example was the fearful riot in the high summer of 1748 when three sailors from HMS *Grafton* were robbed 'of thirty golden Guineas and four gold *Moidores*' while in the Star Tavern in the Strand. The Star, originally an ale-house, was from 1745 run by Peter Wood, a tavern-keeper of Russell Street – a man of bad repute. He had been prosecuted for keeping a disorderly house as early as 1747. In 1748 in conjunction with John Tompson and Sam Howard he was running the Star openly as a brothel, well known for the collusion of its waiters and girls with outside criminal elements. When the sailors complained, they were ejected from the brothel. They went back to Wapping and returned with a number of shipmates, breaking into the Star, destroying all the furniture, smashing all the crockery and cutting all the featherbeds into shreds and setting them on fire. They stripped all the whores and thrust them naked into the street, and for good measure, before departing, broke all the windows. They returned the next evening and 'to the plaudits of a large crowd' proceeded to destroy the next-door brothel, the Crown, and were only prevented from doing more damage by the arrival of a troop of the Royal Horse Guards, who helped to arrest them.

Two of the sailors and a man named Bozavern Penloz (who claimed to be the son of a Devonshire clergyman, but was only a sneak-thief passing by who entered the Star and stole £50 from a bureau) were found guilty and sentenced to be hanged at Tyburn. In October 1749 there was 'a tumultuous assemblage of sailors . . . determined to rescue them' but the presence of the troops 'persuaded them to disperse on the promise that Penloz's body would not be given to the Surgeons for dissection'.

Peter Wood was later to be presented to the Court Leet of the parish and fined £40 for keeping a disorderly house. He then decided to change his occupation from publican to peruke-maker (poor Penloz had been a perruquier too) but later was fined £10 for keeping another bawdy house. A woman named Sarah Wood – possibly some connection – was later to be whipped 'from Katherine Street unto the end of Brydges Street' for a similar offence.

Henry Fielding had witnessed the affray, which may have led him to establish that same year his famous Bow Street Runners, the first properly organized and trained police force in the world. Although at first there were only six of them – and never more than a dozen – they proved very effective as thief-takers within the bounds of Bow Street's magistracy, and they were also utilized in the struggle against prostitution. A random selection from the contemporary Sessions Registers includes Mary Grundy 'who was whipt from east to west in Covent garden', and two keepers of disorderly houses, John States and William Melliford, also to be whipped from east to west but in addition a second time 'from Drury Lane unto Saint Giles'. For stealing and counterfeiting the punishment was death, or transportation to America.

In 1731 a confidence-trickster named Joseph Crook, who passed himself off as Sir Peter Stranger, after spending an hour in the pillory was 'seated in an Elbow-chair where the common hangman cut off both his ears with an incision-knife . . . and then slit his nostrils with a pair of Scissors and seared them with an hot IRON. A Surgeon then applied the necessary steps to stem the flow of

(Opposite) Peter Wood owned the Star Tavern which in 1748 was a brothel. It was ransacked and then burnt down by sailors from HMS Grafton *in a famous riot in which two Covent Garden brothels were destroyed*

The Tars' Triumph *or* The Bawdy-House Battery *depicting the destruction of Peter Wood's Star Tavern and the assault upon its inmates*

blood' – and then all of them went to the Ship tavern at Charing Cross.

Child rape was also very prevalent: whereas rape perpetrated upon a girl or an adult woman was a hanging offence, sexual interference with a child was not deemed to be such an horrific thing, possibly because most of the children concerned were poor orphans who had been hired out for begging or prostitution and so were regarded as vagabonds and *ipso facto* malefactors. It was also generally thought that sexual intercourse with a child was not only 'safe' against venereal disease but 'could bring an old man back to life'! The perpetrators usually escaped with a fine or some expression of condemnation from the Bench.

There was also a marked increase in the 'heinous and detestable Sin of Sodomy, not to be named among Christians' – although Henry VIII, who first made it a capital offence, had no difficulty in calling it 'buggerie' in his Ordinance. By the middle of the eighteenth century the justices were very wary about such cases because of the death penalty; they demanded evidence of 'actual penetration', and even when there were witnesses who had seen the offenders *in flagrante delicto* every attempt was made to reduce the offence to 'attempted sodomy' which merited only a spell in the pillory and a fine – although an acquitted man would find it very hard to live down the stigma.

While many men of rank and wealth were implicated, the great majority of the catamites were found among the lower ranks of soldiers, whose pay was so low that they could not exist without some extra means of income, and from the ranks of working-class boys and men who might otherwise starve.

There was a great scandal in February 1726 when Mother Margaret Clap's Mollies house 'next The Fountain in Clare Market' was raided. Ned Ward had already mentioned this house as early as 1701 so that she had had a long run, although the trial made it clear that the authorities had known of its real nature for many years. The devastation amongst the homosexual community was catastrophic, the defendants coming from all areas of the metropolis and surrounding areas as far away as Kingston-upon-Thames.

The indictment stated that the house bore the character of a place of rendezvous for sodomites 'and for the more covenient entertainment of her Customers she had provided Beds in every room . . . commonly thirty or forty *Chaps* every Night . . . even more on Sunday Nights'. Many were in gangs soliciting within the Piazza of Covent Garden, 'upon occasion assaulting Passengers coming from the Playhouse and Taverns as well as the Coffee-houses and Bagnios. . . . others taken "in the act" in the churches of St Martin-in-the-Fields and St Paul's Covent Garden'.

A principal witness was a teenage catamite, Edward Courtenay, working at the Cardigan's Head public house at Charing Cross and at the same time acting as a 'Molly-cull' within Covent Garden. He identified a number of men with whom he had consorted, and the *London Journal* for June 1727 then reported: 'York Horner and Robert Whale stood yesterday in the Pillory at Charing Cross for keeping a House of Entertainment of Sodomites . . . [and] for attempting to commit sodomy upon one of the youths belonging to the Royal Chapel . . . they were so loaded with Dung and Dirt that they appeared like Bears . . . in short, if the Populace had been suffered to exert their desired Resentments . . . they must have received their Exit upon the spot. They were remanded for further punishments. . . .'

Several were found guilty and hanged; young Courtenay was released because he had turned King's Evidence, but some time later he was again caught and pilloried.

Lesbianism is seldom mentioned. It was colloquially known as 'the Game of Flats', usually indulged in by ladies of the quality in specialist houses such as Mother Courage's in Suffolk Street, Haymarket, and later in the century at Frances Bradshaw's elegant house in Bow Street. The best-known practitioners were Lady Caroline Harrington and her friend Elizabeth 'the Pollard' Ashe. It was regarded as an aberration – indeed, it was not even a misdemeanour.

None of these varied happenings – not even the depredations of the gangs of pickpockets, a scourge akin to locusts – could prevent great crowds coming to Covent Garden looking for enjoyable diversions. A never-failing attraction was the cheerfulness of the market men and women, their wit and *bonhomie*, their salacious repartees, audacious and very audible commentaries on all and sundry, high and low. An even greater attraction was the gaiety and prettiness of the saucy shop-assistants and impudent 'milliners and mantua-makers', as well as the actresses flaunting their more obvious charms and beauties to invite further dalliance. Great excitement would be caused by the presence of some celebrity, or a fist-fight or a quarrel leading to drawn swords and a little bloodletting. An even greater attraction was a Tyburn hanging, for the processions passed often through Wych Street to the Tyburn Road (Oxford Street) and even upon occasion through Covent Garden itself – there was at one time a gallows in Catherine Street. Huge assemblies came from all over London to enjoy the spectacle, shouting abuse, singing ribald songs or pelting the unlucky criminal with dirt and dung.

There would doubtless be the occasional selling or auctioning of wives in the market-place. Before the passing of the Marriages Act in 1754, wives were regarded as one of the husband's chattels. The woman would have a noose round her neck and sometimes her hands tied behind her back. Most often the proceedings were a parody because the successful bidder was usually the wife's lover. The sale was clinched when both men spat on their hands, clasped hands firmly and shouted the price – usually between 5 and 10 shillings. But often a man would sell his wife as his only chattel because he was starving. Nobody knew whether the practice was legal or not so that generally a blind eye was turned to it. In any case, divorce was far outside the reach of the poor.

In 1751, with the passing of the Act Regulating the Commencement of the Year (the switch from the Julian to the Gregorian calendar), there were riots in Covent Garden and Westminster with the crowds shouting 'Give us back our eleven days!' Later in the century there was the excitement at the hustings outside the church during elections.

All this was free except for the price of a coffee or a beer in one of the numerous hostelries.

These occurrences were an important factor in Covent Garden's survival, for in the mid-century there was plenty of competition from other pleasure centres. The Marylebone Gardens were opened in July 1738 and became very popular with 'the middle sort'. A silver token, price 12 shillings, secured admittance for two persons for one year to the concerts and other shows. The Gardens had the advantage at first of being quieter and more respectable, although the approaches were plagued by footpads and highwaymen, so that escorts were needed. Such was the Garden's popularity that two years later the entrance fee was raised to a guinea. One of the greatest attractions in 1747 was the popular singer Mary Ann Faulkner, *inamorata* of Lord Halifax.

The Gardens at Vauxhall, just across the river, also drew away many of the *haut ton* because they were easily reached across Westminster Bridge, newly built in 1750. But the greatest counter-attraction was Ranelagh, opened in 1742, with its great rotunda around which ladies and gentlemen and the greatest 'Toasts' paraded and gossiped and made assignations. The admission fee was half a crown, which included tea or coffee and bread and butter – but no liquor was served. However, the music was not up to much – a distinguished French visitor wrote: '*On s'ennui avec de la mauvaise musique et du thé et du beurre!*' Nevertheless, it weaned away much of the carriage trade from Covent Garden, some of it lost for ever because of the rising importance of the environs of St James, as well as the tremendous increase in coaches due mainly to the great improvement in roads, including the turnpikes or toll roads which enabled the wealthy as well as the rising middle class to travel more easily and widely to such sylvan villages as Knightsbridge and Kilburn, Islington and Sadler's Wells and even further, as far as Hertford and Tunbridge Wells.

The demand for bigger and better coaches created a new industry, and Long Acre became one of the greatest centres of coach-building, employing hundreds of people and finding work in the ancillary trades for such as out-of-work sedan-chairmen. But in contrast, because these coaches could now carry large amounts of heavy luggage, hundreds of labourers and odd-job men were made idle because porters, carriers and packhorses were rendered superfluous.

As poverty grew more intense, crimes of violence increased: the numbers of footpads and highwaymen grew so that it was even dangerous to travel by daylight, Knightsbridge and Hammersmith being particularly vulnerable to hold-ups by highwaymen. Footpads were numerous even outside Marylebone Gardens. Others turned to coin-clipping and counterfeiting – both hanging offences – and several alleys around Clare Market were nests of counterfeiters. There was tremendous activity in the fencing of stolen jewellery, in which occupation a number of Jews were engaged, known for the speed with which gold and silver were melted down and rendered untraceable. At one time Henry Fielding secured the help of the elders of the Jewish community to bring some malefactors to justice, especially if violence had been committed.

By the mid 1740s Jews were no longer strangers – a great number were British-born. Their relationship with Covent Garden's loose ladies was by now quite longstanding – as early as 1701 Tom Brown of Shifnal in his *Letters* had made a prostitue say that she had sold her maidenhead to fifteen customers 'and by the same token seven of them were Jews'. John Gay in *The Beggar's Opera* (1728) has Slammekin, arguing with Jenny, exclaiming, 'I, Madam, was once kept by a Jew, and bating their Religion, to Women they are a Good Sort of People!' Henry Fielding in his *Covent Garden Tragedy* (1745) makes Lovegirlo boast: 'By Jove! I'll force the *Sooty Tribe* to own that a Christian keeps a Whore as well as they!' Hogarth in *The Harlot's Progress*, plate 2, depicts young Moll Hackabout, having been seduced and abandoned by Colonel Francis Charteris, now under the protection of a rich Sephardic Jewish 'fop', the Jewish ambience being shown by a round of matzoth (unleavened bread) hanging on the wall.

The other factor helping Covent Garden to resist the attractions of its competitors was a change in public attitudes towards the theatres. These were about to be revitalized in ways as yet unthought-of, bringing back the 'People of Fascination' as well as the burgeoning mass of 'People of the Middle Sort'.

12. The Theatrical Connection

The Covent Garden of 1737 was in many respects the same as in the time of John Gay and Dean Swift, when a favourite jingle was:

> Prepare for Death if here at Night you roam
> And sign your Will before you sup from home!

In this situation John Rich's splendid new theatre in Bow Street also played a part, bringing in crowds from outside to swell the thronging streets. Rich produced still the dumb-miming type of pantomime entertainment, himself acting as the Harlequin; the roundly pornographic Restoration plays were also presented. But the audiences and their tastes had begun to change: the less sophisticated taste of the middle classes demanded less pornography and more comedies of a sentimental and moral nature, reflecting perhaps an emergent humanitarianism. An anonymous contemporary wit observed: 'England was a highly moral Nation while at the Play'. Both managements and actors failed to react to this changing situation, although John Payne Collier's attack on pornographic programmes should have alerted them.

In 1737 two young and impecunious men arrived from the quiet county town of Lichfield. Neither David Garrick nor Samuel Johnson could afford the coach, so they travelled with one horse, riding and walking alternately. Garrick's father was a Captain of Dragoons on half-pay and Johnson's a not very successful bookseller. Garrick had three halfpence in his pocket; Johnson was the richer by a penny.

Johnson, shabby, uncouth, with pockmarked face, rented a garret in a poor staymaker's house in Exeter Street and was to subsist on bread and water (or even go without dinner) and suffer several years of penury before he rose to great fame as *savant* and lexicographer, deeply concerned with social and political problems. Even when he had moved away from the Garden, he was

THE OLD THEATRE, DRURY LANE.

This Front which stood in Bridges Street, was built by order of Mr Garr
previous to parting with his share of the Theatre.

See Pennants Lond

Publish'd June 1 1794 by N. Smith Mays Buildings St Martins Lane.

often to be seen in the bookshops there, in one of which he met James Boswell.

David Garrick, young and handsome and nine years younger than his friend, made his name quickly and by 1742 was part-manager of Drury Lane Theatre and earning large sums of money. In contrast to Johnson, who had become the epitome of conservatism, Garrick was a theatrical revolutionary and was to outshine his famous predecessors, Charles Macklin and James Quinn, by completing the escape from the old traditions then stifling the life of the theatre.

First he established order in the playhouse by removing the boxes from the stage. In 1749 he advertised that nobody would be allowed to go behind the scenes. This met with opposition from actors who used to fraternize during performances with their friends and supporters, but by hiring burly minders, one at each side of the stage, he enforced his will. Garrick's actors now had command over their own space, free from interference. He brought discipline to rehearsals and encouraged whatever talent there might be. In 1750 he innovated the dropped curtain between acts, so that scene-shifting and scene-shifters were hidden from the audience. He appointed the famous composer Thomas Arne as Musical Director to ensure that the musical intervals should keep the audience attentive, and his own prologues were direct and truthful. Not until much later did he come round to dressing the players in costumes appropriate to the play's period, following Macklin's appearance in kilts and tartans in *Macbeth*, in which play Garrick himself had previously appeared in full Hanoverian officer's rig!

He could not solve the vexed question of remuneration of playwrights and players. This was an overhang from Caroleian times when most authors had been aristocratic amateurs or scholars writing as a pastime, not particularly bothered about payment for their work. But by Rich's time professional dramatists had emerged, who were paid by results. The dramatist was entitled to the proceeds (after the manager's expenses) of three 'benefits' on the third, sixth and ninth performance of his play, so that he was compelled to hawk around the tickets to friends and supporters to ensure a minimum audience, sometimes even before the play was produced. It was humiliating but had the advantage of bringing him in contact with a wide range of theatre-goers.

The greatest sufferers were the actors and actresses. Except for the most illustrious, their wages were always very low, and they were dependent on public goodwill for their annual 'benefit' which was designed to eke out their meagre earnings. In practice this degraded the lower-paid artistes even further, keeping them 'in hopeless serfdom', forcing many of the women into part-time prostitution in order to exist. This helps explain the great increase in the demi-reps who swelled the ranks of courtesans around Covent Garden and why so many of the most famous actresses became so notorious for their amorous exploits. They needed to frequent the coffee-houses, taverns, bagnios and houses of assignation to enhance by their presence the reputation of these places as well as advertising themselves. It was extremely effective. The aristocracy, who had been deserting the Garden in favour of the more traditional offerings at the Italian Opera House – the King's Theatre in the Haymarket, to give it its official title – came swarming back to Covent Garden to enjoy the charms of the sprightly, beautiful and 'modern' young ladies to be found there.

Quite a few of these young ladies, such as Harriet Lamb and Elizabeth Farren, married happily into the peerage, and many others such as Martha Rae and Kitty Fredericks became permanent mistresses to other noblemen. Origin and race were no bar. Beauty, grace and good manners were the only pre-requisites – plus a little luck and sexual willingness.

The largest contingent was Irish. Their charm and gaiety enlivened every stratum of society, and their sexual exploits kept the gossip-mongers and scandal-sheets constantly happy.

First there was Catherine 'Kitty' Clive, daughter of a well-known Dublin lawyer. She had married when only eighteen the actor George Raftor, but the marriage foundered and this charming Irish beauty quickly found rich lovers amongst the fops and beaux, using them to further her theatrical career. For a while she was mistress to Henry Pelham, then Earl of Lincoln, and she had a platonic relationship with Horace Walpole. Indeed, when she retired from a highly successful career she went to live at his mansion in Strawberry Hill, where she died in 1785 well esteemed by everyone who knew her.

Another Hibernian beauty was Mary Ann Faulkner, niece of George Faulkner, 'Prince of Dublin Publishers'. She was an accomplished actress and singer, appearing regularly at Marylebone Gardens from 1747 to 1752, singing 'to the accompaniment of Musick Wine and Plum Cake'. She appeared occasionally at both theatres in Covent Garden, where she numbered among her lovers Sir George Saville and 'Lord Vainlove' – William Holles, Viscount Vane. In 1752 she became mistress to George Dunk, Earl of Halifax, when Lady Halifax (who had brought him a fortune of £100,000 in

172

1741) was dying. Mary Ann was already married to a poor Customs clerk, William Donaldson, who at once began to pressure Lord Halifax 'for Pension and Office'.

She and her brother, Captain George Faulkner, 'a scoundrelly blackmailer', enriched themselves by selling 'Places and Favours' granted by the besotted Halifax. When Lady Halifax died, in October 1753, Halifax declared his intention of marrying his mistress, but his family brought immense pressure to prevent such a *faux pas*. Mary Ann's heyday was during Halifax's term as Viceroy of Ireland between 1761 and 1763, when he acquired the nickname 'Hurgo Dunkara' (a Hurgo, pronounced 'whoorgo', was Swift's name for a Lilliputian nobleman), which epitomized both his high life-style and his sexual obsession. Mary Ann's reputation and rapacity were common knowledge.

In 1769 Donaldson charged the Earl with 'crim.con' with his wife, but he was bought off with a lucrative post in the Customs in Jamaica. The scandal-sheets went to town with the story of *Dunkara and Mariana*, and the liaison broke down, leaving Mary Ann to publish her *Memoirs as Mistress to Lord Halifax* in 1770. Halifax died in 1771 but Mary Ann was still in the news as late as 1785.

Donaldson later returned from Jamaica and invested some of his money in 'spungeing-houses' one of which was in Covent Garden and another in Turnham Green, in which he 'sheltered' Lucy Cooper prior to her death.

Undoubtedly the most famous Irish export was Margaret 'Peg' Woffington, daughter of a Dublin bricklayer. She possessed every blessing that it was possible to bestow upon any woman – beauty, charm, vivacity, wit and a generous-hearted nature, which was expressed by a brilliant smile for everyone she met. She also possessed an Irish temper which could flash out in a moment and be dissipated by a sense of humour equally as quick-witted. Moreover, she could act. She was also sexually very promiscuous but had the *nous* to choose her paramours carefully for maximum sexual enjoyment and financial advantage.

In 1742, at Drury Lane, she met and fell in love with David Garrick, and they lived together quite happily for a couple of years until a bitter quarrel ended the liaison. She continued to play in the theatre without speaking to him, communicating only by the exchange of notes.

Peg alternated between Drury Lane and Covent Garden theatres until in 1747 at Drury Lane she had a stroke and had to be carried off the stage. She was back in Dublin from 1750 to 1754, when she returned to London. Then occurred the famous incident when, playing opposite her *bête noire* George Anne Bellamy, her fake stabbing became a real one.

She was very extravagant and was thus always hard up, and she frequented Moll King's and the other hostelries and upon occasion would be seen enjoying herself in one or other of the well-known brothels. (The Harris List of 1764 mentions a young lady named Peg Woffington but explains that, 'This young tit takes her name from the late celebrated actress . . . but we cannot allow her so great a share of beauty as Peggy had' – an unusually fine tribute post-mortem).

The quarrel with Mrs Bellamy is the more curious because at one time Bellamy's father, the lecherous old Lord Tyrawley, had been turned down by Peggy in splendid fashion. Not only was he worn out but he also had syphilis and she was taking no chances, 'Captain! I accept your Compliments as an *Irish Oak* of sixty years is superior to an *English Deal* of twenty-six; but their Timber is all free from *Vermin* and your's is subject to Perish ere it has obtained its first Verdure!'

In her career Peg Woffington had shared her favours with such notorious wenchers as John Campbell, Earl of Loudon (who would need a Leporello to chronicle all his sexual encounters), the gallant Field-Marshal Edward, Lord Ligonier, 'a very gay dog', Thomas Medlicott MP, 'the licentious Medlycot', and Charles Hanbury Williams, MP for Eton, later Envoy at the Courts of Dresden and St Petersburg, for which services he was knighted in 1744. He committed suicide in 1759, a bitter, frustrated man.

The English contribution to the *filles de joie* was no less glamorous. First and foremost was the lovely, graceful Frances Barton, daughter of a poor soldier of good family – his father had been a prebendary of Westminster – a Guardsman turned cobbler, Christopher Barton. The child had some dire experiences, starting as a flower-girl in Covent Garden market, where she was known as 'Nosegay Fan'. She earned extra money by singing ditties and reciting poems in the Bedford Head and the Piazza Coffee-House. She then went into employment with a French milliner in Cockspur Street where she picked up fine dress sense and a knowledge of French; she also picked up something else, which compelled her to spend a time in the Lock Hospital.

Then Frances worked for a while in Mrs Sally Parkes' brothel in Aldersgate Street and followed her into her much more elegant and famous house in Spring Gardens near Charing Cross. Here she was taken by Mrs Parkes' own lover, a rich Creole, whereupon Mrs Parkes threw her out. In desperation she became a cookmaid in

Robert Baddeley's house but, this proving no way to better herself, she went into Charlotte Hayes' high-class 'house of convenience' in Great Marlborough Street, where she was groomed and polished. Here she became very friendly with gentlemen who frequented the Covent Garden theatres, her talent was recognized, she was 'discovered' and in the summer of 1755 she made her first appearance on the stage at the Haymarket Theatre in the part of Miranda. Shortly afterwards, '. . . she imbrac'd Mr Lacy at Drury Lane.' She was then eighteen years old.

There she met Abington, a trumpeter in the Guards, and he became her music master and her lover. They lived together in the same boarding-house until one evening '. . . the maidservant coming in as usual to warm her bed with a pan of hot coals . . . saluted the posterior of Mr Abington by accident . . . setting the bed on fire. . . .' Miss Barton and her paramour were compelled to leave the house. Soon afterwards she married Abington, who could see that she was becoming a star and decided to take advantage of the situation. The marriage was a disaster, partly because young Fanny was on the make and consorted with many lovers. She needed them because she was a heavy, compulsive gambler and constantly hard up.

The roster of her lovers is impressive. There was that 'unmitigated profligate and even greater wencher than his father the Admiral', Captain Jack Byron, known as 'Mad Jack' for his courageous exploits on the battlefield and as 'the Boisterous Lover' for his exploits in bedrooms. (His only real claim to remembrance is that he was the famous Lord Byron's father.) Another intimate friend was Admiral (later Viscount) Samuel Hood. The House of Lords was very well represented in Frances' collection, although '. . . she did not disdain the embraces of the Commons when her need for money was pressing.' Indeed, about 1760 she was already on the Harris list, which noted that, 'Miss Barton then did not keep a Coach: and was glad to take her place behind the celebrated Miss Lucy Cooper.' She was criticized for 'her shameless attire which exposed her almost entirely naked bosom to lascivious leering glances'.

Frances separated her lovers into 'those whose liberality gave her a life of splendour and those whom she picked-up at random as the humour took her'. The Creole once more appeared on the scene and set her up in a very elegant maisonette in St Martin's Lane, conveniently near to the Covent Garden theatres, but within four months he was recalled to the West Indies and disappeared from her life.

Abington was now becoming a nuisance: frequent public quarrels tended to damage her fast-growing reputation. He was 'persuaded' to accept £500 'on condition that he forbore ever to approach her'. She was then 'in keeping' with a wealthy West of England squire, Mr Needham (father of the future MP for Newburgh); he was probably the 'purchaser' but he died shortly afterwards leaving her a small annuity.

By 1770 Frances was one of the most famous actresses in Britain. In Dublin she was also the leader of fashion, the 'Abington cap' being all the rage amongst the ladies. But despite all her earnings she was always deep in debt because of her gambling and general extravagances, and in 1773 she was again in the Harris list, which reminded her that thirteen years previously she had not been so grand. She now kept 'an elegant house . . . but her salary, tho' genteel is not sufficient to maintain her Table and Manner of living, altho' Mr [Thomas Jefferson] makes it up. . . . She measures Gentility by the weight of her Purse.'

In 1775 Frances returned to London at David Garrick's invitation and appeared at Drury Lane and Covent Garden until 1790 when it was remarked that '. . . her Person had become full and her Elegance somewhat unfashionable.' Meanwhile she had been enjoying the favours of William Petty, Marquis of Lansdowne, in his elegant house in Clarges Street, Mayfair, with a 'settlement' of £50 a week, and she was still living there 'upon a comfortable independency keeping a very elegant Carriage' after her last stage appearance in 1799. Nevertheless, she still found it necessary to be seen at Charlotte Hayes' prestigious 'nunnery' in King's Place and at Nelly Elliott's popular bagnio in Newman Street off the Oxford Road, and even at Mrs Cosway's house of assignation in Stratford Place in Oxford Street. Here she met, among others, Henry Dundas, later to be Lord Dundas. This period of affluence gradually diminished. By 1807 her gambling had brought her low and she was reduced to two rooms at 19 Eaton Square, in which she died in very poor circumstances on 4 March 1815, still esteemed as a great actress.

Another famous actress-whore was George Anne Bellamy, an illegitimate daughter of the incorrigible lecher James O'Hara, Earl of Tyrawley, by a young girl named Searle whom he had enticed from a boarding-school. The child was born in 1731 and was supposed to have been baptized Georgiana but the deaf and not quite sober old priest misheard the whispered instruction and she was known as George Anne all her life. To give him his due, the old Earl always described himself as 'a humorous profligate character' and took a close interest in the welfare of his numerous – and all admitted – progeny, including George Anne and her brother, the later General Charles O'Hara.

Early in her career she fell in love with George Metham, son of a wealthy country squire, who could not marry her because of his father's opposition. When she was pregnant she married a Captain Bellamy, who deserted her after her 'premature' baby was born. She had another son by Metham sometime later.

Baron d'Archenholz in 1773 wrote: '. . . her beauty, her wit, her intelligence, her talents and her generosity and refined manners irresistibly attracted everyone to her', and her friend Barney Thornton eulogized her in his *Drury Lane Journal*: 'Oh! the Mrs Bellamy! the fine, the charming, the Every Thing Mrs Bellamy – the best actress and handsomest Woman in the World!'

George Anne was one of the first to demand the emancipation of women. She was quick-tempered and forceful, able to follow political affairs, at the same time pursuing a highly successful stage career at Covent Garden Theatre. Even ladies of the highest rank maintained social intercourse with her because of her refined manners, her high intelligence and her stand on women's liberation, despite her numerous and highly publicized love affairs.

Her long and involved *affaire* with the rich Government contractor John Calcraft was bedevilled by disputes and quarrels over money, aggravated by her extravagance and promiscuity and his constantly evasive promises to marry her. He was generous to their three children and always, albeit eventually and with great reluctance, paid her debts. Even so, she had one spell in the King's Bench debtors' prison before being rescued. On one memorable occasion her good friend Count Haszlang appointed her his 'housekeeper' to give her diplomatic immunity – but the bailiffs got her in the end.

She counted amongst her intimate friends Sir Francis Dashwood and some of his Medmenham 'friars', such as the 'Wicked' Lord Lyttelton, Philip Stanhope, Earl of Chesterfield, George, Earl Spencer, and the great dancing clown Henry Woodward – who was very good to her in adversity. George Methan, now Sir George Montgomerie-Metham Bart., remained in touch with her but never got around to marrying her. Meanwhile Calcraft was disporting himself with Lucy Cooper and the 'Bird of Paradise' and keeping as permanent mistress the young and lovely Elizabeth Bride, by whom he had several children.

While making some arrangements in 1772 about an annuity for George Anne, Calcraft died, leaving a considerable estate in some disorder. Her stage career was coming to an end and, although she had two excellent 'benefits' in May 1785, her debts overwhelmed her. When Calcraft's executors refused to honour his promise of a substantial annuity, she found herself in the Fleet debtors' prison in 1786. Her father had died in 1773 and her daughter Caroline had 'long forsaken her'; most of her friends had been alienated. She died 'in great poverty and Misery' in 1788.

One of the most bizarre actress-courtesans was Elizabeth Ashe, 'a small pretty Creature . . . between a Woman and a Fairy', daughter of John Ashe, one of His Majesty's Commissioners of Customs – although she always claimed that she was the illegitimate daughter of Admiral Lord Rodney and the Princess Amelia. When very young she was often in Covent Garden mixing with the *haut ton*. In 1751 she married the scapegrace Edward Wortley-Montague but he left her a year later because of her promiscuity. Ten years later she married Captain Robert Falconer RN but before long she was carrying on a lesbian relationship with the equally profligate Lady Caroline 'Polly' Harrington (also a frequenter of Covent Garden 'stews'). The friendship was broken when Miss Ashe became the mistress of Count Josef Franz Xavier Haszlang, Bavarian Envoy to London, who was very well liked in all circles in London Society as a pleasant, helpful and compassionate man. Lady Harrington, one of the most powerful Society hostesses, claimed that 'her character was demolished' by her friend's actions. Despite her two marriages, Elizabeth was always known as 'Little Ash', and Horace Walpole nicknamed her 'the Pollard Ash', observing that 'she had had a large collection of amours' before she died, still gay and happy, at the age of eighty-four.

Even more bizarre is the story of George Bubb-Dodington, Baron Melcombe, and his black mistress. George Bubb was the son of a rich self-made builder and had added the Dodington name on the death in 1720 of an uncle who had property in the Piazza. He lived there until 1730, when the lease was taken over by John Rich 'for the Theatre'. From 1698 until 1737 Nico Strawbridge resided in Russell Street next door to Will's Coffee-House. She was a beautiful, imperious and intensely jealous young woman who became Bubb-Dodington's mistress sometime about 1730. George was absolutely besotted with her and would kneel before her in public; moreover, he had promised her 'under a Bond of Twenty Thousand Pounds' that he would never marry anybody but her. (He kept secret from her that in 1725 he had married his ex-mistress Katherine Behan.) In 1740 George, who amongst other things fancied himself a poet and a Wit, composed a long poem which ended:

Tho' many are the Beauties
And many who excel
Yet Strawbridge, sweet Strawbridge
Shall bear away the Bell!

George had by then ingratiated himself into the Prince of Wales' circle, lending him large sums of money which he never reclaimed. The Prince, Frederick Louis, was estranged from his father and was deliberately kept short of funds for his own gambling and wenching exploits, and even for his day-to-day expenses. George was 'an obsequious toady' angling for a peerage.

He introduced 'his jetty mistress' into the highest Society, where she was well received, but she died suddenly in 1742 without ever knowing of her lover's duplicity. (Curiously enough, Kate Behan, his wife, was until her death in 1756 always thought to be George's mistress.) In 1761 he was created Baron Melcombe of Melcombe Regis but did not enjoy his honour long, for he died in the following year. Melcombe Street, hard by St Marylebone Station, is his most lasting memorial.

To complete the tally, there were a number of Jewish actresses who made their mark and were much courted by beaux and fops. The earliest on record was the beautiful, well-educated and charming Hannah Norsa, a daughter of the owner of the Punch Bowl Tavern in Drury Lane, Isaac Norsa, scion of a famous Italian-Jewish rabbinical family, which had numbered eminent singers in its ranks. She made her debut at Covent Garden in 1732 when she was twenty and was an immediate success.

At the Haymarket in 1736 Hannah met Sir Robert Walpole, shortly afterwards becoming his mistress and being dubbed 'Lady W's Vice-Regent'. It was alleged she lent Walpole £3,000 upon his promise to marry her when he was free, and she lived with him in great style at his mansion at Haughton, being styled Mrs Haughton, but in the event he neither married her nor repaid the loan.

Horace Walpole recorded that in 1746 he met 'the father of my brother's concubine, an old Jew, Issachar. . . . And was well impressed with his wit, humour and manner', but soon afterwards the liaison ended and Hannah resumed her stage career under John Rich at Covent Garden. By 1749 '. . . she was much reduced in Fortune . . . living on John Rich's charity.' She died in 1785.

Better known was Eleanor Ambrose, one of the three gifted daughters of Isaac Abrahams, a Portuguese Jewish merchant. All three were beautiful, well-educated, musical and well mannered, speaking French and Italian.

179

A later view by Maurer (1753). Lord Archer's house is at the rear far left. In the right-hand corner is the Shakespeare's Head. Mother Douglas's bagnio is under the tenth arch from James Street, which is shown bisecting the piazza

Eleanor made her debut briefly at Drury Lane and then turned demi-rep, her lovers including Sir Francis Blake Delaval, Admiral Lord Howe, Admiral Lord Rodney, Sir Robert Walpole and the Earl of Harrington. These and others kept her so well occupied that she did not resume her stage career until 1761, at Drury Lane, where she appeared regularly until 1782, being known to all as 'Nosegay Nan', with a voice described as 'famous'. She also appeared occasionally at Covent Garden, striking up a friendship with Charles Macklin and becoming his mistress for a while. Her sister Maria was Sir Edward Walpole's mistress for many years, and the liaison only ended with his death in 1784. The youngest sister Nancy was also an actress at Covent Garden but early in 1783 (*vide* the *Rambler* magazine) Macklin dismissed her – 'a fortunate circumstance for that young lady' who was being pursued by a rich admirer in Hammersmith who was to marry her. Nancy had spent

some useful formative years in Mrs Prendergast's exclusive 'nunnery' in King's Place, 'being greatly admired for her gentle manners and education'.

At one time when things were low, Macklin took Eleanor and Nancy and their mother to Dublin 'to restore their fortunes', and there they enjoyed the abundant hospitality of a young Irish rake, Sir Henry Echlin, Bart. Returning broke to London, they were rescued by Sir Francis Blake Delaval, who set up the sisters and their mother in a small house in Marylebone, 'taking the sisters' earnings as singers in payment for an allowance made to Nancy'. Eleanor resumed her stage career at Drury Lane from 1787 to 1789, when she retired to the small house, dying there in 1818, being then in her eighties.

There are very few references to Jewish prostitutes in the Garden. The Harris List for 1773 advertised 'Miss Robinson, a Jew . . . who could be found at the Jelly-shops', 'a spirited woman . . . Elizabeth Waterman who is really Miss Jacobs . . . at the King's Arms in Catherine Street', and 'Dutchy', 'a pretty girl with glossy black hair . . . a daughter of some of the Tribes of Israel, Dutch by birth and speaking broken English . . . at Crown Court in Russell

Street'. (Her father strongly rejected his daughter's mode of life and had disowned her.)

In the 1779 edition Harris refers to Miss Baruk, 'a smart little Jewess who has given up the Sons of Circumcision for the substantial blessings of Christianity . . . she is about 21, good features, fine eyes, always very merry and good humoured'. Her father, a respectable schoolmaster in Autres Place, was angry and broken-hearted that his daughter had turned into 'a Christian whore'. There was also Miss Levi, who at the age of seventeen was operating from the Denmark Coffee-House in Brydges Street, when she 'renounced her Levitical friends for the sake of a Christian Attorney, who gave her inward proofs of the new faith . . . she has a sprightly disposition, good teeth, fine eyes which are very bright . . .'. By 1779 she had already been 'on the game' for five years.

In contrast the three quite respectable Abrams sisters were able to make their way to success without resort to dubious practices. Harriet, at her debut at Drury Lane in October 1775, was hailed as 'an English soprano of Jewish descent'. The *Drury Lane Journal* said that she was very young, with a sweet voice and fine 'shake' and was received with great applause, although the *Public Advertiser* of the same date ended its luke-warm criticism with the words: '. . . the number of Jews at the theatre is incredible.' When her two sisters grew up, they sang as a trio in concerts at grand houses arranged by Madame Blubber, and they had good benefits between 1792 and 1795, when they played with Haydn. Gillray depicted them 'trilling away in the corner' at one of Lady Bucking-hamshire's gambling parties in 1794. All lived to great ages.

Dr Johnson, surveying the social scene, called the swaggering beaux and rakes whoremongers 'who deal with women like a dealer in any other commodity . . . as an ironmonger sells iron-mongery', and later, as a comment upon the myth of gentlemanly behaviour, he remarked: 'Most vices may be committed very genteelly; a man may debauch his friend's wife genteelly; he may cheat at cards genteelly.' He was, however, not averse to pretty actresses. He was a highly sexed man and often tempted, but eschewed both prostitutes and brothels, relieving himself by onanism.

By the mid-century some of the glitter was departing from Covent Garden. Henry Fielding remarked in 1752: 'Within the memory of many now living the circle of *People of Fascination*

(Opposite) Stow's plan of Covent Garden, 1755

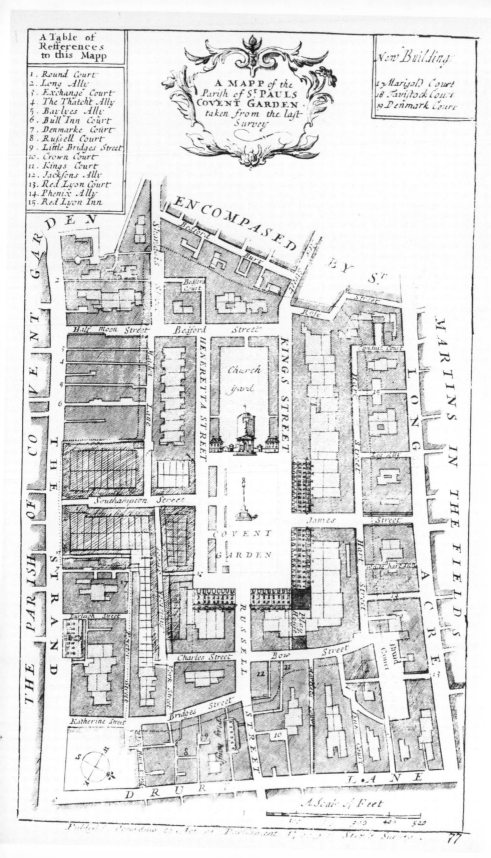

A Table of Refferences to this Mapp

1. Round Court
2. Long Ally
3. Exchange Court
4. The Thatcht Ally
5. Baylyes Ally
6. Bull Inn Court
7. Denmarke Court
8. Russell Court
9. Little Bridges Street
10. Crown Court
11. Kings Court
12. Jacksons Ally
13. Red Lyon Court
14. Phenix Ally
15. Red Lyon Inn

A MAPP of the Parish of St PAULS COVENT GARDEN taken from the last Survey

New Building

17 Marigold Court
18 Tavistock Court
19 Denmark Court

COVENT GARDEN

THE PARISH OF

MARTINS IN THE FIELDS

ENCOMPASED BY St

LONG ACRE

Shandois Street

Bedford Bury

James Street

Rose Street

Bedford Court

Half moon Street

Bedford Street

Walter Lane

HENRETTA STREET

Church yard

KINGS STREET

Chandois Court

Hart Street

Southampton Street

COVENT GARDEN

James Street

Charles Church Court

THE STRAND

Russell Street

Bow Street

Hud Court

Wm leigh Street

Charles Street

Drury Lane

York Street

Marquis Court

12

11

13

Katherine Street

Bridges Street

8

9

10

RUSSELL STREET

DRURY LANE

A Scale of Feet

Published according to Act of Parliament 1720 by Stow Survey.

77

included the whole parish of Covent Garden . . . but [now] . . . the circle contracted to Leicester Fields and Golden Square. Hence *People of Fashion* retreated . . . to Hanover Square whence they were driven to Grosvenor Square.'

As if by design from on high to hasten the decline, Peg Woffington died on 28 March 1760 'wasted away to a Skeleton'. King George II died on 25 October of the same year; *Mother* Douglas died 'in her House under the Piazza' on 19 June 1761 and John Rich on 26 November, likewise in his house in the Piazza. Of these four Mother Jane Douglas' demise has the greatest significance here because she was the last of the great bawds in Covent Garden to cater for the nobility and gentry in an elegant but rumbustious style which suited the early Hanoverian period. Those 'houses' which remained accommodated a less exalted clientele with fewer pretensions, with the sole exception of the elegant and sophisticated French-style seraglio being run in the Little Piazza by Mrs Elizabeth Gould.

13. Mrs Elizabeth Gould

High in the reputation of Covent Garden procuresses was the woman known as Mrs Gould. She was born Elizabeth Gold, about 1720, and first comes into the light as the ratepayer of 5 Bow Street, adjacent to the theatre, in 1742. Nothing is known of her antecedents. The house in Bow Street was clearly a small brothel of no particular eminence, but she was obviously a woman of parts with an eye to the future. She anticipated the changes in the Garden and had early decided to emulate the example of Jane Goadby who was the first to open up in London a Parisian-style bordello to cater for the growing army of wealthy men extending their sexual education by foreign travel. Mrs Goadby's luxurious house in Great Marlborough Street was the forerunner of the even more palatial 'nunneries' to be opened near the royal palace of St James by mid-century. But Mrs Gould's was the only one in Covent Garden in due course.

She was a handsome woman of imperious mien and, more importantly, possessed of a good head for business. She had early decided that 'The Sins of others would be her Sin' – a golden phrase coined more than a hundred years earlier by that princess of whoredom Donna Britannica Hollandia.

The aristocracy were beginning to desert Covent Garden so far as their sexual requirements were concerned, although they would continue to visit the theatres and coffee-houses for other diversions. There was a need for a well-appointed, quiet, 'respectable family-style house' for the wealthy citizens and merchants of the City of London who were not at ease amongst the noble snobs in St James – indeed, most of them would not be admitted into such High Society, however wealthy or influential they might be.

This attitude also created difficulties for the wealthy and important members of the Ashkenazi Jews – generally called German Jews – who had fled from the European pogroms. Starting as artisans and small businessmen they had raised themselves by their bootstraps into the rapidly growing 'middle course of people'

Mrs Gould decided to cater for these 'tired businessmen' who wanted some peace and quiet and a little sexual diversion after a hard week in the City. Accordingly everything was geared to this group, and the *cuisine* was of the highest order, with only the finest wines and liquors being served by well-trained liveried flunkies. Their sexual needs were to be taken care of by hand-picked young ladies of the very best quality of beauty and charm and the greatest discretion. 'She would not engage any woman who was addicted to Intoxication or who used Bad Language' – indeed, none such would even be admitted to the establishment. All the young hostesses to be well dressed and well mannered with 'understanding of gentlemen's need's; all could dance and many had a knowledge of a foreign language. Virgins would be secured for those exigent and rich enough to pay for such extravagance. For all these delights, however, larger and more suitable premises were needed. Meanwhile, sometime between 1745 and 1755, Mrs Gould had married a Mr Leese and in that name had leased various properties in and around Covent Garden.

The chance came when 'distiller' John Bradley, a gin-shop proprietor and property speculator, wanted to lease the upstairs premises of his gin-shop at the corner of Russell Street and the Little Piazza. (Jane Douglas had occupied these premises when she came to the Garden in 1735.) It had been part of Matthew Lovejoy's infamous hummums. In March 1759 Mrs Leese took a lease from Bradley and moved in. According to the *Nocturnal Revels*, in the financing and preparation 'She had the backing of an Eminent and Wealthy Jewish Notary Public.' This must have been Moses Moravia, a ship-owner and ship-broker well known on the Exchange, who until 1752 had been an esteemed pillar of the Jewish community and a regular man-about-town. In June 1752 he and two others were found guilty of conspiracy to defraud an insurance company and were sentenced to a year's imprisonment, a large fine and to be stood in the pillory. Upon his release he returned to bill-broking and rehabilitated himself; he died in 1767 in somewhat strained circumstances because of riotous living and gambling.

Mrs Gould proceeded to equip the rooms as one of the most luxurious brothels in London. One great advantage was the two entrances, the essential pre-requisite demanded by Madame de Gourdan of Paris, Mrs Gould's mentor, one being the 'open door' for those not ashamed to be seen patronizing such an establishment, and another, around the corner, catering ostensibly for ordinary customers of a shop. Mrs Gould's entrance was at Russell Street, and the covert one was through Bradley's gin-shop. However, she eschewed Madame de Gourdan's advice to have a section devoted to the needs of the guests' servants and coachmen. She concentrated on 'the quality' and rich merchantry, although persons of eminence in other spheres were not excluded if they had money enough.

Accordingly the wealthy London Exchange brokers, City merchants and bankers were wont to come on Saturday evenings and stay over until Monday morning, enjoying peace and quiet; for further relaxation there was a gambling salon in which the stakes were very high. All disturbances or jarring incidents were avoided.

One of Mrs Gould's earliest clients was Moses Mendez, who spent more time in Covent Garden than in his City bill-broking business. He was but one of the many of 'the Sons of Circumcision' or 'Levites' who represented the City gentlemen of 'the middle course'.

Her young ladies had no fear that their profession would damage their prospects of marriage or a good and long-lasting 'settlement'. They were encouraged to save their money and maintain complete silence as to their activities and their clients. In this way, both they and Mrs Gould, by maintaining a low profile, never seem to have fallen foul of the law's minions, although sometimes, a fraught occasion could arise.

In 1762 it was reported in the *Memoirs of the Bedford Coffee House* that the comedian Sam Foote – then nicknamed 'Frontana' – had ruined his credit with the Covent Garden bagnio-keepers by his behaviour at Mrs Gould's. He had one evening brought a lady there and 'enjoy'd the supper and the accommodations so much that he stayed for a couple of weeks'. Mrs Gould, 'imagining him to be a Man of Fortune', let him run up a bill until he sent down one evening 'to borrow some Gold . . . which she lent him but made enquiries and discovered that he had no money . . . so she gave him a Bill and ordered him to leave'. Foote replied that he had ate and drunk at her house for almost three weeks, 'for which you have the conscience to charge me near Forty Pounds . . . which I shall not pay. If you arrest me I shall lay an Information against you for keeping a public brothel.' To get rid of him and avoid a scandal, Mrs Gould 'gave him the Bill receipted . . . altho' she never got a Farthing of it', but Foote was never admitted again.

The 1763 edition of these memoirs, discussing a charge of £5.14. for an overnight session with one of the Bedford's ladies, acidly remarks that Mrs Gould 'would have charged double . . . [and]

discovered some necessary articles such as a *Birch* to light your Fire with, a dozen or two of *Jellies*, White Gloves and Cold Creams . . . and a string of etceteras'. It is not clear whether the birch was intended to light a coal fire or to ignite the flames of passion – although flagellation *chez* Mrs Gould should not be excluded.

In March 1769 disaster struck the Little Piazza when the hummums all went up in flames, the entire façade of the buildings collapsing into rubble. W. C. Evans, the comedian, states that Mrs Gold then moved to Bow Street, presumably back to her original premises, since *The Meretriciad* (1770) says that she was still pursuing her career. She is last heard of in *Nocturnal Revels* (1779), which states, almost with reverence, that, '. . . she had recently retired with a handsom fortune.' Mrs Leese died on 24 May 1784 and was buried in the church of St Martin-in-the-Fields, and no more is heard of Parisian-style bordellos in Covent Garden.

The face of the Piazza reflected the changes, for now there were at least two commercial interlopers. Abraham Langford had taken over Christopher Cock's fine auction gallery, and Charles Moran, a bookseller, now had a shop. The management of several hostelries had also changed.

Callaghan's Coffee-House was now part of Haddock's bagnio being run by Sophia Lemoy. Charles Macklin had taken over Lucy Earle's establishment, calling it the Piazza Coffee-House which, after his bankruptcy in 1754, was taken over by Richard Maltby, and again in 1768 the management fell into the hands of Elizabeth Richardson (presumably) the wife of the ex-head waiter at the Shakespeare's Head. The Shakespeare's Head was flourishing under Packington Tomkyns, and Joe Selthe's old Sam's Coffee-House on the corner with Russell Street was now licensed as a public house. In the Little Piazza John Rigg, who had started as a 'cupper' in the cellar under Mrs Douglas' 'House of Civilitie' now leased the whole house, while next door Richard Vincent was soon to give way to Matthew Lovejoy. Testimony to their survival is found in William Hickey's *Diary*.

Hickey claimed to have discovered the joy of carnal copulation in the Garden when he was fourteen years old, when he 'picked up a girl under the Piazza . . . went up three pair of stairs in a dark narrow court off Drury Lane, where he offered her half-a-guinea (all he had) but she would only accept five shillings altho' she had not even a sixpence in her possession . . . then she took his dear little maidenhead'. He visited her several times later, although his sexual education was effected by a much older woman, Nanny Harris, in a court off Bow Street, 'where she fed him lobsters,

The great fire of 20 March 1769 which destroyed all the hummums *in the Little Piazza, including the* bagnios *of Matthew Lovejoy and Elizabeth Gould and* Distiller *Bradley's gin-shop. In the rebuilding the ruins of the colonnade were demolished and not replaced. (From an etching by W. Grimm)*

oysters and Rum Punch' from 1762 and again when in 1765 she moved to Cecil Street in the Strand.

Throughout 1765 and 1766 Hickey was often in the Shakespeare's Head, usually with two girls, and at the Bedford Head. At the Piazza Coffee-House, Maltby's, 'one could always be sure of a drink and a Doxy', or eating at Slaughter's and then going to 'the Old Frow's brothel at the top end of Bow Street' (Mrs Hamilton's) or to Mrs Cocksedge's 'next door to Sir John Fielding's'.

In January 1766 Hickey celebrated being articled to Mr Hayley the solicitor with a drinking debauch where he met Edward Thurlow – a future Lord Chancellor – whose usual haunt was Nandos' in Fleet Street. In November he participated in the whip-round to help Lucy Cooper, and in March 1768 discovered 'a diabolical den called *Wetherby*'s in the narrowest part of Little Russell Street' and Marjoram's – formerly run by Mother Jane Murphy in Tavistock Street, remarking that Ned Shuter was a favourite at both places. John Marjoram was to be found in Southampton Street from 1775 to 1787, with his diabolical reputation undented.

Another of Hickey's haunts was Stacies's – the Bedford Arms had been by then taken over by Dick Stacy – where he would drink himself into a stupor and manage to stagger over to Wheatherby's or to the equally disreputable Cross Keys, likewise in 'the narrowest part' of Little Russell Street. (This throwaway remark helps to pinpoint the locations of these dens.) When Nancy Harris died, 'a martyr to sexual and venereal diseases', he grieved for a few days and then sought out his long-time little friend Sally Brent and regaled her at Maltby's 'at considerable expense'. He boasted that he had no need for harlots because' . . . many fine women upon the Town would have been only too glad to accommodate him for nothing', mentioning among others Madame la Tour, then Lord Melbourne's mistress. Nevertheless, a few days later he went to the Shakespeare's Head with two well-known harlots, 'Priss' Vincent and Mary Newton, both concert singers and part-time actresses, but on his way over to Stacie's he was waylaid and robbed. His assailant, one of his table companions, was later transported to Botany Bay.

In 1768 the magistrate Saunders Welch reported to Sir John Fielding that of the inhabitants of Covent Garden '. . . a quarter were illiterate Paupers, helpless against their Fate, living in filthy obscene squalor, crowded together, starving and freezing in Winter. . . . [he had] visited houses where dead bodies had laid for days . . . they had all died of starvation . . . such people had to resort to crime just in order to exist. . . .' Many of the assaults and robberies were commited by gangs of homosexuals, who turned violent when their overtures were rebuffed. Because of the increasing poverty sodomites had multiplied and – as with others who were starving – crime was the only way out. In 1766 a chapbook *The Fruit Shop* has the verse:

> GO WHERE YOU WILL, at every Time and Place
> SODOM confronts and stares us in the Face;
> They ply in Publick at our very Doors
> And take the Bread from much more honest Whores . . .
> For Pleasure we must have a GANYMEDE,
> A fine fresh HYLAS, a delicious Boy
> To serve our Purposes of beastly Joy. . . .

A further discouragement to potential visitors was the activity of the press gangs, bands of men armed with cutlasses and led by

(Opposite) Sir John Fielding, blind half-brother of Henry Fielding

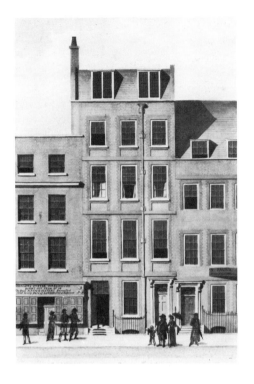

The Bow Street Public Office when removed across Bow Street to its present site. It was only legally established at a magistrate's court in 1792

Royal Navy officers who crimped men from ale-houses and streets and even from churches, whence bridegroom and male congregants were sometimes carried off. Families were broken up and ruined. Originally roving round the ports or anywhere where seamen congregated, the press gangs now ranged inland, and Covent Garden was an obvious target.

Finally, the Society for the Reformation of Manners about 1770 had this to say: 'Covent Garden is the Great Square of VENUS, and its purlieus are crowded with the practitioners of this Goddess. One would imagine that all the prostitutes in the Kingdom had decided on this neighbourhood . . . for lewd Women in sufficient numbers to people a mighty Colony . . . are not wanting . . . these Houses have become the Resort of abandoned Rakes and shameless Prostitutes. These and the Taverns afford an ample supply of Provision for the Flesh . . . and for this the *bagnios* are near at hand. . . .'

There were of course hundreds of establishments catering for the

(Opposite) A satire on the drunken constable whose duty was to carry out the proclamation against vice and drunkenness enacted by George III

A
PROCLAMATION
AGAINST
DRUNKENESS

needs of the less affluent men seeking some means of releasing their sexual frustrations. Thousands of impecunious young – and old – men could not afford the charges made in 'clean' brothels and had perforce to seek the services of ambulant harlots operating from rooms in lodging-houses.

Times were also bad for poor women and girls, for whom there was comparatively few outlets for earning a decent living. Domestic service was akin to slavery, and mass-production factories were yet to come. Living-conditions within the boundary of the parish of St Paul's, Covent Garden, were horrific.

By the middle of the century the problem had reached vast proportions. Even young rakes and would-be rakes had to settle for something less comfortable. A first-hand report from a very famous and reliable source sheds considerable light on the situation. The young reporter was James Boswell.

14. The Adventures of a pair of Rakes

James Boswell was twenty-one on 29 October 1761, and his father, Lord Auchinloch, had promised him a year in London if he passed his Bar examinations, which he did in July 1762. His father then gave him an allowance of £100 for the year, which meant that young James would have to be rather economical.

Boswell soon found lodgings in Downing Street, paying twenty-two pounds the year to include a breakfast of toast or rolls and tea from his own stock. He also had to pay for his own coals and candles. After breakfast he would walk to his chambers in the Temple and take his dinner at about 3 p.m. in a chop-house 'ordinary' for about 18d, and about 6 p.m. he would take his tea in a coffee-house. There he could sit, talk or read the newspapers for as long as he wished.

A little later Boswell was compelled to move to cheaper lodgings nearer to town, to make ends meet, because he could not ask his father for more money, and he got by with making frequent visits to friends and relations, where he was usually able to get a meal. He was very friendly with his cousin Alexander Montgomerie, tenth Earl of Eglinton, a well-known rake and sportsman, who moved in the highest Court circles as well as the lowest Covent Garden dives and theatres. One of his cronies, Sam Derrick, showed Boswell around and explained the situation to this 'country cousin'. He was introduced to such famous lechers as John Wilkes MP ('Wilkes and Liberty') and the poet Charles Churchill. He also met David Garrick, then managing Drury Lane Theatre, the singer John Beard, then managing the Covent Garden Theatre, and the comedian Sam Foote, then running the Haymarket Opera House. He lived in hopes of meeting willing actresses – but they only looked for beaux with money.

Then on the morning of Tuesday 25 November 1762, Boswell

195

woke up with the realization that he had been in town 'for some time without female Sport'. (He was not a virgin when he came to London: he had already used the services of Edinburgh's most famous bawd, 'Lucky' Spence, and had seduced one of his father's maids, whose son was born in December 1762.) Thus Boswell went into the Strand and picked up a girl, and they went 'into a narrow court with the intention to enjoy her in *armour* but she had none. I toy'd with her and she wondered at my size . . . I gave her a Shilling . . . I resolved to wait cheerfully until I got some safe girl or was liked by a Woman of Fashion.' (It is interesting to note that he thought the whore should supply the condum: generally speaking it was the man's responsibility to supply the 'armour'.) He was always worried about getting gonorrhoea.

Boswell was set upon being economical as he could not afford 'First-rate Dames' (nor the fees of London surgeons, 'which run very high'), so when he had a love affair with the actress Mrs Lewis (Louisa) who had a small flat in Covent Garden, he wooed her carefully but thriftily. She kept stalling him off for several weeks, then borrowed 2 guineas and let him consummate his desires on 12 January 1763, at which he was in raptures. Four days later he became alarmed at the 'little heat in that Member sacred to Cupid', realized that he had caught gonorrhoea and had to have treatment by his friend Dr Douglas. He was very angry with Louisa, who had thought that her bout had been cured: it was for that reason she had stalled him. She very punctiliously repaid him his loan.

Later in the year he went to listen to 'Sam Foote's comicalities' and that evening engaged in a 'brutish exertion with a low Wretch' on Westminster Bridge, this time in 'armour'. A week later he visited the Shakespeare's Head, where, although he had no money, he was to 'toy with two pretty young ladies' and enjoy 'high debauchery' – a remarkable feat for a penniless man – and there is no talk of 'armour'. The next day he picked up 'a fresh agreeable girl named Alice Gibbs' who preferred his advances 'without armour', although he had been at great pains to follow Mrs Phillips' instructions that her 'engines' were always to be washed before use.

On 4 June, the King's Birthday', he went into the Strand and 'picked up a little profligate Wench and gave her Sixpence . . . for which she allowed me Entrance, but refused Performance'. Justifiably incensed by this breach of contract he pushed her against the wall, whereupon she screamed and 'some soldiers and whores' came to her aid and threatened him with violence. He remonstrated, saying, 'Should not a Half-pay Officer roger for Sixpence?', explained the situation and left, after roundly abusing the girl. No soldier or whore would have dared to argue with an officer, and certainly not over a whore.

Boswell then (again) swore a resolution that, 'He would have no more rogering in England, except with Mrs . . . in my own Chambers', but coming up the Strand on 1 August he was tapped on the shoulder by 'a Fine Fresh Lass . . . an Officer's daughter . . . born in Gibraltar' and went home with her, 'armour' and other precautions thrown to the wind.

With this adventure he closed his diary. Three days later he was back in Edinburgh, once again to consort with local whores until he returned to London in 1772.

The other expert was the precocious womanizer, William Hickey. When, at twenty-one, he returned to Covent Garden after a brief exile in India, he lost no time in resuming his debaucheries with old as well as new acquaintances. He was now a member of the Madras Club at the Shakespeare's Head. His boon companions were a young American named Osborne, young Hayter – the son of his principal, an associate in the East India Company, Lieutenant Fredericks, and a wealthy young rake named Rhoan Hamilton. They called themselves, and behaved like, *Mohawks*. In the winter of 1771 after a drunken spree two of them spent a night in the Round House – Hickey implying that he was only an observer and not a participant. Three years later they created 'an outrage' in Covent Garden as a result of which Rhoan Hamilton 'paid all his debts and decamped'; Mr Hayter sent his son 'to rusticate in Holland'; young Osborne 'declared himself bankrupt and was sent back to America!' and Lieutenant Fredericks 'was killed in Action (in America) within the twelvemonth'.

Hickey was still living it up with some of the foremost 'Toasts of the Town', although often using the less expensive services of Sally Brent, even though from 1774 he was 'under treatment from Dr Hayes for a venereal disease'. Another was that Sally Hudson first advertised by Harris in 1764, now operating from Margaret Street after she had 'prudently saved £200 as Third Girl' in a fashionable bagnio (she was soon to open her own establishment in the Piazza and rise to fame as 'Mother' Hudson by 1780). Another was Clara Hayward, by now a famous actress as well as demi-rep, who openly boasted that she had received her training at Mrs Nancy Banks' school in Curzon Street and that her 'finishing-school' was Charlotte Hayes' famous establishment in Great Marlborough Street, from which she had been 'rescued' at considerable expense by Evelyn Meadows, later Duke of Kingston. She was then busily amassing money and valuable presents from a string of noble lovers. As late as 1784 she was described as one of 'the *Great Impures* . . . still lovely, lively and laughter-loving and in great demand for all social functions'.

Hickey renewed acquaintance with Mary Sturgess, previously known as Polly Jones 'a fine woman plump and lusty, with good skin and lovely eyes', with an elegant house in Cumberland Court off Drury Lane, and with the Larkins sisters, both Drury Lane actresses augmenting their earnings by intimate relationships with wealthy, theatre-haunting rakes. One of them claimed that when attending 'the late Earl of Chesterfield . . . his *caprice* was to have his eyes licked by a female tongue'.

Mary Newton was a concert singer of considerable merit, appearing often at the Marylebone Gardens and between 1747 and 1760 at Drury Lane; she was then (from 1738 till about 1766) living in a suite of rooms in Tavistock Street in which she entertained her clients. Elizabeth 'Priss' Vincent was also a popular singer at Marylebone Gardens, being billed as the Principal Vocalist from 1763 to 1766, but she was even more popular in the Shakespeare's Head at stag parties because of a 'rather special trick which she could be persuaded to perform for gentlemen only'. She was still going strong in 1781. Hickey also claimed to have been an 'old flame' of the lovely 'little Lamb' Harriet Powell, who later became Countess of Seaforth, when she was an inmate of Charlotte Hayes' 'nunnery': she would have been only about fourteen then!

As an indication of contemporary good manners and behaviour amongst the upper classes, Hickey's description of a Lord Mayor's banquet to which he had been invited is very revealing. The ceremony was dignified and superb but, 'Far different was the scene in the hall, where in five minutes after the guests took their stations at the tables the dishes were entirely cleared of their contents, twenty hands seizing the same joint or bird, literally tearing it to pieces . . . the roaring and noise was deafening and hideous, increasing as the liquor operated, bottles and glasses flying across from side to side without intermission. Such a Bear Garden I have never witnessed except on my first visit to Wetherby's . . . this abominable and disgusting scene continued until near ten o'clock when the dancing commenced. . . .'

The contents of these contemporaneous diaries clearly disclose the deep contempt with which in Georgian times young men regarded womenfolk. In public they considered them expendable play-things, some expensive and some cheap, to be taken up as pets for longer or shorter periods, then – if they were lucky – to be pensioned off with a 'settlement' but more than likely to be jettisoned. Enjoying the favours of a 'Toast' was just a notch in one's social ascent, which accounted for the merry-go-round by which the same group of aristocrats would purchase in turn the favour of a particular 'High Impure'. If she were outstandingly beautiful and very clever, she could make enough to ensure a comfortable end, and if she were a popular Drury Lane actress, she might, if she played her cards right, go on to old age. But more of them were dead or worn out by the time they were thirty-five or forty.

The tone of the Covent Garden bagnios was a mirror of the decline in manners. In 1764 Lord Pembroke recommended Casa-nova to go to 'a good brothel in the Strand' which turned out to be the Star, still owned by Peter Wood. Casanova asked the waiter to bring him a woman: the waiter explained that a number were available but the arrangement was that the gentleman would give each a shilling if he did not choose her. Casanova later told Pembroke that it cost him 20 shillings without result as he did not fancy any of them. His Lordship explained that it was a well-known ploy: the waiter sent in first the least desirable ones to allow them to earn a shilling, from which his commission was deducted.

On another occasion Casanova was introduced 'to a bagnio in the Strand where a rich man can sup, bathe, and sleep with a fashionable Courtesan . . . it makes a magnificent Debauch . . . and only costs six Guineas!' This was Haddock's original bagnio, the Turk's Head, now owned by Mother Olivia Harrington and known by all in 1764 as 'a fine place of resort'. Hickey's brother Henry was involved there in a drunken affray in 1770 when a man was killed; Henry fled abroad and died in Madras in 1774. It was usually known as Harrington's bagnio and was again in the news in 1778 when it was robbed, the robbers being caught and hanged. In 1789 there was a reference to 'a Messuage lately in the tenure of Mrs Harrington'. The year 1764 also witnessed the girl destined to be the next 'Toast of the Town' for about twenty years; her name was Betsy Coxe.

15. Betsy Coxe and other Votaries

One evening in Covent Garden in 1762 Captain Fox was accosted by a very pretty young girl, who took him to her room in Windmill Street. She was ill, diseased and utterly poverty-stricken and had been forced onto the streets because the landlady was badgering her for the rent. This little girl, 'born in profound obscurity' and at that time an orphan, was Elizabeth 'Betsy' Green. She had been born locally about 1748 of poor and illiterate parents and ill-treated and abused by all until the captain, who felt a certain compassion, took charge of her for a few weeks.

Fox mentioned the matter to his friend Lord Lyttelton, who agreed to take her off his hands. This was the blackguardly lecher who became known in later life as 'the Wicked Earl Lyttelton'. He treated the child so badly that after a fortnight Captain Fox took her away and put her into the care of Charlotte Hayes, 'under whose care and tuition her wonderful beauty was brought out. . . . No age or clime has ever produced such a perfect model of voluptuous beauty. Her confinement was neither tedious nor severe, but it wore off her extreme vulgarity, rust and general awkwardness. Moreover her language needed to be purified of offensive barbarisms.

When Betsy was seventeen, Charlotte introduced her as 'a Delicious Young Girl' to some chosen gentleman friends, and she became the 'Toast' of many clubs. Three years later she yielded to Colonel John Coxe, whose name she adopted when it was said that, 'No man has even indulged a mistress so lavishly.' He had to go abroad very frequently and as soon as his back was turned 'She assembled all her most abandoned companions of either sex and converted his house into a temple of debauchery . . . of orgies of *Bacchus* and the rites of *Priapus* . . . his choicest wines and viands were squandered by this rabble.' This went on for four years until his patience snapped and he threw her out.

Betsy then took lodgings in Curzon Street, Mayfair where she was 'protected' by Lord Falkirk, who later became Earl of Alford. She then became known as 'the very *Rage* of London' but the owners of the house got fed up with the noise and disturbance caused by so many visitors, so she moved over to Mother Nancy Bank's house nearby, where 'her turbulent attitude' exasperated the bawd's patience, causing her to move about 1769 to Long Acre.

Betsy's appearance and fine contralto voice soon got her onto the stage at Drury Lane, usually in parts where she could wear male attire, but the money was poor. Through her friendship with Sally Hudson – another of Nancy Banks' star boarders – she found a steady protector in the young Henry Nevill, still a student at Oxford, who was later to become the second Earl of Abergavenny. In her role as the acknowledged 'Beauty of Long Acre' she was chosen to open the brilliant ball at the Pantheon in January 1776. The Master of Ceremonies, in accordance with his published principles, forbade this but was persuaded to change his mind when swords were drawn by a couple of young bloods – one of them the Duke of Fife – and Betsy became the belle of the ball and London's finest 'Toast'.

All this had gone to her head, and by now she had become a veritable termagant. 'Let a waiter at Ranelagh delay providing her with Tay, or a link-boy for her Coach . . . and to the rage of Moorfields she will add the language of Billingsgate and the discipline of Hockley-i'-th'-Hole!' (This enclave in Saffron Hill was then regarded as the very sink of iniquity and depravity in all London.) Nor was her behaviour any better in the resorts in the Piazza, where in 1780 her name was often linked with those of the Earl of Craven and Thomas Howard, Earl of Effingham. Drink and debauchery were now taking their toll but still she was reckoned to be one of the thirteen 'Most Celebrated Courtesans' in London, in 1780 – three years later she was down to number nineteen, in the list of 'Most Fashionable Votaries of Venus'.

In 1785 the *Rambler* recorded that poor Betsy had been abandoned by her Hibernian lover, who had left her indigent, so that '. . . she is eleemosynarily dependent upon the Sisterhood.' Clearly this was not much help because her name next appears in the Harris List 1788 being described as 'formerly the *Toast* of the *Bucks* at Bath, but now to be found at Mrs Kelly's *seraglio* in Duke Street together with her old chum, Sally Hudson. She died, 'in abject poverty' on June 14, 1814 at the age of 79.

A strong contender for the highest place was her contemporary, Mrs Jane Lessingham, who at one time was referred to 'a Thaïs of

Sam Derrick and (opposite) his faithless, promiscuous mistress, the famous comedy actress Jane Lessingham

the First Rank.' She early 'felt a strong propensity for the stage' and owed her start to the loving coaching of Sam Derrick, with whom she was sharing 'a poor tenement in a floor two pairs of stairs high in Shoe Lane', not far from the Old Bailey. Both were desperately poor and subsisted on her small earnings as an actress. For a while they had lived in the house of the famous 'oculist' John Taylor, but they were asked to leave when 'she proved not to be his wife.'

Derrick, popularly known as 'the Poet', was intimate with everyone connected with the Covent Garden stage and took great pains to prepare Jane for her first appearance in 1756. She was an immediate success, but one result was that she became mistress to Thomas Harris, who became a proprietor of the theatre soon afterwards. She bore him three sons, and he built her a house on Hampstead Heath. That was a good time, when Harris, at his prime, was called 'the King of Clubs', and she, esteemed as a comic actress, was dubbed 'the Queen of Clubs'.

Although Jane owed everything to Derrick's training and care, she proved very ungrateful. During his relatively brief period of prosperity when MC at Bath, when once he called upon her the manservant declared that, 'His mistress knew no-one of that name.' Derrick, enraged, pushed his way in and confronted her: she then threatened to call the constables. When, in early 1769, Sam Derrick was in direst need, she refused to help him. Shortly afterwards he died, leaving a so-called Will and Testament express-

ing thanks to all the Covent Garden madams and whores who had helped him 'when he had not shoes for his feet'; he especially mentioned Charlotte Hayes and Lucy Cooper.

Jane Lessingham suddenly deserted Harris 'for a naval gentleman', Admiral Edward Boscawen, but in 1775 was 'taken into protection' by Henry Addington, soon to become Mr Justice Addington and later Lord Chief Justice of England and Earl of Sidmouth. He was already nicknamed 'the Amorous Justice'. He made her a present of a 'snug house' in Marylebone Grove, which was quickly dubbed by Covent Garden cognoscenti 'Bunters' Hill' (a 'bunter' being the poorest ambulant whore) in recognition of her reputation. In September 1717 she was the centre of a *cause célèbre* during which she was described as 'a pompous celebrated actress and a plump lascivious harlot' but this seems not to have disturbed her relationship with the Justice. She was then forty-two years old.

Jane continued her stage career: like Betsy she was wont to wear male attire while on stage, but she also wore it when frequenting the Covent Garden coffee-houses and taverns. Then suddenly she deserted the Justice for a young Covent Garden actor (thought to have been the handsome John Palmer), who was known disparagingly as 'the Tea-pot Actor'. The Justice's anger at this humiliation was unbounded: it was reported that he 'never mentioned her name thereafter except by the most opprobrious appellations'.

There is no further mention of her in the theatrical publications or the scandal-sheets or lists of Cyprians. She died in 1801, described by Musgrave as 'Actress and Courtezan'.

Both of these 'Votaries of Venus' were often to be found at the house of a woman deemed 'the second edition of Lucy Cooper' because in many respects she imitated Lucy's charm and vivacity but without her vulgarity. She was Frances Herbert, 'a fine stately woman, tall and elegant, of fair complexion and white teeth', who about 1760 was keeping 'a very reputable brothel in Play-house Passage in Bow Street' elegantly furnished with much silver plate on a good sideboard – '. . . her *nymphs* were tolerably good pieces.' Miss Herbert had been the mistress of a rich City gentleman who had funded her establishment and was her most frequent companion there until she fell in love with another of her clients, a young *beau garçon* with broad shoulders, which caused a *frisson* amongst the other clients since up to that time only a very few had been admitted to her embraces – most of the visitors being elderly gentlemen in the Sinking Fund Office. Among them was Thomas Bradshaw, MP for Saltash, a Lord of the Admiralty popularly known as 'Black Harry' and of dubious reputation. He was also one of the fashionable 'Macaronis' whose ultra-fashionable dress, gait and manners were deemed to be the hallmark of the most polished gentleman. Bradshaw was much taken with the beauteous Fanny and wanted to marry her. To that end, in about 1770, he set her up in an elegant 'genteel house in Queen Anne Street . . . in an honourable way'. In 1774 he was suddenly taken ill and died while in Bath. From about 1770 she had adopted his name and was henceforth to be known as Fanny Bradshaw, although still operating from her house in Bow Street, and it would seem that Bradshaw, regarded as 'a notorious Procurer and sycophant', in 1772 had a financial interest in that establishment.

With Fanny Bradshaw's departure to the more salubrious area of Queen Anne Street, the era of the 'Great Bawds' in Covent Garden ended. While there still remained a large number of so-called reputable brothels, there was now nothing, apart from the theatres, to attract the *haut ton*. The market was encroaching more and more onto the centre square, and market-men and wholesalers were taking over premises hitherto occupied by fashion and 'millinery' shops.

Even the coffee-houses were deteriorating, and much of their meretricious allure had been lost: many now accommodated Cock and Hen Clubs, 'the lowest and most disreputable places . . . where there was much Smoking, Swearing and singing of Filthy Songs'. It was said that, 'One woman in every three had to sell her body for bread, or starve.' In 1774 'Pickpockets made no scruple to knock people down with bludgeons . . . no later than eight o'clock in the night . . . in the Piazza in Covent Gardens; they come in large bodies armed with *cuteaux* and attack whole parties of people coming from the Coffee-houses and Theatres.'

A first-hand account of contemporary behaviour is given in the *Bucks' Midnight Ramble* (1774):

> At Midnight when each *Buck* was drunk
> And each had got his roving *Punk*
> We damned all puny Asses.
> Mischief was then our Desire
> To chuck the *Waiter* on the Fire
> And break the Bowls and Glasses.
>
> The uproar reared, each Whore was fled
> And all the *Waiters* gone to bed
> The Landlord sued for quiet.
> 'Keep it up' was all their cries
> Those *Doggs*, they came with their Eyes
> Then they'd kick up a *Riot*.

The *Chairs* and *Tables* went to rack
And on their *Muns* my Fist went smack
Which set the *Froes* a-crying;
From their Heads the Blood did pour
Aloud their Cries all Gallows *Whore*
'Why! damn ye, Bob's a-dying'.

In *Heaps* they lay upon the Ground
With broken Heads, black Eyes around
Like Oxen in a slaughter;
Rolling, Bob recovered soon
Sweet, slily, crept out of the Room
And *swived* the Landlord's Daughter.

The Candle's out and the Fire dim
And every thing so queer and grim
Much like a scene of Trouble:
Into a *Rattler** all they got
And bilk'd the Landlord of his Shot
And tipp'd the Whores the double!

Another cause for anxiety was the growing number of homo-sexual prostitutes. Baron von Archenholz during his visit in 1773 said that Englishwomen were so lovely that he found it easy to understand why Englishmen held 'a certain unnatural vice in the utmost abhorrence . . . they speak of it . . . with such horror that . . . it is better to suffer death at once for the Fury of the Populace is unbounded'. One ploy was blackmail.

In the summer of 1779 the Honourable Charles Fielding and his brother (sons of the Earl of Denbigh) walking through Covent Garden were accosted by two homosexual pimps. The brothers drew their swords, took the men into custody and charged them with attempted assault and blackmail, because it was essential to defend themselves against even the imputation. Their normal wenching was socially acceptable but the merest suspicion of sodomy meant social death just as actual sodomy could mean physical death.

On 12 June 1790 the Honourable Mr Cuffe and his friend Lord John Netterville were importuned in Covent Garden by a thug named Charles Jones, a 'well-known sodomiticall prostitute' who had followed them 'shouting and ranting and accusing them of committing an indecent offence and demanding money from them as blackmail'. The two men, horrified, hurried home, pursued by 'a mob of homosexuals. They complained to the Bow Street magis-

* A 'rattler': a hackney-cab, which rattled on the cobbled streets.

206

An errant female brought before the constable in the Watch-House by a 'Charley' – the popular name for a watchman, still used well into the nineteenth century

trate, when it was disclosed that Frank Vaughan *alias* Charles Jones *alias* 'Fat Phyllis' was known to the officers as a 'frequenter of Masquerades [at the theatre] always in female attire and is extremely effeminate and much painted . . . as also are his companions'.

In the winter of 1785 the 'Agents of the Bow Street Court' arrested fifteen men, 'several being Persons of Consequence and one of Noble rank', charging them with the worst kinds of sexual debauchery. They were caught 'in the act of nursing and feeding . . . new-born babies (large dolls)'. Indeed one of the 'mothers' was so realistic that the agents had released 'her'. Although all were acquitted, the mob outside the court burnt them 'in effigy . . . without respect to their Rank'. The agents also raided the White Lion Mollies house in Long Acre and two men, Hepburn and White, were sentenced at the Old Bailey for 'this horrid brutish crime . . . the name of which must not be pronounced amongst Christians'.

Footmen and flunkeys and soldiers were the main offenders – between 1760 and 1770 it was calculated that every thirteenth man in service was a flunkey of some sort. Poor men who had been press-ganged into the armed forces and received little or no pay 'were compelled to sell their Arses as some Women sold their C . . . s'. In 1770 the pressgangs had raided several 'houses of ill fame' in Covent Garden and Drury Lane and carried off not only bullies and pimps but also 'several respectable Citizens . . . paying their visits normally to their regular whorehouses'.

In 1794 a 'Club of Paederasts' which used to gather in the Bunch of Grapes in Clare Market every Monday night 'for the most hideous and unnatural purposes' were taken before the Bow Street magistrates. Eighteen men still dressed in women's clothes appeared in court. It was charged that each had a woman's name to disguise their identities even from each other: 'Miss Fanny', 'Countess Papillion', 'Lady Golding' and so on. They had a terrifying experience. A huge crowd was gathered outside the court and although they were guarded by a troop of soldiers they were pelted with stones, dung and mud, being powerless to escape injury because they were all handcuffed in pairs like a chain-gang. Here, too, all were acquitted because of 'lack of evidence'.

16. More Lists of Cyprians

Towards the end of the eighteenth-century an unknown writer had remarked that, 'Dishonour was a sure Passport to Celebrity . . . thanks to the News-paper Men every frail Beauty might wake up one Morning and find herself famous!'

There was a continuous demand in all types of publications for news of salacious goings-on and as a corollary magazines or pamphlets giving more intimate details on the lines first carried out by Jack Harris. Indeed, in 1773 there was published another edition under his name, which (unwittingly) discloses that Covent Garden was no longer the same magnet as before; out of 150 'Cyprians' mentioned, only fifty-one lived in or around the Garden. Moreover, to give it weight, the names of well-known ladies who did not need any such advertisement were put in as fillers.

Chief among the practising bawds in Bow Street were now Mrs Freeland, Mrs Barsey and a man named Carter whose bagnio was cheek-by-jowl with the magistrates' office. The Long Acre bagnio has several mentions, as has Mrs Pledwell (or Plodwell) who had a smaller establishment at the rear. A woman named Gifford appears in Market Court, off Drury Lane; she was very likely the second wife of the actor Henry Gifford.

Places of assignation are now the 2 shilling gallery at the Playhouse, the Denmark Coffee-House, Haddock's Turk's Head bagnio in Charing Cross (run now by Olivia Harrington), and the Cat Tavern in the Strand, which commanded considerable opprobrium: 'The Master of *The Cat* was a Bailiff's follower, and his wife was equal in polite accomplishment. This agreeable jolly couple fatten upon the miserable gains of a few wretched women to whom they will often lend five or ten Guineas but in return these poor girls are obliged to be there every and all day spending their money – or the Marshalsea's the word! To paint them in their true light would almost exceed belief. . . .'

*A gallant is making his proposi-
tions to a* Cyprian. *Haddock's*
bagnio *is under the fourth arch.
Both Jack Harris and H. Ranger
were long dead by 1773*

At Mr Carroll's in Tavistock Street could be found such as Miss
Smith, who was 'Cold as the Ice itself; She admires nought but
Pelf', while Miss Lewis at 11 Market Row was content with small
profits and quick returns, clearing between £2 and £3 a week and
never losing a customer but when *gonorrhoea simplex* kept her from
her lodgings.

Miss Tamar Gordon, 'a Northumbrian lass at the Long Acre
bagnio', had a figure and limbs like Venus herself but she was as
'cold as a Dutch woman', and Sophy Weston (who patronized both
Mrs Barsey's and Mrs Anne Freeland's establishments in Bow
Street) 'drams it too much'. Miss Robinson, who was rather tall,
slim and genteel, with dark-brown hair and large dark eyes and
frequented the local jelly-shops, was 'a Jew who has no objection to
a bit of Christian flesh but not in Shylock's way . . . she choses her
lovers carefully'. Her minimum charge was £1.

In 1779 there appeared a two-volume book of anecdotes which,
although primarily dealing with the famous 'nunneries'
flourishing in King's Place, St James, also contained many valuable
nuggets of information about the state of affairs in contemporary

Covent Garden. It was entitled *Nocturnal Revels*, 'Sketches and Portraits of the Most Celebrated *Demi-reps* and Courtesans of this Period'. The publisher was one M. Goadby, otherwise unrecorded but clearly someone very close to the famous bawd Jane Goadby in Great Marlborough Street who brought the Continental-style bordels to London about 1750.

It tells us that the opera-singer Caterina Galli was 'still well-preserv'd after thirty years, tall and genteel' and a woman of intrigue who had been pursued 'all over Europe by the little Jew Mendez, a Paragon of *Foppery* . . . even to France, Lyons, Venice and the Hague'. He was only five feet tall but he had told her that, 'Little Dogs have long Tails', to which she had riposted, 'Even if you were all Tail you would not be half as long for me!'

The Honourable 'Jack Spindle' used to boast of more vices than all the other bloods and beaux in the Inns of Court and would brag of his amours with fruit-girls and cheap harlots; he thought it was of uncommon merit to debauch a common prostitute with a guinea. 'He was only twenty-five but you could think he was sixty.' This description goes a long way to explain the motivations of this most vicious nobleman who left a trail of sorrow and misery to hundreds of innocent girls as well as experienced women.

A good deal of the information given was taken from another Harris List published in the same year. Once again, out of about 150 items only forty-eight deal with Covent Garden and the Strand, the rest being a hotch-potch ranging from south London to Hammersmith with no particular concentrations and few startling revelations.

It does reveal that one of the young ladies causing the sad downfall of the Honourable Mr Damer was a sixteen-year-old nymphomaniac from Piccadilly who was then at Black Harriet's 'nunnery' in King's Place, a little plump brunette with fine hazel-coloured eyes who would never say no to any young fellow. Damer would stay with her sometimes for as long as a fortnight and was very generous.

Most interesting is the story of Isabella Wilkinson, whose family had been long established around Sadler's Wells area and were known as entertainers of various kinds. Isabella was the star attraction as a dancer on the wire rope at the Sadlers Wells theatre for many years and often appeared at the Covent Garden theatres. During a time when she had broken her leg, she 'rusticated' in various Covent Garden coffee-houses and bagnios, where she had a good clientele; she also visited the King's Place 'nunneries' to assuage the needs of various diplomats. At Drury Lane she usually danced the role of Columbine, at which '. . . she was unexcelled' but by 1779 the vignette said: 'Tis true her bulk is rather a hindrance to her agility which may in some measure excuse her not being able to get off the ground . . . but she is very decent in what she performs . . . she still continues to tipple to excess. . . .'

The tally of places of assignation is remarkably varied. 'At the Hair-dresser's in Hart Street'; 'At the Glass-shop in James St'; 'At the Barber's in Newport St.'; 'At the Cheesmonger's in Church St. Soho'; 'At the Coal-shop in Berwick Street'; 'At a Stocking-shop in Long Acre'; 'At the Turner's in Russell St', and at 'Chymists, Grocers, Chandlers, Perfumiers, Watchmakers and Taylors', at a bun-shop and – the ultimate degradation – the coalsheds in several locations including Wardour St, near Soho. Some of these shops were mere fronts, but others were tradesmen taking a rake-off from the 'bunters'.

There are references to German, French, Dutch and Belgian girls all plying for hire; one claimed to be the daughter of an indigent German baroness who kept house for her in a Marylebone Street; one, known as Lady Rosehill was certainly entitled to be so called.

David Carnegie, younger brother of the Earl of Carnegie, an ensign in the 25th Regiment of Foot, was styled Lord Rosehill. In 1767 he went to Maryland and there married Margaret Cheer, omitting to mention that on 27 January 1767 he had married Christina Cameron 'born in wedlock' to Captain Alexander Cameron, at Fortwilliam in Scotland. In 1773 she was calling herself Mrs Hamilton, the name of her protector in the interim, but now 'The public has enjoyed her.' She was a close friend of the famous courtesan known as 'the Honourable Charlotte Spencer', who had been the intimate companion of Lord Spencer Hamilton and whose name she had adopted. Charlotte at this time was living in Long Acre.

One small piece of arcane information to be gleaned from these sources was that conjugal visits were allowed in the King's Bench debtors' prison, 'both licit and illicit', a fork with the tines upwards being stuck to the cell door to indicate the purpose for which the place was being used and that the occupants should not be disturbed.

In 1779 also yet another Harris List was published, in which the names of a number of willing ladies mainly residing in Cumberland

(Opposite) Isabella Wilkinson the funambulist or dancer on the wire at Sadler's Wells where she was long the star attraction. At Drury Lane she danced the jig. A famous demi-rep greatly esteemed by the diplomatic corps

Court and the Pit Passage are given. In the cluster of courts around Bow Street and Drury Lane lived a very large number of actors and actresses. They were summoned to rehearsals by the beating of a drum – living there was much cheaper than hiring a coach to bring them in when needed.

The following year saw the publication of *Characters of the Present Most Celebrated Courtezans* prefaced by a eulogy of 'The Erudite and Philosophical Mr Harris of the Covent Garden Lists'. It contained thirteen names of reigning beauties, all courted and patronized by high society, but sadly only a few of them were based on Covent Garden. Stage stars such as Mrs Baddeley and Eleanor Ambrose and Elizabeth Farren – 'of great beauty but little talent' – were included, as also was Betsy Coxe, 'whose contralto voice is more often heard in the *bagnios* than on the stage of Drury Lane' but the others were best known in St James, although they came frequently to flaunt their charms in the Covent Garden theatres, usually to enhance the prestige of their escorts.

There were more lists to come: the *Rambler* Magazine of April 1783 gave a list of 'The Most Fashionable Votaries of Venus' which, however, contained the names of only six of those of 1780. Amongst those added were Lady Dorothy Worseley, Mary 'Perdita' Robinson (the Prince of Wales's mistress), the well-known actress-courtesan Margaret Cuyler, and 'the Avians' – a group of courtesans bearing the names of birds. There were Mary Sarah Adcock, 'the Goldfinch', Mrs Irvince, 'the White Swan' of Berners Street, Gertrude Mahon 'the Bird of Paradise', Polly Greenhill, 'the Greenfinch', and Mrs Corbyne, 'the White Crow'. Rather unkindly it reported that Betsy Coxe 'was in decline'.

Margaret Cuyler claimed to be the illegitimate daughter of 'a Gentleman of Fortune' and to have spent her youth in St James's Palace mixing with the young princesses – certainly she had come from a good family and was accepted in high society, but she quickly became corrupted both in manners and in morals. In 1767 she eloped with the young Colonel Cornelius Cuyler of the Guards, posing as his wife and living 'in splendid fashion in London, Paris and Dublin'. She was then only about fifteen. Since he was frequently abroad on military missions, time lay on her hands and she sought sexual gratification amongst the bloods around her. The Colonel apparently did not object to these *affaires* so long as they were with 'Persons of the Quality.' When he was posted to India he settled £300 a year on her, for life. By this time, however, she was having an *affaire* with Thomas Metcalfe of the Bengal Lancers, to whom she showed great affection, even to

Margaret Cuyler, prominent actress at Drury Lane and faithless mistress to Colonel Cornelius Cuyler and Thomas Harris, the theatre's manager

Mrs Mary Corbyne the White Crow, *one of 'the Avians', and a top toast of Regency London*

pawning her jewels to help equip him for his service in the West Indies. She was also being pursued by the young Lord Binning, Charles Hamilton, but his father, the Earl of Haddington, 'paid her generously' to break this liaison. Meanwhile Metcalfe had introduced her to Thomas Harris, then manager at Drury Lane Theatre, and she had become his mistress and the mother of two children. When in 1777 Colonel Cuyler returned and 'was on the point of taking up with her again', he learnt 'that she had been polluted by a Bourgeois' and changed his mind. He had by then earned the *sobriquet* of 'the Complying Colonel'.

By 1779 Margaret had started her stage career at Drury Lane, where she was to work regularly as a comic actress, with occasional appearances at the Haymarket Theatre, until 1800. She was still moving in aristocratic circles and was a particular friend of 'the Bird of Paradise', visiting from time to time Mrs Matthews' elegant establishment in King's Place when she needed money to pay her gambling debts.

Hickey, who had met her with Metcalfe at Mrs Cornelys' in Soho Square and at various times at the Bengal Club at the Shakespeare's Head as well as other hostelries in Covent Garden, opined that

Margaret Cuyler was only an 'understrapper' on the stage and of no great pretentions as an actress, and 'she was a great *Jack Whore*' without manners or beauty, but that Major Metcalfe 'was deeply enamoured of this woman'.

In 1785 she was living with Lady Douglas in Lansdowne Road, Kensington, planning to set up a 'Greek shop' (a faro-house) in Covent Garden to augment her salaries as an actress. The *Secrets of the Green Room* (1795) said that she was 'of hasty violent temper . . . the terror of the Green Room . . . but of a generous warm heart . . . she continues on the stage only for the salary.'

The faro-house appears to have packed up in 1793 because at that time she was living in semi-retirement in Margate, and in 1808 she was living in the Isle of Man with an 'Hibernian refugee' but she still kept in touch with her old love, Metcalfe, until he was drowned in 1813 when returning home in the ill-fated *Île de Paris*. She died in 1814.

Some enterprising publisher revived the Harris Lists in 1788 and ran them annually until 1793, from an address in Little Bridge Street, Drury Lane, but there are hardly any references in them to Covent Garden. It proves, however, that the very mention of Covent Garden in the titles was a great draw to all those seeking sinful entertainment, although the contents made it clear that Covent Garden was no longer 'the Grand *Seraglio* of the Nation'.

In 1790 Charlotte Loraine published her *Memoirs*. In 1788 Harris had described her as 'the *Agreeable Jewess* . . . a very desirable companion . . . who drank little and swore less . . . was well-educated and well-mannered'. She claimed that her downfall was caused when a procuress introduced her to William Poulteney, tenth Earl of Bath, at the Playhouse in Bow Street. When he died in 1764, the young John Fitzpatrick, Earl of Upper Ossory, took her into keeping, but she ran off with a captain of the Guards. She was then living in Goodge Street, off Tottenham Court Road. The new romance was short lived.

Charlotte spent much of her time mixing with theatrical people, getting bit-parts from time to time, until she met and married a Mr Hazzlewood 'who had an income of £300 a year, kept two maids and a foot-boy, but had no Carriage'. This latter deprivation was, naturally, insupportable, and after bitter quarrels the marriage foundered. From this point she observes a discreet reticence about her activities, but she was clearly active within the theatrical circuit for in 1795, as Mrs Hazzlewood, she published *The Secret History of the Green Room* – a *chronique scandaleuse* of the relationships between the actresses at all the theatres and the nobility.

Her account of Frances Abington is a mixture of adulation and spite, remarking that Abington – then nearing the end of her career – had left the honours to Elizabeth Farren, although Farren, while copying Frances' style, was never in the same class.

Betsy Farren was the daughter of a well-known surgeon in Cork who had married a Liverpool-born girl, and as a child she was sent to Liverpool, making her debut as an actress when she was only fifteen. She was so poor that the other actresses lent her various articles of apparel to enable her to go onto the stage. She was an immediate success and made her first London appearance at the Haymarket in 1777, when she was eighteen. She went over to Covent Garden and Drury Lane but made rather less impression upon those more sophisticated audiences.

At Covent Garden she met 'the British Demosthenes', Charles James Fox, who introduced her into the highest society. One evening this tall, imperious beauty met Edward Stanley, twelfth Earl of Derby, 'a vindictive little man' who had refused to divorce his wife, Lady Elizabeth Hamilton, after her *affaire* with the Duke of Dorset in 1778. Lord Derby persuaded the two reigning Society hostesses, Lady Dorothy Thompson and Lady Cecilia Johnston, to become young Betsy's patronesses and groom her for higher things. Lady Derby died in May 1797, and immediately afterwards he married Elizabeth Farren. The marriage was a success. She managed to bury any hint of a sexual relationship with Fox, who was a wencher *par excellence*, and resolutely ignored all those who had known or helped her in her penurious days, by adopting a most haughty demeanour, which in turn made her and her diminutive husband the butt of constant jokes and caricatures.

Another vignette was of the famous actress Jane Powell – usually known as Harriet Powell but not to be confused with the lovely Lamb who became Countess of Seaforth. Jane was the daughter of an army sergeant at Chatham Barracks. She was desperately poor 'and compelled by necessity to be involved in every disgrace and distress that can befall her sex'. First she was a slavey in a Chatham family under conditions so onerous that she decamped with a soldier named Farmer and spent the next few years as a camp-whore in the barracks until one of the officers helped her to get to Covent Garden, where she had the good fortune to meet John Philip Kemble, who gave her a start as an actress, but she still had to supplement her income by becoming a demi-rep. She had a great success as a dramatic actress at Drury Lane and married William Powell, then the prompter and later the manager of the theatre. Thereafter she was known as Harriet Powell. Powell died in 1769.

A Peep at Christies;—or—Tally-ho, & his Nimeney-pimmeney ta the Morning

She was one of the sought-after demi-reps, amongst her clients being HRH Prince Ernest, Duke of Cumberland, and Charles, Earl of Cornwallis. In her later years she was one of the 'Top Toasts' in the King's Place 'nunneries'. She died in 1829.

Another young lady who commanded a great deal of notoriety was Mary Darby, daughter of an affluent merchant in Bristol, where she was born in 1758. A pretty child, genteelly brought up and educated, her comfortable home life was broken up when her father lost his fortune and had to move about 1770 to London, where Mrs Darby opened a boarding school for young ladies in Chelsea. In 1772 Mary moved into a residence in fashionable Marylebone, and soon afterwards the parents separated, the father going to America.

At Marylebone her life changed dramatically. She met and married – at the age of fifteen – a young clerk, named Thomas Robinson, who had ideas above his station and means, so that they frequented the Covent Garden theatres and coffee-houses, running into debt so quickly that in 1775 both of them were in the King's Bench prison, whence they were rescued by David Garrick, who had made Mary's acquaintance the year previously.

Garrick arranged her debut at Drury Lane in 1776 when as Juliet she was an instant success. Robinson, educated at Harrow and of good family but 'aping the rich and aspiring to be a man of Fashion', turned into a lazy, dissipated young man, but the neglected bride was quickly taken up by George Robert Fitzgerald, 'a rumbustious Irish Ruffian and a great favourite with well-born ladies' (he was executed for murder in 1786) and then by Thomas 'the Wicked' Lord Lyttelton, who enjoyed her in tandem with Betsy Coxe.

George, Prince of Wales, then just eighteen, saw one of her performances at Drury Lane and immediately fell in love, importuning her and sending love-letters signed 'Florizel'. She was four years older. He swore undying love and promised her a settlement of £20,000. From this time Mary was known as 'Perdita', from the part of that name in *The Winter's Tale*. The love-affair of 'Florizel and Perdita' became public property, causing considerable anger and anxiety to George III, especially because in 1780 the Prince came of age and had his own establishments. He was also heavily in debt and being pursued by moneylenders.

The actress and demi-rep Elizabeth Farren finally married the diminutive Earl of Derby. She was an indifferent actress but a pretentious snob

On 20 August 1781 the King wrote to his Prime Minister, Lord North: 'My Eldest son got last year into an Improper relationship with an actress, a Woman of indifferent Character and he sent her Letters and made foolish Promises. Colonel Hotham has settled to pay the enormous sum of Five Thousand Pounds for their return.' By this time, however, the Prince's affections had cooled and he was already infatuated with Mrs Fitzherbert. After some rather unpleasant and undignified haggling Mary was compelled to settle for an annuity of £500, half of which was to go to her daughter 'for life', and as compensation for Mary's 'resignation of a lucrative Profession'. It was not a very princely settlement, because from that money she had to keep her mother, who died in 1793 at Mary's house in St James Place, as well as the daughter, and Thomas Robinson! George 'visited her occasionally for old times' sake'.

The settlement was woefully inadequate, and (*vide* the *Rambler* Magazine) 'She was soon in distress and available for other offers.' Amongst her lovers were George Capel-Conyngham, Viscount Malden, 'the Irish Owl' – otherwise Arthur Murphy the dramatist, and several other gentlemen in the Prince's entourage, until in 1787 she was taken into protection by Colonel Sir Banastre Tarleton. From about 1784 she had been in ill health, suffering from 'fevers, rheumatism and arthritis' and before her death she was a helpless cripple. She died on Christmas Day 1803, but the story of 'Florizel and Perdita' keeps her memory alive to this day.

The story of Lady Dorothy Worseley is rather different. Apart from being one of Barney Thornton's favourites and a close colleague of George Anne Bellamy in the struggle for female emancipation, she was 'a Person of the Quality' by birth, a scion of the House of the Flemings, earls of Wigtown.

As Lady Dorothy Seymour Fleming, born about 1750, by the time she was eighteen she was frequenting the Covent Garden bagnios and coffee-houses for her many amorous adventures. She was also well known as a writer and poet. As an 'advanced' female, she married in 1775 Sir Richard Worseley, seventh baronet, a Fellow of the Royal Society and a Clerk to the Privy Council, where he was known as 'Sir Finical Whimsy'. It was a marriage of convenience for him because she brought a very handsome dowry, but it was equally convenient for her because it allowed her to continue her literary, social and sexual activities. Sir Richard likewise pursued extra-marital adventures.

This situation lasted until 1782 when Sir Richard sued for a divorce citing as co-respondents Captain George Morris Bissett of the Hampshire Militia, Henry Herbert, tenth Earl of Pembroke, Lord Deerhurst, Lord James Graham, heir to the Duke of Montrose, and the Honourable Charles Williams Wyndham. A very great deal of dirty linen was washed in public, including allegations of venereal disease passed from one to another, and in the end Sir Richard was awarded damages of one shilling because of his own bad reputation.

Immediately thereafter Lady Dorothy resumed her maiden name, Fleming, and also her former varied activities. She lived for a while in Paris 'in genteel poverty' but could also be found in Covent Garden gambling heavily. In 1782 she published a satirical poem, *The Whore*, which was a trenchant attack on male attitudes as well as a blast for women's liberation from man-made shackles. The introduction commends the reader to the amorous activities of 'Liberated Worshippers of the Cyprian Goddess' mentioning as supporters *inter alia* Lady Penelope Ligonier and Lady Henrietta Grosvenor.

> Of all the *Crimes* condemn'd to Woman-kind
> WHORE, in the Catalogue, first you'll find.
> This vulgar Word is in the mouths of all
> An *Epithet* on ev'ry Female's fall.
> The *Pulpit-thumpers* rail against the WHORE
> And damn the Prostitute: What can they more?
> Justice pursues her to the very Cart,
> Where for her Folly she is doom'd to smart.
> Whips, Gaols, Diseases – all the WHORE assail
> And yet, I fancy, WHORES will never fail . . .
> Yet Everyone of Feeling must deplore
> That MAN, vile MAN first made the Wretch a Whore.

After being mentioned in the *Rambler*'s list in April 1783, Lady Dorothy went abroad again, returning from time to time to England. In 1799 she was living in the fashionable village of Brompton, still being received by Society hostesses for her views and wit, until in 1805 in Paris she married Louis Cochet and vanishes from history.

One Covent Garden celebrity who could not make any of the lists was the Amazonian beauty weighing about forty stone known as 'the Royal Sovereign', who lived somewhere off the Strand. She was a particular favourite of the Duke of Norfolk but was also 'to be seen by all Admirers at Six pence the time'. Her nearest rival was a neighbour 'who could only reach thirty stone'. The two ladies achieved a measure of fame in James Gillray's caricature of 27 May 1792 *Le Cochon et les deux petits*, where they are embraced by Charles

The forty-stone Royal Sovereign and her companion, Nelly Hutton who weighed only just under thirty stone with their noble patron Charles Howard, Duke of Norfolk. Another client was the famous highwayman Thomas Ward, later hanged at Tyburn (James Gillray, 1792)

Howard, eleventh Duke of Norfolk. They were regarded as 'Natural Curiosities': both frequented the Garden and despite their bulk practised as courtesans.

17. The Nurseries of Naughtiness

By the last quarter of the eighteenth century Covent Garden's reputation as London's 'sin city' had dropped. It was still the haunt of pleasure but much of its continued allure was due to the splendid efforts of a number of brilliant actor-managers, whose plays with handsome actors and beautiful actresses and singers still drew the crowds. While the nobility and gentry, their ladies and their mistresses still brought glamour to the Garden, when the performances were over they took their coaches and went westward to St James and its luxurious 'nunneries'.

Moreover, the Garden was getting a reputation for roughness of a much more dangerous nature than before, and many potential customers stayed away. Still, there was much to be seen and enjoyed. There were Punch and Judy shows (which because of the American and French Revolutions now had political thrust), sword-swallowers, giants and dwarfs performing curious antics, girls selling oranges, fruits, nuts and flowers, ballad-sellers, pie-men offering a bewildering variety of goodies, even milkmaids milking their cows in the streets to supply fresh milk. To add to the noise and bustle there were now elegant, large coaches containing lovely imperious ladies and sumptuously attired gentlemen to be gazed at or hooted, their horses forcing their way through the crowds. There were gallants and macaronis prowling for young girls to seduce.

There were also the poorest and saddest of all creatures – old prostitutes worn out and diseased, some perhaps still young in years but looking like fifty and sixty, earning a few pence by running errands for the new young courtesans. Many were ex-market women – the type which the French called *marcheuses* – finished with life and holding on till death released them mercifully.

The Piazza and Russell Street were surrendering to the

Amongst the many traders was this famous sausage vendor.
Her message was:

You little rogues, go off to play
I give no sausages away
But if you within do choose to call
Two shillings buys the pan and all

wholesale fruit and vegetable merchants, whose demands for space grew ever more fierce, but Tavistock Street and Long Acre were hives of fashionable shops and workshops, in front of which apprentices beckoned passers-by to enter and buy their wares. Tavistock Street was choked with coaches whose occupants wanted the most fashionable hats or mantuas or dresses. Amongst the milliners was Lord Thurlow's protégée Miss Christian 'who was so ugly as to be a Wonder' but his Lordship's support ensured her success. There was Thomas Paulin, the mercer at the sign of the Statue of Queen Elizabeth and the haberdasher Mr Gordon at 'Ye Golden Fan and Crown', and Mr Jackson's dress-shop at the Habit Warehouse. It was reckoned to be one of the sights of London.

But nestling discreetly in Tavistock Row was one of Mr Harris' recommendations: 'Miss Phyllis: a Fine Crummy plump-made Dame, a veteran in the Mysteries of *Venus*, whose chief Trade is with elderly Gentlemen . . . the Waiter at Maltby's *Bagnio* sends a note to her in Tavistock Court . . . she is rated at but twenty-six but we are of the opinion that she has at least sunk Ten years. . . .'

Russell Street was not completely devoid of light ladies. In 1788 there was Miss Green at 32 Little Russell Street and Miss Milton and Mrs Townshend at 23 Russell Street, besides a beauty just named Emma 'at a Black Hairdresser' or 'at the French *Sooty Frizeur*'. Poor Emma had suffered a mishap which had needed treatment with 'Murcury' and in the following year took refuge in Mother Gray's bosom 'next the Opera House' in Bow Street, where Mother Gray welcomed all visitors with a glass of 'Usquebaugh'.

By this time too Long Acre had become a fine shopping centre, but it was most famous for its twenty-five coachmakers and the superb coaches they made for the nobility and gentry. In demand was a hinged flap on the rear seat under which a chamber-pot was placed. One had just to remove the cushions to utilize the convenience, and it was not necessary to ask the driver to stop. Unfortunately for Covent Garden, however, their fine, well-sprung coaches had made travel so much more easy that people could visit places of amusement further afield, even as far as Hampstead and Knightsbridge, to which custom and large sums of money were diverted. Moreover, ten minutes' walk took the traveller to Leicester Fields, where many doxies and 'houses of resort' could now be found.

The Garden was also facing a new type of competition from such places as The Pantheon in Oxford Street, which had opened in January 1772 with a great fanfare of publicity as a concert hall and ballroom, designed to attract a more respectable but still wealthy

Prostitutes at this time were frequently pickpockets, quite apart from the stealing of valuables from drunken or beaten-up clients. Fanny Murray's Memoirs *mention her meeting every Saturday at the Shakespeare's Head at 'The Whores' Club' to pay Jack Harris his commissions and also to divide the spoils. The penalty for pickpocketing was hanging, although by 1796 transportation to Botany Bay was substituted, because juries refused to condone the death sentence. Cruikshank, 1796*

class of people. The Master of Ceremonies had announced before-hand that no courtesans or actresses would be admitted, but a first-hand account stated: 'The Company were an *olio* of all sorts. Peers and Peeresses, Hons and Right Hons, Jew-brokers and Demi-reps, Lottery-insurers and Quack-doctors.'

That was the night when the constables at the door had refused to admit the reigning actress Sophia Baddeley until her escort, Sir William Hanger, drew his sword against them, and when the MC refused to allow Betsy Coxe onto the floor to dance the cotillion with her squire, Captain Scott of the Guards. Since Charlotte Hayes and two other bawds, Mary Mitchell and Mrs Ferguson, were present with their attendant 'nuns', Captain Scott remarked to the manager that, 'If you turn away every woman who is no better than she should be, your Company will soon be reduced to a Handful!' Kitty Fredericks, who was accompanied by the Duke of Fife, was not molested in any way, although she was the most famous courtesan in London.

The other competition came from the marvellous concerts and balls given by Mrs Cornelys at her mansion in Soho Square, which royalty occasionally attended and where the most refined and elegant assignations could be made by such powerful ladies as the Countess of Harrington and her clique, who acted as unpaid procuresses. It was here that the Chevalier Giacomo Casanova met the Earl of Pembroke, who recommended him to go to the Star. Here too he met the lovely elegant Swiss Jewess 'La Charpillion' who was to cause him such disappointment and frustration.

Still, there were a great many who needed the sorts of diversions for which Covent Garden had become famous. Voltaire had earlier remarked *à propos* the 'English Sundays . . . there were no Concerts, no Operas, Card-playing was forbidden . . . People go to Churches and to Prostitutes'. Most of these 'forbidden' amusements could always be found somewhere in the Garden. In 1787 George III had issued yet another Proclamation, this time 'Against Vice' with a call for the urgent suppression *inter alia* of 'loose and licentious books and pictures'. In 1793 it was reported that 'Rich shop-keepers in the Piazza exhibit obscene Prints, thus attracting the Idle'.

Yet another diversion was to be found in the Garden: brothels specializing in flagellation.

Flagellation was, of course, nothing new but as a general rule 'the English perversion', as it was called, was the profession of the 'Posture Molls' who both gave and received, visiting clients in brothels and taverns or privately in their homes. One of the earliest mentions is in 1724, when the Middlesex Court dealt with the case of Peter Borges and Susannah Hutchins, charged with stealing money from an un-named 'person of the quality'. Susannah was further charged with stealing 4 golden guineas and a golden moidore, but she vehemently denied this, saying that the money was payment for whipping the plaintiff 'in consequence of which she had worn out a pennyworth of rods'. When told to carry on, she asked for more money to buy some more rods, whereupon he had threatened 'to swear a Robbery' – a dreadful threat which carried a death penalty.

The Judge accepted the word of the 'person of quality', whereupon Susannah 'pleaded her Belly'. A Panel of Matrons subsequently ascertained that she was not pregnant and she was remanded for sentence. At this point it was disclosed that the plaintiff was His Excellency Baron Carl Sparre, the Swedish Ambassador, who, realizing that the poor woman was likely to be hanged, withdrew all the charges. Susannah was reprieved and both were given pardons. This is one of the very few cases of flagellation brought into court.

The sisters Anne and Eleanor Redshawe had, as early as 1743 opened in Tavistock Street 'an extremely secretive . . . discreet *House of Intrigue* . . . [for] the Highest *Bon Ton* . . . catering for Ladies in the Highest Keeping'. The wealthy married ladies 'came in disguise to amuse themselves' but it was later disclosed that one of its primary functions was to supply flagellants, for which they had a special arrangement 'for Ladies of Refinement experienced in this field' with Mrs Matthews, one of the most prominent 'abbesses' in King's Place. In 1750 the sisters moved over to Bolton Street, Piccadilly, where they were still to be found in 1766.

In 1777 flagellation became a more open topic with the publication by George Peacock, of 66 Drury Lane, of a series of books eulogizing the art, the most famous being Mary Wilson's two-volume *The Exhibition of Female Flagellants*, extolling the great virtues of men being whipped by women. She had started in Covent Garden about 1760 but by 1777 was operating from Tonbridge Place, King's Cross, before moving to more modern and elegant premises in Bond Street and later to Hall Road in St John's Wood. In 1787 she sold the 'goodwill' to the even more famous Theresa Berkeley, and she emigrated to Paris in 1800.

At the same time Peacock published *Fashionable Lectures*, based on the principle

A ROD's the best Invigorator
A ROD applied upon the Rear!

claiming that it was better than 'Cantharides or *Viper's Broth* to give new vigour to flagging spirits.

The object of the exercise was to advertise the valuable services of Mrs Susannah Birch who had started in Exeter Street about 1762. One of the books was *Madame Birchini's Dance*, 'A Modern Tale with original Anecdotes', and another was *A Treatise on the Use of Flogging in Venereal Affairs*. Madame Birchini also plugged her 'Observations on the Pleasures of the Birch administered by the lovely Hand of a Favourite Lady'. *The Meretriciad* (1770) recommended Mrs Birch's 'Martial Truncheon' rhapsodizing in the following stanza:

Birch for the Bum: ye floggers here resort . . .
All kinds of Instruments, all kinds of Ware
To raise your Passions . . .

She was still operating in 1790 from an address in Chapel Street, Soho.

An elderly Jewish beau in Drury Lane, dressed like a young man in a blue coat, his waistcoat laced with gold and a cocked hat. An old maid opens the door, on the lintel are the words 'Kind and Tender Usage', while a pretty young prostitute peers invitingly from the window

Best known perhaps is Mrs Collett, who established her flagellation house in Covent Garden about 1766. She made no attempt to hide its function – after all there was nothing illegal about whipping between consenting adults. Every sort of gadget was available, and the quality of the clients was very high, the most noble being the Prince Regent in 1788. A contemporary pondered: '. . . it is not known whether the Royal Wrist wielded the Whip or whether the Royal Buttocks submitted to it!' After her death, her niece Mrs Mitchell carried on the institution until well into the nineteenth century.

By 1793 the Bow Street magistrates were openly blaming prostitution on gross overcrowding and rack-renting, saying further that '. . . the most respectable girls and women were . . . forced onto the streets', and the general poverty was so dire that '. . . there was a Pawn-shop at the corner of every alley . . . charging thirty per cent on goods left with them.' Concurrently they remarked on the immense increase in theft, counterfeiting, coin-clipping and pickpocketing all frequently linked with prostitution. All were hanging offences until George III, mainly as a result of the American Revolution, changed the punishments to transportation to Botany Bay, regarded by most malefactors eventually as a fate worse than death.

By 1770, however, the scope of prostitution in the Garden had narrowed down to Drury Lane and its *congeries* of courts and alleys such as Martlet Court, Cumberland Court and Pit Passage, which were real 'whores' nests'. The two theatres still drew the visitors, who included growing numbers of members of the Jewish community, now very much anglicized. There were already a number of Jewish traders in the vegetable and fruit-markets, and Jews were well regarded in theatrical circles not only as players but as writers and composers of lyrics and as designers. They were also suppliers of jewellery, dresses and trinkets to the actresses – the jewellers were usually nicknamed Lazarus after a well-known one in Berwick Street who used to grant credit to them, they were well liked because they would buy back the goods when, as very often, the players were down on their luck. For some reason, too, the Drury Lane bagnios were popular with Jewish clients.

Indeed, by the end of the century these penchants of the 'Sons of Circumcision' or 'Mordecais' as they were good-humouredly known were often recorded or caricatured. There is a print by Carington Bowles in 1772 captioned *Beau Mordecai Inspir'd* at the door of a Drury Lane brothel which has the phrase 'Kind and Tender Usage' on the lintel, and a pretty girl beckoning him within.

The behaviour of some of the members of the community aroused considerable anxiety amongst the elders, for the Mosaic laws forbade Jews to have congress with alien women and prostitutes – although from time immemorial the injunction had been often disregarded because Jewish prostitutes were very few and far between. In 1784 the elders of Bevis Marks Synagogue were compelled to strengthen the terms of their original ordinances because they were being breached so often. Their pious objections were being frustrated by discreet houses like those of Mrs Gould in Covent Garden. There was, however, not much they could do about it.

One of the pleasant diversions of wealthy lechers was the so-called 'Auctions of Cyprians' usually held in a tavern or in one of the high-class bordellos. The June 1783 issue of the *Rambler* gives a hilarious account of one such entertainment when the lovely but very diminutive 'Bird of Paradise' – Gertrude Mahon – was put up, the bidders being Count Haszlang, Sir Banastre Tarleton, Sir John Lade and 'Old Mordecai from St Mary Axe'. On other occasions there were usually several young ladies in the pool: it was a means of establishing prices for services – for example, it was asserted that the Honourable Charlotte Spencer's minimum charge was £50 per night. In another issue of that same year the *Rambler* reported that, 'The Late Master Russell left £50 each for six Virgins, this being the price that Mother Douglas had long since established . . . on a Virgin.' Drury Lane was still renowned for its 'Drury Virgins', who could sometimes be relied upon to give their clients the 'Covent Garden Disease' at such low-class places as the Ship Tavern, which in 1790 advertised 'Persons of all sexes are wedded and bedded at any hour of the Night or Day at small Expence and without a Licence'.

Nearby Catherine Street was busily catering for the great mass of frustrated men now coming in from the country areas in the wake of the nascent industrial revolution, trying to find gainful employment in the Great Wen. In one of the even more sleazy alleys between Catherine Street and the Aldwych, originally known as Eagle and Child Court but more usually as Eagle Court, one Mother Sarah Woods carried on a very successful business. She had been charged in August 1777 before Sir John Fielding with 'harbouring young girls from eleven to sixteen . . . for the purpose of sending them nightly to parade the streets . . . after she had kept them hard at work keeping her house clean all day . . . some half-naked and drunk . . . the Watch had picked up a girl of twelve . . . with others of Mrs Woods' servants . . . and a man parading with them to prevent them running away with their Cloaths'. She absconded, but bobbed up again and in 1788 was advertising her 'nymphs' in the Harris List from an address in Leicester Fields.

In August 1777 Sir John had also sentenced a Covent Garden bawd named Ann Morrow to stand in the Charing Cross pillory. She was so badly treated by the mob that '. . . her death (in Bridewell) was expected hourly, she having lost the sight of both eyes.'

George Alexander Steevens describes the scene in 1780:

> On Bulks and in Alleys we often meet with girls of twelve and thirteen years of age lying in a most despicable condition: poor Objects with a pretty Face. A Pimp will pick them up and take them to a Bawdy-house wherein the poor Wretch is stript, washed and given Cloaths. These are called *Colts*. The Pimp gets paid a Pound or two for his trouble: the girls have thus been bought and must do as the Purchaser pleases . . . . I have known a girl pay £11 for the use of a Smock and Petticote which when new did cost only six Guineas. The girls are obliged to sit up every Morning until Five o'clock to drink with any straggling *Buck* who may reel in in the early Morning and bear with whatever behaviour these drunken Visitants are pleased to use – and at the last endure the most Impure connexions. . . .

After referring to the times when he was younger, he goes on:

> But all is changed. The fine Women are descended to street-walkers and ignominious Houses like *The Cat* in Exchange Alley where every enormity is nightly practised: low-bred, debauched and . . . infamous vulgarity . . . the Women are now a set of the most ignorant depraved offensive and disease-ridden prostitutes whose whole Conversation is made up of the grossest Obscenity, too rank to be heard by any others than Coal-porters . . . the Refuse of Suttling-tents and Seaports. . . . We no more meet hearty and jolly droll fellows. . . .

The Buck's Delight, a collection of lewd songs and ballads published about 1778, disregards such disagreeable aspects as described by Steevens. One ballad in particular is dedicated to a lovely 'barberess' called Sally 'living at the Three Hairs in Brydges Street . . . up two flights of stairs . . . [who was] clean nice and neat and whose price was just half-a-crown'.

> A Charming girl lives here in Town
> Not far from Covent Garden,
> Were I worth twenty-thousand Pound
> She should have every Farthing. . . .
> Her Breasts heave high; with rolling Eye
> She's quite the THING I'd have her;
> Were you to see, above her Knee
> You'd swear she was the SHAVER.

> If anyone should want to know
> The girl that's here intended,
> To Brydges Street they need to go–
> There they will be befriended.

Another ballad extols the prowess of the highwayman John Rann, better known as 'Sixteen-string Jack' because he wore that number of ribbons to his jacket when other fops displayed only a dozen. He was well known in the Garden for his carousing as well as for his gallantry towards the ladies whom he held up on Hounslow Heath. He was hanged at Tyburn in 1776 still flaunting his ribbons and accompanied from Covent Garden to the gallows by a huge crowd of admirers.

The ballad linked his name to the well-known Covent Garden courtesan Margaret Caroline Rudd. She was the daughter of a respected Dublin surgeon, Patrick Young, and had married in 1762 Lieutenant Valentine Rudd of the 62nd Regiment of Foot but left him in 1770 to live with Daniel Perreaux, by whom she had three children. The brothers Perreaux enjoyed good repute as respectable gentlemen, Robert being a surgeon, but in 1774 they were arrested and charged with conspiracy and the forgery of a bill for £7500 drawn on Drummond's Bank. Margaret was also charged with conspiracy and was lucky to be acquitted; the brothers were hanged in 1776.

She then turned to prostitution and was launched on a higher career by the profligate Lord Irnham, 'the King of Hell', and later 'protected' by John Kerr, Earl of Ancram. Years later James Boswell admitted that he had approached her in 1776 'with some considerable wariness' and when he met her again at a social gathering in Scotland in 1785 she was known as Mrs Stewart, 'claiming that her mother was a natural daughter of Major Stewart of Ballymore'. Boswell then wrote: ''Tis tantalizing now in the circumstances . . . [when it was inexpedient] to approach her amorously'. Although she gave him her address in London where she was then known as a high-class procuress, Boswell does not record whether he ever made use of her services.

During most of the Garden's history the Cyder Cellar at 20 Maiden Lane, at the corner of Half-Moon Alley, is mentioned as the ultimate sink of iniquity; when all other drinking-dens were closed, it still stayed open. It was not always so: when it was opened about 1730, it was a sort of concerthall where men and women could drink and join in sing-songs while drinking cider, deemed to be less iniquitous than ale and beer and spirits. There were several rows of tables and platform at the end of the large, narrow room on which anyone could sing or even declaim. It very quickly degenerated into a hell-hole, and the 'artistes' would lead in loud and lewd songs for the audience to follow. In mid-century under Robert Derry's management it reached a nadir of obscenity.

The earliest Harris lists carried a prefacing article entitled 'A Night at Bob Derry's' which encouraged the presence of all 'Cyprians'. Here in 1763 Boswell spotted Sir Thomas Apreece, son of Moll King's elegant admirer; in 1776 William Hickey thought it worse than Weatherby's, although in 1780 George Alexander Steevens described it as 'a House for all frolic-loving men'. Who and what Bob Derry was is unknown, but in his cellar could be found the highest in the land mixing with the very dregs of the criminal underworld. the 'Top Toasts' as well as the destitute 'bunter'. There was constant disorder and frequent mayhem and on occasion even murder. It was the rake's last port of call, and the prostitute's last chance of a cully in an unsuccessful night.

It was from Bob Derry's that in 1790 Daniel Mendoza sent his challenge to Richard Humphreys to meet him 'in the Park or at The White Hart . . . with three friends each on the following Monday at six o'clock' a meeting that was to turn bruisers into boxers and give birth to a new sport.

Bob Derry's Cyder Cellar (to distinguish it from another Cyder Cellar further along Maiden Lane established about mid-century which later became first a church and then a synagogue) maintained its evil reputation until it was demolished in 1858.

By this time, however, the Piazza had shed most of its sinful reputation. The taverns and coffee-houses were replaced by hotels. Lord Archer's fine house was now Evans Hotel; Charles Macklin's Piazza Coffee-House was now the Piazza Hotel; the Bedford Arms was to become the Imperial Hotel, and the rebuilt hummums the Old Hummums Hotel. The former fashionable milliners' and haberdashers' shops in Russell Street and Tavistock Street had been taken over by wholesalers and retailers of fruit and vegetables, and most of the light ladies pushed along to St Giles and Tottenham Court Road and Soho.

For close on two centuries the market dominated the scene and the surrounding streets, deprived of these wantons, and their establishments became dreary areas of no interest to pleasure-seekers.

Today Covent Garden has been renewed and revived as a lively meeting-place with plenty of diversions undreamed of by eighteenth-century 'People of Fashion'. There are bright and clean cafés, restaurants and public houses, and even night-clubs and

On the site of the hummums in the Little Piazza Mr Hewitt built his hotel. Note the effigy of the lion which had formerly graced Button's Club in Russell Street

AUCTO SPLENDORA RESURGO.

Whereas, some evil disposed Person or Persons have raised a report that

The Old CIDER Cellars,

inMaiden Lane, Covent Garden are closed

The Proprietor begs most respectfully to inform the Public in general, that the above **ESTABLISHMENT IS OPEN,** and pledges himself that no exertion shall be wanted on his part to merit a continuance of that support, which this ESTABLISHMENT has enjoyed for the last Century.

CHOPS, STEAKS, SUPPERS, &c.

Harmonic Meetings every Evening;

The attendance of Gentlemen will be quite sufficient to say, that the ESTABLISH-MENT IS OPEN. — *was opened in the year 1720.*

The entrance to Bob Derry's infamous Cyder Cellar (opened originally about 1720) in Maiden Lane, as it was about 1800

discos. There are fine attractive shops and stalls and a busy flea-market as well as a fascinating museum. There are diversions ranging from Punch and Judy shows for the children to impromptu West Indian bands and sing-songs in which all may join. There are still many reminders of the Garden's frolicsome past.

Sadly the marvellous Piazza has almost completely disappeared, although Lord Andrew Archer's handsome mansion at 43 King Street – in which one of 'Pharaoh's Daughters' long and successfully fleeced the unwary ensigns – beautifully restored with its adjacent pillared portico displays its Georgian elegance. John Rich's Covent Garden Theatre, now the magnificent Royal Opera House, still enjoys it royal patronage and attracts thousands of opera buffs from all over the world to its prestigious performances. Garrick's Drury Lane Theatre is now only one of a cluster in nearby Aldwych and the Strand. St Paul's Church still watches solemnly over the Garden's morals, even while today's buskers perform under its colonnade as their predecessors did of yore.

Where stood the hummums is the splendid Museum of London Transport, and Mrs Gould's high-class establishment at 11 Russell Street is replaced by a gleaming modern café. A lovely, huge greenhouse full of flowers stands on the site of Mother Jane Douglas' famous 'House of Civil Reception', and along Maiden Lane Bob Derry's Cyder Cellar is covered by a highly respectable, well-known philatelic establishment. Law and Order are still – and much more effectively – maintained by the successors to John Fielding's Bow Street Runners, operating from the Bow Street Magistrate's Court, opposite the Royal Opera House, so that the pleasure-seeker today enjoying the scene need not fear such eighteenth-century hazards as footpads and press gangs. For bagnios the visitor will have to try elsewhere, and likewise for the courtesans!

Despite the great changes, Covent Garden's ambience is little changed: with a little imagination the visitor, walking around or sitting with a quiet drink will quickly visualize the scene as it was in the eighteenth century.

Bibliography

Anon., *Effigies & Parentage of Sally Salisbury* (London, 1722)

Anon., *Account of the Tryall of Sally Salisbury* (London, 1723)

Anon., *Scotch Gallantry Display'd or The Life and Adventures of Colonel Fr(ancis) Ch(arter)is impartially related* (London, 1730)

Anon., *Tom King or 'The Paphian Grove' incl. The Humours of Covent Garden* (London, 1738)

Anon., *The LIFE & CHARACTER OF MOLL KING late Mistress of King's Coffee-House in Covent Garden* (W. Price, near the Sessions House in the Old Bailey, London, 1747)

Anon., *The Memoirs of the celebrated Miss Frances Murray* (J. Scott, Paternoster Row, London, 1759)

Anon., *Betty's Fruit Shop* (J. Harrison, near Covent Garden, London, 1765)

Anon., *Memoirs of The Shakespeare's Head* (F. J. Noble, London, 1755)

Anon., *Characters of the present Most Celebrated Courtezans* (M. James, Paternoster Row, London, 1780)

Anon., *The Whore: A Poem written by a Lady of Quality (in A Collection of Poems & Satires) attrib. to Lady Dorothy Worseley* (C. Moran, London, 1782)

Anon., (Sam Derrick?), *Memoirs of the Bedford Head Coffee-house by A Genius* (H. Single in the Strand, London, 1751)

Archenholz, Baron Johann Wilhelm von, *Pictures of England* (translated from the German edition of 1770) (Dublin, Byrne 1791; London, 1788)

The British Mercury, or Annals of History Politics & Manners in England, publ. in English. (Hamburg, 1787–92)

Bleackley, Horace, *Ladies Fair and Frail* (Lane, London, 1909)

Blyth, Eric, *Memoirs of the Life of the Duke of Queensberry. Old Q* (Weidenfeld, London, 1967)

Boswell, James, *London Journal 1763* (OUP, Oxford, 1969)

Brown, Thomas of Shifnal, *Letters from the Dead to the Living* (London, 1702)

    Cheats of the Town (London, 1706)

    Letters of Severall Occasions, ed. A. L. Hayward, (New York, 1927; London *c*.1700)

Burford, E. J., *A Pleasant Collection of Bawdy Ballads and Verse* (Penguin, London, 1982)

Chancellor, E. Beresford, *Annals of Covent Garden* (London, 1930)

Cleland, John, *The Memoirs of Fanny Hill* (London, 1748)

Dawson, Nancy, *Authentic Memoirs of the Celebrated Miss Nancy Dawson* (London, 1762)

Dormer, Joseph, *The Female Rake or 'A Modern Fine Lady'* (London, 1736)

Dryden, John, *Satyre on the Players* (London, 1691)

Dunton, John, *The HE-Strumpet 'A Satyre on Sodomites* (H. Bragg, Paternoster Row, London, 1707)

Finch, B. E., and Green, Hugh, *Contraception through the Ages* (Owen, London, 1963)

Galt, John, *The Lives of the Players* (F. Hill, Boston, USA, 1831)

Goadby, Mary, *Nocturnal Revels, or The History of King's Place* (London, 1779)

Grose, Francis, *A Guide to Health, Beauty, Riches & Honour* (Hooper & Wigstead, London, 1796)

Harris, Jack, *List of Covent Garden Ladies or The New Atlantis* (H. Ranger, London, 1764 and editions of 1773, 1779, 1783–88)

Harvey, A. D., 'Prosecutions for Sodomy in England' in (*Historical Journal*, Vol no 4. pp. 939 ff) (London, 1978)

Hazzlewood, Charlotte, *Secret History of the Green Room* (T. Sabine, London, 1795)

Hickey, William, *Memoirs*, ed. A. Spencer (London, 1948)

Jones, Louis C., *Clubs of the Georgian Rakes* (Columbia University, New York, 1942)

Lorraine, Charlotte, *The True & Entertaining History of Charlotte Lorraine afterwards Mrs Hazzlewood* (T. Sabine, London, 1790)

MacMichael J. H., *The Story of Charing Cross* (Chatto, London, 1906)

Marshall, Dr Dorothy, *The English Poor in the 18th century* (Routledge, London, 1926)

Melville, R. Leslie, *Life & Work of Sir John Fielding* (Williams, London, 1934)

Mountaigue, James, *Old Bailey Chronicle in The Newgate Calendar* (Randall, London, 1783)

Pepys, Samuel, *Diary* (R. Latham & W. Matthews, Yale, 1970–76)

Petherick, W., *Restoration Rogues* (Hollis & Carter, London, 1956)

Phillips, Hugh, *Mid-Georgian London* (London, 1964)

Steevens, George Alexander, *Adventures of a Speculist* (B. Bladon, London, 1788)

Stow, William, *Remarks on London* (St Aubyn, London, 1722)

Tanner, Dr Anondyne (pseudonym), *Life of the Late Celebrated Elizabeth Wiseburn known as Mother Whybourn* (London, 1721)

Thompson, Edward, *The Meretriciad. A Satire* (London, 1765 and 1770)

Thornton, Bonnell, *Termagant – or Madame Roxana in Covent Garden Journal* (London, 1752)

Uffenbach, Baron Zachariah von, *London in 1710* trans. W. Quarrell and Margaret Moore (Faber, London, 1934)

Ward, Edward 'Ned', *The London Spy* including 'A History of the London Clubs' (Sawbridge, London, 1709)

Williams, E. N., *Life in Georgian England* (Batsford, London, 1962)

Wilmot, John, Earl of Rochester, *A Panegyrick vpon Cundums* (London, 1674)

> *Poems for Severall Occasions* (London, 1732)

Young, Sir George, *'Poor Fred': The People's Prince* (OUP, Oxford, 1937)

Index

Abergavenny, Henry Nevill, 2nd Earl of (1755–1845), 201
Abington (née Barton), Mrs Frances, (1737–1815), 174–6, 217
Abrams sisters:
  Elizabeth (1770–1830), 182
  Harriet (1758–*c*. 1822), 182
  Theodora (1775–1834), 182
Acts of Parliament, *see* Proclamations
Adam, Robert (1728–1792), 10
'A Day's Ramble' (1698), 26
  see also Dennis, John
Adcock, Mary Sarah ('the Goldfinch'), 214
Addington, Mr Justice Henry, Earl of Sidmouth (1757–1844), 204
Addison, Joseph (1672–1719), 26–9, 150
Adventures of a Young Gentleman, The (*c*. 1745), 91
Aga Hamid, H. E., the (1765–1773), 125
Agas, Ralph, 4
Aldwych (Alde-Wyke), 1, 231
Alford, Sir John Graeme, Earl of (1700–1773), 201
All-Night Lads, 58
Almonds for Parrotts (1708), 146
Ambrose sisters:
  Eleanor Ambrose (*c*. 1730–1818), 179, 214
  Maria, 179–81
  Nancy, 179–81
Amherst, William Pitt, Viscount (1773–1857), 141
Ancram, John Kerr, Earl of (1737–1815), 233

Apreece, Thomas (?–1762), 60, 88, 234
Apreece, Sir Thomas Hussey (1744–1833), 88, 234
Archenholz, Baron Johann Wilhelm von (1741–1812), 206
Archer, Lord Andrew (1747–1778), 141, 160, 234, 237
Archer, Lady Sarah (1741–1801), 141
Aretino, Pietro (1492–1556), 102
Argyle, John Campbell, 5th Duke of (1723–1806), 67, 100
Armistead, Mrs Elizabeth (1751–1842), 72
  see also Fox, C. J.
Arne, Dr Thomas, 159, 171
Arthur's Club, 135
Ashe, Elizabeth, 'the Pollard' (1730–1812), 166, 178
Ashkenazim, 185–6
  see also Jews
Atkyns (Atkins) Sir Richard, Bt. (*c*. 1700–1756), 82–3
'Auctions of Cyprians', 99, 231
Aylmer, Admiral Lord Matthew (1658–1720), 94

Backside (Holywell St, St Clement's), 1
Baddeley, Mrs Sophia (1745–1801), 93, 214, 226
Bagnios (the first), 17, 18
Ballad of Nancy Dawson, The, 125
Banks, Mother, Nancy, 197, 201
Bankside (in Southwark) the, 5
  see also Winchester, Bishop of
Baptiste, Alexandre, 93
Barrodale, John, 8

Barry, Elizabeth (1658–1713), 15, 47
Barsey, Mother, 209–10
Baruk, Miss, 182
Bath, William Poulteney, 10th Earl of (1694–1756), 216
Baths, Bathing, *see* Sanitation
Bathurst, Allan, 1st Earl of (1684–1775), 68
'Bawdy-house bottle', a, 62
Beaumont and Fletcher, 14
Bedford Arms Tavern, the, 86, 93, 98, 100, 107
Bedfordbury (formerly *The Berrie*), 71
Bedford bagnio, the, 107
Bedford Head Coffee-House, the, 94, 100, 107–12, 125, 174
Bedford Head Tavern, the (in Henrietta St), 88
Bedford Head Tavern, the (in Maiden Lane), 107
Bedford Head Tavern, the (in Southampton St), 107
Bedford House, 3, 5–8, 13, 33, 157
Bedford family, *see* Russell
Bedford Street, 12, 88, 125, 134
   see also Half-Moon St
Beefsteak Society, The, 100, 108
Beggars' Opera, The, see Gay, John
Belfield, Earl of (1708–1774), 108
Bellamy, Mrs George Anne (1731–1788), 75, 93, 154, 174–8, 220
Belle Chuck, 49
Bellew, Ann, 74
Benefits (performances for actors), 171, 172
Bengal Room, The, 97, 215
Ben Jonson's Head, the, 93, 105, 117–22
   see also Wetherby's
Bennett, Mrs Lydia, 44, 45, 47
Bentinck, Lord William (1649–1709), 48
Berkeley, Mrs Theresa, 228
   see also Flagellants
Bermudas, the ('A Whore's Nest'), 12
Betterton, Thomas (1635–1710), 15
Beveridge, William, Bishop of Bath & Wells (1637–1708), 42
Bevis Marks Synagogue, 231
Biddulph, Mrs Elizabeth, 78
   see also Careless, Betsy

Bingley, George Fox-Lane, Lord (1696–1773), 68
Binning, Charles Hamilton, Lord (1753–1826), 215
   see also Haddington, Lord
Birch, Mother Susannah (*alias* 'Birchini'), 149, 228
Bird Market, James St., 159
Bird, Mother, 69
   see also Needham
Bird, Miss *alias* Johnson, 105
'Bird of Paradise, the', 214, 215, 231
   see also Mahon, Gertrude
Birkenhead, Sir John (1616–1679), 42, 144
Bissett, Captain George Morris (1757–1821), 221
   see also Worseley, Lady
Black-a-Moor, The, 56
   see also King, Moll
Blagney, Mr Justice Jacob (?–1733), 48
Blakeney's Head, the Lord, 135
   see also Dillon; Lotteries
Blue Aprons, 19
Blue Posts Chocolate-House, The, in Exeter Street, 73
Blunts and Tatlers, 88
Bog-houses, 32
Bolingbroke, Frederick St John, 2nd Viscount (1734–1787), 48
Bombay Room, The, 97
Boscawen, Admiral Sir Edward (1711–1761), 204
Boswell, James (1740–1795), 60, 98, 147, 195–7, 233, 234
Bow Street, 11, 13, 57, 73, 74, 93, 109, 112, 119, 132, 141, 152, 166, 185, 188, 189, 204, 206, 208, 237
Bow Street Runners, 160, 208, 237
Boxing, 88, 234
Bradley, John (?–1770), 73, 186
Bradshaw, Mrs Frances (née Herbert), 166, 204, 205
Braun, Georg, & Hogenburg, Franz, maps, 5
Bray, Rev. William, DD, MA (?–1644), 11
Brent, Charlotte 'Sally' (1735–1802), 197
Bride, Elizabeth (1746–?), 177
   see also John Calcraft

Bridewells – Houses of Correction, 19,
44, 48, 72
see also Tothill Fields
Bridgeman, Sir Orlando Bt.
(*c.* 1730–1764), 117–19
Brogdanones, 159
Brown, Thomas, of Shifnal, 35, 90, 168
Browne, Richard, 3
Brydges Street, 11, 15, 73, 86, 105, 137,
162, 182, 232
Brydges, Catherine (*c.* 1593–1657), 6
see also Chandos
Brydges, Giles, 3rd Baron,
(1547–1594), 6
Brydges, James, 1st Duke of Chandos
(1673–1744), 117
Bubb-Dodington, George, Viscount,
178–9
see also Melcombe
Bucks' Delight, The (1778), 232
Buck's Midnight Ramble, The (1774), 205
Buckingham, John Sheffield, Duke of
(1648–1721), 49
Buckinghamshire, George Hobart,
Earl of (1731–1804), 142
Buckinghamshire, Albinia (1738–1816)
Countess of, 142, 143, 182
see also 'Madame Blubber';
Pharaoh's Daughters
Buggery, 16, 164, 165
see also Homosexuals
Bull Head Tavern, the, formerly the
Bull and Butcher in Clare Market,
32
see also Spiller, James
Bull Inn Court and Bull Inn Tavern,
the, in the Strand, 12
Bunch of Grapes, the, in Clare Market,
a 'Mollies House', 208
'Bunters', 234
Burgess, Mother Margaret, 59, 71
see also Flagellation
Burgess family, 71
James, James St (1720–1740)
John, Bow St (1727–1733)
Thomas, Drury La (1711–?)
William, Russell St (1711–*d.* 1753)
Burgess, Peter (Borges), 227
see also Flagellants; Hutchins, Susan;
Sperre, Baron Karl
Burleigh (Burghley) House, 4, 8

see also Cecil
Burney, Mrs Fanny (1752–1840), 30
Bute, John Stewart, Earl of
(1713–1792), 67
Butler, Mother Elizabeth
(*c.* 1730–1825), 86, 88
Button's Coffee-House (Daniel Button
c. 1662–1731), 26–9, 107
Byron, Mr (a Creole), 174–5
see also Parkes, Sally
Byron, Captain John 'Mad Jack'
(1756–1791), 175

Caesar's Head, 12
see also Sare
Cage, The, in Covent Garden, 130
Calcraft, John (1726–1772), 118, 177–8
see also Bellamy
Caledonien, the, *see* Buttons
Callaghan's Coffee-House, in the
Piazza, 74, 141, 188
Campbell, James, 100, 102
Cane, Mother Mary (?–1754), 71
Capel-Cunningham, 220
see also Malden, Lord
Cardigan, George Brudenall, Earl of
(1670–1732), 48, 50
Cardigan's Head, the, Tavern, 74, 165
see also Mollies
Careless, Elizabeth 'Betsy'
(*c.* 1700–1739), 52, 76, 78, 79, 92,
98, 108, 130
see also Biddulph
Carnegie, David, 212
see also Rosehill, Lord
Carpenter, George, Lessee (?–*c.* 1785)
of Covent Garden, 85–6
Carpenter's Coffee-House, *see* 'The
Finish'
Carroll's Bagnio, 210
Carter, Abraham 'Sam's', 141
Carter's Bagnio (Abraham Carter), 209
Casanova, Chevalier Giacomo G.
(1723–1798), 199, 227
Casey, Laurence (*Little Cazey*), 57, 79
Cassilis, Lady Susan 'Lady Castleless'
(1699–1763), 140, 141
Castle Tavern, the, Henrietta St, 82
Castlemaine, Lady Barbara Palmer,
Duchess of Cleveland
(1641–1703), 70, 89

Cat, the, Tavern in Exchange Alley, 209

Catalogue of Jilts, A (1691), 102

Catey, Mother, 59, 72

Catherine Street (Katherine Street), 10, 11, 18, 20; (gallows), 162, 166, 231

Cecil Street, Strand, 189

Cecil, Thomas, Earl of Exeter (1542–1623), 5

Cecil, William, Earl of Burghley (Burleigh) (1520–1598), 4

Chamberpots, 10, 19, 62, 130
see also 'Member's Mug'; Sanitation

Chandos family, see Brydges

Chandos Street, 12, 18, 26, 50, 71 and *passim*

Chapman's Coffee-House (*c.* 1671), 26
see also 'Will's'

Characters of the Present Most Celebrated Courtezans (1780), 214

Charing Cross, 1, 232 and *passim*

Charles I (1600–1649), 6, 13

Charles II (1630–1685), 11, 14, 15, 17, 21, 42

Charles Court, 67, 89

Charles Street, 67, 86, 102, 137

Charteris, Col. Francis (1675–1732), 47, 70, 168
see also Needham, Elizabeth

Chelsea, 1, 219

Chesterfield, Philip Dormer Stanhope, Earl of (1694–1773), 68, 100, 147, 177

Child Rape, 164

Chocolate-Houses, 72–4, 122, 156

Chudleigh, Lady Elizabeth, Duchess of Kingston (1720–1788), 81

Churchill, Charles (1731–1764), 111–14, 118

Civil War, 11, 13, 14

Clap, Mother Margaret, 33, 62, 165
see also Homosexuals

Clare, Charles O'Brien, 6th Earl of (1699–1761), 32

Clare Market, 30–32, 122, 165, 168, 208
see also Homosexuals

Clay, Francis (?–1738), 159

'Clean Brothels', 191

Cleland, John (1709–1789), 134

Clive, Catherine 'Kitty' (1711–1785), 172

'Club of Paederasts', the (1794), 208

Coates, Robert 'Cock-a-doodle-doo Coates' (?–1848), 114, 115

Cock, Christopher, Auctioneer (?–1748), 159, 188

Cock, the, Tavern in Charles Street owned by Mother Wilkinson, 18

Cockeslane off Snow Hill: an 'assigned place', 5

Cock and Hen Clubs, 205

Cockpit, the, Theatre, 14

Cocksedge, Mother, 189

Colborn, William, 109

Cole, Mother, 134

Collett, Mrs, 230
see also Flagellation

Colson, Israel, 149
see also Phillips, Constantia

Concerning Decency, by Sam Rolleston, 100

Condoms, see Phillips, Constantia

Congreve, William (1670–1729), 154

Constables' Ramble, A (1762), 131

Convent Garden Eclogue, The (1735), 92
see also Hanbury Williams

Conyers, Sir Gerard, judge (1661–1737), 52

Cooper, Lucy (1725–1772), 92, 93, 98, 108, 117–121, 124, 175, 204
see also Weatherby

Coote, Gen. Sir Eyre Coote (1726–1783), 126
see also Dawson, Nancy

Corbyne, Mrs Mary, 'the White Crow', 214

Cornelys, Mrs Theresa (1723–1797), 215, 227

Cosway, Mrs, 176

Cotton, Elizabeth 'Nancy', Courtesan (?–1769), 54, 73, 74

Courage, Mrs, a 'house for lesbians', 99, 166

Courteney, Edward, 165
see also Homosexuals

Court of Cupid, The (1765), *see* Thompson, Edward

Courtesan, The (1770), 107

Covent Garden Cyprians, *see* Harris, Jack

'Covent Garden Disease', the, 231

Covent Garden Market, 16, 17, 85, 86

see Carpenter, George

Covent Garden Morning Frolick, A,
engraving by Boitard, 79

Covent Garden in Mourning (1757), 62

Covent Garden Satyre (1756), 114, 132

Covent Garden Theatre (Theatre
Royal), 124 and *passim*

Covent Garden Tragedy, A (1745) by
Henry Fielding, 168

Coxe, Elizabeth 'Betsy' (*c.* 1748-1814),
199–201, 214, 219, 226

Coxe, Col. John, 200

Craven, William, 6th Earl of
(1739–1791), 201

Crazy Tales (*c.* 1716), 43, 149

Creoles, 174, 175

Cresswell, Mother Elizabeth
(*c.* 1625–1684), 21, 42

Crew, Nathaniel, 3rd Baron, 18
see also Durham, Bishop of

Croft, Richard (?–1742), 96

Cromwell, Oliver, Lord Protector
(1599–1658), 11, 13, 35

Crosdell, Ann, 86
see also Carpenter's

Cross Keys, the, Tavern in Bedford St,
88
see also Bedford Head

Cross Keys Tavern, the, in Little
Russell St, 115, 190

Crown, the, a brothel in the Strand,
162

Crown Court, Russell St, 181
see also Albertini

Cuffe, The Hon. Mr Jonah, later
Denning-Wheeler (1765–1833),
206–7

Cumberland Court, Drury Lane, 198,
214, 230

Cumberland, Prince Ernest, Duke of
(1771–1851), 219

Cumberland, Prince Henry Frederick,
Duke of (1745–1790), 125

Cumberland, Prince William
Augustus (1721–1763), 130–1

Cundums, 131, 144–9
see also Phillips

Cuyler, Col. Cornelius (1740–1819),
214

Cuyler, Margaret (1752–1814),
214–16

Cyder Cellar, the (*c.* 1720–1858), 12,
80, 118, 233–4, 237
see also Derry, Robert

Damer, Hon. John (?–1770), 116, 211

Darby, Mary, *see* Robinson 'Perdita'

Darking, Mary, 73
see also Haddock

Dashwood, Sir Francis Bt.
(1708–1781), 68, 177
see also Hell-Fire Club

Davies, Thomas (1712–1785), 98

Davis, Mary 'Moll' (*c.* 1640-post 1678),
42

Davis, Elizabeth 'Little Infamy'
(*c.* 1745–1794), 106, 108

Davis, 'Poll' (*c.* 1740–1781), 105
see also Shuter, Ned; Dawson,
Nancy

Dawson, Anne 'Nancy' (*c.* 1720–1767),
61, 62, 73, 81, 92, 93, 98, 105–6,
122–6

Day, Thomas, 17

De Gourdan, Madame, 186–7
see also Gould, Mrs Elizabeth

Delaval, Sir Francis Blake Bt.
(1727–1771), 82, 180–1

De la Roche, Elizabeth, 82

De Leyre (Lyre), William, Assessor, 2

Demi-Rep, The (1766), 109
see also Thompson, Edward

Denmark Alley and Denmark Coffee-
House, The, 13, 182, 209

Dennis, John (1657–1734), 'A Day's
Ramble' (1698), 26

Dennison, Elizabeth and Richard
(fl. 1700–1780), 68–70
see also Hell-fire Stanhope

Derby, Edward Stanley, 12th Earl of
(1752–1825), 10, 217
see also Farren, Elizabeth

Derrick, Samuel (1724–1769), 106,
110–12, 202–4

Derry, Robert (*c.* 1700–?), 80, 118, 124,
234, 237

De Sevigny, Marquise Marie
(1626–1696), 146

Dewberry, Joseph, 140, 141
see also Mordington

De Veil, Justice Sir Thomas
(1683–1746), 62, 152

Dicing, 135
  see also Gambling
Dillon, Mary, 138
  see also Mordington
Dillon, Mother Catherine née O'Neill,
  135
Dillon, Peter (husband to above), 135
Dingley, Henry, 3
Dirty Lane, *see* Bow St
Dissolution of the Monasteries (1539),
  3
Dixon, Mother, 71
  see also Cane
Dodd, Rev. William, DD (1729–1777),
  126
Dog and Bitch Yard, 89
Donaldson, William (?–1780), 120,
  160, 173
  see also Faulkner
Dorset, Frederick John Sackville, 3rd
  Duke of (1745–1799), 67
Douglas, Mother Jane (*c.* 1700–1761),
  75, 78, 97, 111, 128–134, 140, 146,
  184, 231
Doves of Venus, The (1642), 13, 74
Drewerie, 1, 5
  see also Drury Lane
Drury, The Hundreds of, A
  sub-division of a county, 19, 65,
  150
  see also Drury Lane
Drury Lane and Theatre, 1, 5, 10, 11,
  15, 19, 24, 30, 69, 154, 155, 171,
  173, 180, 181, 198, 201, 211
  and passim
Drury Lane Journal, the, 74, 177, 182
Drury Place, 5
Drury, Sir Robert de (?–1495), 5
Drury, Sir Roger de (?–1408), 5
'Drury Virgins', 231
Dryden, John (1636–1700), 15, 16, 26
Dubery, Sarah, 141
Dublin, 104–5, 215
  see also Ireland; Macklin
Duffus, George, homosexual (?–1722),
  32
  see also Mollies Houses
Dukes Place, a 'Whores' Nest', 36, 47
Duncombe, Peter, 26
Dundas, Henry, Visc. Melville
  (1742–1811), 176

Durham, Bishop of, Nathaniel Crew,
  3rd Baron Crew (1633–1721), 18
Dutch Sam, 88
Duval, Claude, 18

Eagle Court (Eagle & Child Ct), 231
Earl's Court, 67
Earle, Lucy, 80, 188
  see also the Turk's Head
East India Company, 97, 131, 197
Eastsmith, Mother, 133
Echlin, Sir Henry Bt. (1740–1799), 181
Edgecumbe, Richard (1716–1761), 108
  see also Mount Edgecombe
Edward VI (1537–1553), 3
E and O (Evens and Odds), 135
  see also Gambling
Effingham, Thomas Howard, Earl of
  (1746–1791), 201
Egan, Pierce, 88
Eglinton, Alexander Montgomerie,
  10th Earl of (1723–1769), 195
Egremont Charles Wyndham, Earl of,
  (1710–1763), 78, 106
'Elephant & Castle, The', Sophia
  Charlotte, Countess von Platen
  (1673–1725), 37
  see also George I
Elizabeth I (1533–1603), 4
Elliott, Eleanor 'Nelly', 176
'English Perversion, The', 227
Essay on Woman (1763), 83
  see also John Wilkes
Essex Serpent Tavern, The, 159
Eton School, 53, 96
Evans, W. C., hotelier (?–1854), 100,
  188, 234
Evelyn, John (1620–1706), 14
Exchange Court or Alley, 13
Exeter Exchange, 105
Exeter House, 4
Exeter Street, 73, 122, 228
Exhibition of Female Flagellants, The
  (1777), 228
  see also Wilson, Mary

Fair Penitent, The (1775), *see* Abrams,
  Harriet
Falkirk, Lord, 201
  see also Alford, Earl

Fallopio, Gabriele (1523–1562), 144
   see also Cundum
Faro-houses, 135–43
Farren, Elizabeth (1759–1829), 172,
   214, 217
   see also Derby, Lord
Fashionable Lectures (*c.* 1780), 228
   see also Birch, Mrs;
   Flagellation
'Fat Phyllis', 206–8
   see also Homosexuals; Vaughan alias
   Jones
Fat Priestess, 60
   see also Moll King
Faulkner, Mary Anne (*c.* 1725–1771),
   167, 172
   see also Donaldson; Halifax, Lord
Featherstone, Nancy, 78
Female Flagellants, The, 228
Ferguson, Mrs Mary, 226
'Field of Blood, the', 58
Fielding, Lt. Col. Hon. Charles
   (?–1746), 206–7
Fielding, Lady Frances, later Countess
   of Winchilsea (*c.* 1710–1734), 82
Fielding, Henry (1707–1754), 57, 76,
   111, 114, 152, 153, 156, 157, 162,
   168, 182
Fielding, Sir John (*c.* 1720–1780), 100,
   114, 119, 189, 190, 231, 232, 237
Fife, James McDuff, Earl of
   (1729–1809), 201, 226
'Fighting Israelites', the, 88
   see also Boxing; Jews
Finch, Hon. John (1692–1763), 50–2
   see also Salisbury, Sally
'Finish, The', 85–8
   see also Carpenter's
Finish, The, a tavern in James Street,
   86
Fire and firefighting, 115–16
Fisher (Fischer) Catherine Maria,
   'Kitty Fisher' (1738–1767), 120
Fitzherbert, Mrs, 220
Fitzroy, Lady Caroline, *see*
   Harrington, Lady
Fitzwilliam, John Williams, 1st Earl
   (1719–1756), 128, 131, 134
   see also Douglas, Jane
Flagellation, 43, 71, 91, 111, 227–30
Flashers, 136

Fleece Tavern, the (*c.* 1667), 11
Fleet Street, 1, 80, 189
Fleet Marriages, 54
Fleet Prison, 88, 178
Fleming, Lady Dorothy Seymour
   (*c.* 1750-post 1808), 75
   see also Worseley
Floral Street, *see* Hart Street
Floyd, Mr, 111
   see also Derrick
Football, 159
Foote, Samuel (1720–1777), 82, 86,
   134, 187, 196
   see also Haymarket Theatre, The
Footmen, Union of, 152
Fordyce, Mrs Kitty, 93
Forman, Simon (1552–1611), 102
Fortescue, Sir John, Lord Chief Justice
   (1394–1436), 3
Fountain Tavern, the, in Russell St, 32
Fountain Tavern, the, in Clare Market,
   32, 165
   see also Mollies houses
Fox, Charles James (1749–1800), 72,
   134, 217
   see also Armistead
Fox, Admiral, 200
Fox-under-the-Hill, the, 85
Franklin, Benjamin (1706–1790), 160,
   161
Fredericks, Catherine 'Kitty' (*c.* 1750-
   post 1784), 108, 172, 226
Freeland, Mrs Anne, 209–10
French Revolution, The, 223
French Sooty Frizeur, the, 225
Fruit Shop, The (Betty O'Neale), 190
Fry, Alexander, 141
   see also Callaghan's Coffee-House
'Fullams' (Loaded Dice), 135
Furness, Mary, 112
   see also the Bedford Arms

Gage, Thomas Hall, Viscount
   (?–1754), 60
Galli, Signora Caterina Ruini
   (1723–1804), 99, 211
Galloway, Sir Edward, 137
Gamberini, Signora Elizabeta
   (1731–*c.* 1785), 125
Gambling and Gambling houses, 12,
   34, 65, 135–43, 156, 187

Gambling – *cont.*
  see also Faro-Houses
'Game of Flats, the', 92, 165
  see also Lesbians
Gardiner, Sarah Ann (*c.* 1690–1739),
  94, 107–9
Garfield, John (*c.* 1630–?1664), 102
  see also The Wand'ring Whore
Garrick, David (1717–1779), 93, 100,
  169, 171–3, 176, 219, 237
Garth, Peter, 47
Gay, John (1685–1732), 43, 90, 128,
  135, 150
  see also The Beggars' Opera, 125, 153,
  168;
  The Petticoat, 146;
  Trivia (1716), 65, 68
Gent, G. A., *The Rake Reform'd*, 90
Gentleman's Magazine, The, 67, 74, 79
George I (1660–1727), 37, 136
George II (1683–1760), 37, 40, 48, 60,
  92, 184
George III (1738–1820), 86, 219–20,
  230
George IV (1762–1830), 100, 219
  see also Prince Regent (from 1788)
Gifford, Mrs, 209
Gifford, William, *see* Carpenter's
Gillray, James (1757–1815), 149, 182,
  221
Goadby, Mrs Jane (*c.* 1720–?), 72, 133,
  185, 211
Gold, 'Polly', 105
Golden Cat, the, Tavern, 119
Golden Cup, the, 159
'Golden Fan & Crown, Ye', 225
Golden Fan and Rising Sun, The, 148
  see also Phillips
'Goldfinch, the', 214
  see Sarah Mary Adcock (*c.* 1735-post
  1795)
  see Wilson
Goldsmith, Oliver (1728–1774), 111,
  114
Gong-farmers, 10
  see also Sanitation
Gonson, Sir John (?–1765), 56, 62, 70,
  132
Gordon, Tamar, 210
Gossipers' Shilling Club, the, 114
Gould, Mrs Elizabeth (*c.* 1710–1784),

(Mrs E. Leese), 111, 112, 133,
  184–8, 237
Gould, Henry, judge (1710–1794), 81
Gould, Jack, a Market-Man, 86
  see also Carpenter's
Gower, Sir Samuel (?–1757), 152
HMS *Grafton*, 161–2
  see also Woods, Peter
Graham, Lord George, MP
  (1715–1747), 130
Graham, Lord James (1755–1830), 221
Gray, Mother, 225
Great Fire of London, 15, 16
Great Plague, The, 15, 16
Greek shops, 135, 216
  see also Faro-houses
Green, Elizabeth 'Betsy', *see* Coxe,
  Betsy
Green, Mother, 58, 72
Green Canister, the, 146–9
  see also Phillips
'Greenfinch, the' (Miss Greenhill), 214
Green Hatch and One Lamp, the, 131
  see also Misaubin
Green Man, the, 53
Griffiths, Mother Margaret 'Nan', 59,
  71
Grosvenor, Lady Henrietta, Countess
  (*c.* 1745–1828), 125, 221
Guardian, The (1713), 29
Gwynn, Nell, 15, 90

Hackman, Rev. James (1752–1779),
  102, 112
Hackney carriages, 160, 167, 206
Haddington, Thomas Hamilton, 7th
  Earl of (1720–1795), 215
  see also Binning, Lord
Haddock, Mrs Elizabeth (?–1751), 58,
  64, 72–4
Haddock, Richard (?–1748), 122
Haddock's bagnios, 188
  see also Lemoy, Sophia; Saunders
Haggs of Hell, 58
Haines, Richard, 30
Halifax, George (Montague) Dunk,
  2nd Earl of (1716–1771), 70, 167,
  172
  see also Faulkner
Half-Moon Alley, Passage and Street,
  11, 12, 145–9, 233

Half-Moon Tavern, the, 12
  see also Le becq
Hall, Mother Elizabeth, 67
Hamilton, Mother, 'An old Frow', 189
Hanbury-Williams, Charles
  (1708–1759), 132, 133, 174
  see also Douglas, Jane
Hand and Pen, the, the Marriage Shop,
  12, 13
Handel, George Frederick
  (1685–1759), 154
Hanger, Sir William (1744–1814), 226
Harington, Sir John (1561–1612), 10
Harpers in Covent Garden, 160
Harrington, Lady Caroline, Countess
  of (1722–1784), 166, 178, 227
Harrington, William Stanhope, Earl of
  (1719–1779), 178
Harrington, Mother Olivia, 75, 199,
  209
  see also Casanova
Harris, John, 'Jack' (*c.* 1710–1765), 75,
  81, 98, 102–7, 125, 126, 181, 182,
  197, 201, 209, 211–16
Harris, Henry, 17
Harris, Nancy, 112, 188, 190
  see also Hickey
Harris, Thomas (*c.* 1740–1820), 202,
  215
  see also Lessingham
Hart Street (now Floral Street), 32, 33,
  72, 94, 96; Pillory in, 33;
  Hairdresser in, 212
Haszlang, Count Franz Xavier
  (1709–1797), 177–8, 231
Hat and Beaver Coffee-House, 141
Haveland, Daniel, 74
Haveman, Mother, 72
Haverstock Hill, 59, 62, 126
  see also Moll King; Nancy Dawson
Hawksbee, Calvin, 141
  see also Sam's; Carter, Abraham;
  Selthe
Haydn, Franz Josef (1732–1809), 182
Hayes, Charlotte 'Santa Carlotta'
  (*c.* 1725–1812), 114, 117, 176, 187,
  198, 200, 204, 226
Haymarket Theatre, 45, 99, 154, 156,
  172, 215, 217
  see also Foote; Heidegger
Hayward, Clara (*c.* 1740–?), 197, 198

Hayward (Heywood) Mother
  Elizabeth and Richard, 58, 60, 65,
  67
Hazard Club, The, 97
Hazzlewood (née Loraine) Charlotte,
  216, *Secret History of the Green
  Room*, 216
Heasman, Henry, 94
Heathcock Alley and Court, 13
Heathcock Tavern, the, 13
Heidegger, J. J. (1659–1749), 45
  see also Haymarket Theatre;
  Whyburn
Hell-Fire Club, The, 67, 68, 117, 118
  see also Dashwood
'Hell-fire Stanhope', 68, 70
  see also Dennison, Elizabeth
Henley, Robert, barrister (1708–1772),
  48, 76, 78
  see also Northington, Lord
Henrietta Street, 10, 72, 81, 88, 89, 94
  and *passim*
Henry III (1207–1272), 3
Henry VIII (1491–1547), 3, 32, 164
Herbert, Frances (Mrs Bradshaw),
  204
Herbert, Henry, *see* Pembroke, Earl of
Hickey, William (1749–1830), 86, 98–9,
  112, 115, 119, 121, 188–90, 197–8,
  215, 234
Hill, Miss, 75
Hills, Trevor, (1693–1742), Viscount
  Hillsborough, 68
Hobster, Mary, and Hobster, Stokes,
  (?–1774), 109–12
  see also the Bedford Head
Hockley-i'-th' Hole, 201
Hogarth, William, painter
  (1697–1764), 56, 92, 100, 112, 114,
  131, 168
Hole-in-the-Wall Tavern, the, 18
  see also Duval, Claude
Holland, Dame Elizabeth, 185
Holmes, Admiral Charles (1711–1761)
  and his daughter Holmes,
  Elizabeth (1741–?), 133, 134
  see also Douglas, Jane
Homosexuals *see* Mollies houses and
  Sodomy
Hood, Admiral Samuel, later Viscount
  (1724–1816), 175

Hopkins, Mother Elizabeth (?–1721), 67
Horner, Yorke (?–1728), 165
Horseley, William, 140, 141
  see also Mordington
Hospitals, *see* Lock
Houses of Correction, *see* Bridewells
Houses of Male Resort, *see* Mollies houses
Howard, Julian, 99
Howe, Admiral Viscount Richard (1726–1799), 180
Hudson, Sarah 'Sally', 197, 201
Huguenots, 12, 116
'Hummums, the', 17, 18, 115, 188, 237
  see also Bagnios
Humorous Lieutenant, The, 14
Humphreys, Richard (*c.* 1760-post 1800), 234
  see also Apreece; Boxing
Hundreds of Drury, The, *see* Drury Lane
'Hurgo Dunkara', 173
  see also Halifax, Lord
Hutchins, Susannah, 227
  see also Sperre, Karl

Imperial Hotel, 115, 116
Indian Kings, 159
Infants Office, the, in St Giles, 21, 70
Ireland & Irish, *see* Dublin
'Irish Owl, the', 220
  see Murphy, Arthur
Irnham, Simon Luttrell, Viscount (1713–1787), 233
Ironside, Mr, 29
Irvince, Mrs, 'the White Swan', 214
Islington, 167
Italian Opera House, the (the King's Theatre in the Haymarket), 172
  see also Heidegger

Jacobs, Mrs, 181
Jacobs, J., 131, 147
  see also Douglas, Jane
James I (1566–1625), 6, 8, 124
James II (1635–1701), 41
  see also York, Duke of
James Street, 86, 159
  see also Clay
Jefferson, Thomas, 176

Jelly Houses, 75, 93, 181, 188, 210
  see also Baptiste
Jennison, Robert, 152
Jews, 16, 35, 36, 47, 88, 89, 104, 105, 109, 118, 144, 168, 179, 182, 185, 210, 227, 230
Jiggs, 82, 106, 124
Johnson, Mary 'Moll', 105
Johnson, Dr Samuel (1709–1784), 98, 111, 112, 157, 169, 182
Johnston, Anne, 73, 74
  see also Haddock
Johnstone, Lady Cecilia née West (1727–1814), 217
Jolley, Mother, 67
Jones, Charles, 'Fat Phyllis', 208
  see also Homosexuals
Jones, Mr, 33
  see also Mollies
Jones, Inigo (1573–1652), 6, 7, 11
Jones, Nancy, 117
  see also Cooper, Lucy
Jones, 'Polly', 198
  see also Sturgess
Jones, Winfred, 90
Journey Through England, A (1722–24), 29
  see also Mackay
Journeyman Bakers, 96

Katherine Street, *see* Catherine Street
Kelly, Mother, in Duke Street, 201
Kemble, John Philip (1757–1823), 88, 94, 217
Kennedy, 'Poll' (*c.* 1730–1781), 124–7
  see also Dawson, Nancy
Kennels (Sewage channels), *see* Sanitation
Kensington, 1
Kenyon, Mr Justice Lloyd (1732–1802), 142
Keppel, Admiral Augustus (1725–1786), 102
Key, the Thomas Key Tavern, later the Half-Moon Tavern, 12
  see also Le becq
Kilburn, 167
Killigrew, Thomas (1612–1683), 14
'Kind and Tender Usage', 230
King, Mary and Thomas: Tom King's (1694–1739), Moll King's, Mary

King (1696–1747), 53–65, 73, 80, 85, 92, 108, 114, 117
see also King, William
King of Clubs, the, 202
see also Harris, Thomas
King of Hell, the, 233
see also Irnham, Lord
King's Arms, the, in Catherine St, 181
see also Waterman
King's Arms Tavern, the, in Drury Lane, 67
see also Jolley, Mother
King's Arms Tavern, the, in the Little Piazza, *see* Lovejoy
King's Bench (Court & Prison), 88, 98, 103–4, 119, 131, 177, 212, 219
King's Head, the, in the Piazza, 130
see also Douglas, Jane
King's Head Tavern, the, in Russell St, 65
see also Hayward
King's Place, St James, 211, 215, 228
King Street, 11, 73, 86, 134, 159 and *passim*
King, Thomas (1730–1805), 55
King, William, 58, 62
Kingston, Evelyn Meadows, Pierrepoint, Duke of (1711–1773), 198
see also Chudleigh
Kinnoul, George Hay, 7th Earl (*c.* 1690–1758), 68
Kinsey, Stephen, (1748–1816), the Bedford Head, 112
'Kitten, the' (*c.* 1720–1745), 108
Kneller, Sir Godfrey (1646–1723), 28
Knightsbridge, 45, 47, 167, 225

La Charpillon (1746-post 1780), 227
see also Casanova
Lade, Sir John Bt. (1759–1838), 231
'Lady in Mourning', (*c.* 1720), 62
Lamb, Harriet, later Countess of Seaforth (1750–1779), 172, 198
Lambert, George (1710–1765), 100, 108
Langford, Abraham (1711–1774), 133, 149, 188
Langhorne, William (1721–1772), 71
Lansdowne, William Petty, Marquis of (1737–1808), 176
Laroun, Capt. Marcellus, 57

Lazenby, Robert, 17
Leadbetter, Mrs, 159
Le becq, Jean and Lebeck's Head, 12
see also the Key Tavern
Lee, Miss Peggy, 108, 109
see also Lincoln, Lord
Lee, Mary, Slingsby, Lady, 15
Leeches, Vendors of, 160
Leese, Mrs Elizabeth, 186
see also Gould, Mrs
Legge, Thomas, Covent Garden Satyre (1756), 114, 132
Leinster, James Fitzgerald, 1st Duke of (1722–1772), 100
Lemoy, Sophia (1700–1767), 73, 74, 122, 188
see also Haddock
Lepell, Mary 'Molly', Lady Hervey (1700–1768), 90
Lesbians, 92, 165, 178
Lessingham, Mrs Jane Hemet (1735-1800), 201–4
Lethercote Richard (Leathercoat), 90
Levi, Miss, 182
Levites, 36, 187
see also Jews
Lewis, Mrs 'Louisa', 196
see also Boswell, James
Lewis, Mother, 59, 72
Lewis, 'A Cundum-maker', 147
Lewis, Thomas, 29
Lewkenor's Lane (later Charles St), 102
Lichfield, George Henry Lee, 2nd Earl of (1690–1742), 68
Light of Israel, The, see Daniel Mendoza
Ligonier, Field Marshal Edward, Earl of (1740–1782), 174
Ligonier, Lady Penelope (1749-post 1785), 221
Lillipushes, 159
Limberham, a, 49
Lion, The, effigy, 28, 29, 102
Lincoln, Henry Fiennes-Clinton, Earl of (1720–1794), 67, 108, 172
List of Cyprians (1743), *see* Walpole, Horace
Little Cazey, 79
see also Casey, Laurence
Little Peggy, 108
see also Lee, Peggy

Little Piazza, 17, 72, 74, 78, 86, 112, 115, 126, 128, 186, 188
see also Hummums
Load of Hay, the, later The Noble Art public house, 62
see also King, Moll
Lock Hospitals, 44, 117, 157, 174
London Journal, The, 52, 73, 78, 96, 140, 165
London Mercury, The (1721), 136
London Spy, The (Edward 'Ned' Ward), 30, 32, 165
Long Acre, 1, 3, 6, 13, 89, 167, 208, 212, 225
Long Acre, Stocks in, 212
Long Acre Bagnio, 209
Long, Robert and William, 89
Long Vocation, The (*c.* 1700), 32, 35
Loraine, Charlotte (Mrs Hazzlewood), 216, 217
see also Secrets of the Green Room
Lord Mayor's Banquet, a, a description, 198
Lotteries, 135
Loudoun, John Campbell, Earl of (1705–1782), 174
Lovejoy, Matthew, 73, 112, 126, 186, 188
Low, David, 94, 97
Luffingham, William, 112
Lumley Court, 13
Lyon's Head Tavern, the, 10, 24, 94, 96
Lyre (or Leyre), William de, 2
Lyttelton, Thomas, 'The Wicked' Earl (1743–1779), 200, 219

Macaronis, 205, 223
'Macaroni Preacher, the' (Rev. William Dodd, LLD), (1729–1777), 126
Mackay (Macky) John, 29
Mackintosh, Martin, 'Orange Deb', 33
Macklin, Charles (1697–1797), 171, 180, 181, 188
Macklin's Coffee-House (1754) later the Piazza Coffee-House, 234
Maclean, James, the Gentleman Highwayman (1724–1750), 83
Madame Birchini's Dance, 149, 228
see also Birch, Mrs
see also Flagellants
'Madame Blubber', 142, 143, 182

see also Buckinghamshire, Lady
Maddocks (Maddox), Mrs, 80
Madras Club, 97, 197
Magistrates (stipendiaries), 153
Mahon, Gertrude, 'the Bird of Paradise' (1752–1809), 214, 231
Maiden Lane, 12, 74, 80, 134, 148, 233 and *passim*
Malden, George Capel-Conyngham, Viscount (1757–1839), 220
Maltby's Coffee-house and Richard Maltby, 125, 188, 190, 225
Manners, Hon. John, Captain (1730–1792), 108
Mansfield, David Murray, Earl of (1727–1796), 54, 131
Marcheuses, Les, 223
Marinet family, *see* Douglas, Jane
Marjoram, John and Marjoram's Tavern, 189
Marks, Ruth, 36
Marranos, 36
see also Jews
Marriages Registration Act (1689), 19
Marriage Act, The (1754), 166
Marriage Shops, 12, 13, 55 and *passim*
Marshall, Ann and Beck, 90
Marshalsea Debtors' Prison, 49, 147
Marsham, Lady Elizabeth (1692–1750), 48
Martlet Court, 121, 122, 230
Marvell, Andrew (1621–1672), 12, 107
Marygold Court, 13
Marylebone Gardens, 167–8, 172, 198
Mascorades & Ridottos, An Act Against (1721), 136
Matthews, Mrs Catherine, 213, 228
Matveyev, Andrei Artamonovitch (1666–1725), 34
see also Russia
Maynard, Charles, Viscount (1752–1824), 81
see also Parsons, Annabella
'Maypole, the', (Countess Ehrengard Melusina von der Schulenberg (1667–1743), later Duchess of Kendal, 37
Meade (Mead) Dr Richard MD (1673–1754), 43, 131
see also Whyburn

Meadows, Evelyn (Pierrepoint), 174, 198
  see also Kingston, Duke of
Medlycott, Captain Thomas (*c.* 1720–1795), 174
'Medmenham Friars, The', 177
  see also Dashwood, Sir Francis
Megg, Mary (?–1672), 89
Melbourne, Penistone Lamb, Viscount (1744–1828), 190
Melcombe, George Bubb-Doddington, Earl of (1691–1762), 179
  see also Strawbridge
Member's mug, a, 62
Menassah ben Israel (1604–1657), 35
  see also Cromwell, Oliver
Mendez, Dr Fernando (*c.* 1640–1724), 42, 144
  see also Jews
Mendez, Moses (*c.* 1690–1758), 99, 109, 187, 211
  see also Galli
  see also Jews
Mendoza, Daniel (1764–1836), 86, 234
  see also Apreece
  see also Jews
Meretriciad, The (1765 and 1770), 98, 114, 118, 119, 121, 126, 188, 228
Messiah, The (by Handel), 154
Metcalfe, Major Thomas (1745–1813), 214–16
Metham, George, 177
Middleton, Charlotte, Countess of Warwick, 26, 27
Midnight Spy, The (1733), 90
Misaubin, Dr Jean, MD, LRCP (*c.* 1660–1734), 116, 131
  see also Rock, Dr Richard
Mitchell, Mary and Richard, 109, 114, 226
Mogg, Mary 'Molly' (*c.* 1700–1776), 90
  see also Gay, John; Jones, Winfred
Mohocks, Scourers, Nickers, 34, 35, 68, 107, 136
Mollies houses, 21, 30, 33, 122, 150, 165, 288
  see also Clare Market; Homosexuals
Moll King's Row, Hampstead, 62
Monk, *Mother*, 72
Montague, John, 'Mad Jack', 57, 79
  see also Sandwich, Earl of

Moors (euphemism for Blacks), 36, 62
Moravia, Moses (*c.* 1700–1767), 186
  see also Gould, Mrs; Jews
Mordington, George Douglas, Earl of (*c.* 1680–1741), 137–8
Mordington, Lady Mary (*c.* 1684-post 1745), 138–40, 156
Morrow, Ann, 232
Morton, Mr John, 34
  see also Muscovite Ambassador
Mount Edgecumbe, Viscountess Sophia (1768–1806), 142, 143
Muilman, Henry (?–1772), 146–8
  see also Phillips, Constantia
Muilman, Mrs 'Salvador' (?–1789), 149
  see also Phillips, Constantia
Murphy, Arthur (1727–1805), 'the Irish Owl', 220
Murphy, Mother Jane, at Marjoram's, 189
Murray, Frances née Rudman (1729–1778), 79–84, 92, 103, 120
Murray, David, 1st Earl of Mansfield and Lord Chief Justice (1727–1796), 54, 131
Muscovite Ambassador, 34
  see also Matveyev
Musin-Pushkin, Count Alexei Semyonovitch (?–1817), 99
Mytton (?Milton), Richard, 96

Nando's Coffee-House, 189
  see also Thurlow
Nash, Richard, 'Beau' (1674–1762), 79, 106
Nasty Nursery of Naughtiness, The, see Thornton, Bonnell
Naughty-packs, 13
Needham, Francis John, MP (1748–1832), 176
Needham, Mother Elizabeth (*c.* 1680–1731), 32, 50, 59, 69–71
Neil, Alice, 159
Netterville, John 6th Viscount (1744–1826), 206
Nevill, Henry, 2nd Earl Abergavenny (1755–1845), 201
New Atalantis, The, 103
  see also Harris
New Bagnio, The, see Haddock
New Crazy Tales (1783), 50

New Dispensation Society, The *see*
  Bonnell Thornton
Newgate Prison, 62, 138
New Street, Covent Garden, 11
Newton, Mary, 115, 190, 198
  see also Hickey
Newton, Eleanor and William, 122
  see also Dawson
Nickers *see* Mohocks
Night Soil *see* Sanitation and
  Gong-farmers
Noble Art, The, a Public House, 62
  see also King, Moll
Nocturnal Revels, The (1779), published
  by M. Goadby, 186, 188, 211
Nokes (Noakes) James (*c.* 1630–1692),
  15, 16
  see also Homosexuals
Norden, John (1548–1625), 6
Norfolk, Charles Howard, Duke of
  (1746–1815), 221
  see also 'Royal Sovereign'
Norsa, Hannah (1712–1785), 109, 179
  see also Jews
Northington, Robert Henley, Earl of
  (1708–1772), 48, 82
'Nosegay Fan', 174
  see also Abington, Mrs
'Nosegay Nan', 180
  see also Ambrose, Eleanor
Noses-slit, 162
Nurseries of Debauchery (1724), 152

**Obscene-print Sellers in Covent
  Garden**, 227
O'Connor, Timothy, 141
Offley, William (Offley's
  Eating-house), 88
O'Kelly, Capt. Dennis, 117
Olivier's Alley *see* J. Jacobs
Old Bourne, the (Holborn), 1
Old Hummums Hotel, The, 234
Old Q *see* Queensberry, 121
Old Welsh Ale House, The (later the
  Bedford Head) in Maiden Lane,
  107
O'Neill, Mother Catherine *see* Dillon
'Orange Deb' (Martin Mackintosh), 33
  see also Homosexuals
'Orange Moll', 89
  see also Megg, May

Orford, Earls of *see* Walpole
Orkney, George Hamilton
  (1666–1733), 70
Osborne, Mr (an American) *see* Hickey
Osborne, *Mother* Sarah (1647–1732),
  aliases Roberts and Vincent, 69
Osorio-Alarcon, Cav. Giuseppe
  (*c.* 1700–1774), Sardinian
  Ambassador, 58
Ossory, Earl of, 48
  see also Upper Ossory

Page, Mother, 59, 72
  see also Moll King
Palmer, Barbara, *see* Castlemaine
Palmer, Edward, 8
Palmer, John (1742–1798), 118, 204
Palmer, Sir John (?–1553), 3
Panegyrick upon Cundums, A (1674),
  146
Panel of Matrons, The, 65, 227
  see also 'Pleading the Belly'
Pantheon, The, 84, 201, 225, 226
Paphian Grove, The (1738), 58, 67, 71
Papier-mâché, 159
  see also Clay
'Paragon of Foppery', the, *see* Mendez,
  Moses
Park Place, St James, 70
Parkes, Mother Sally, 174
Parliament, *see* Proclamations
Parsons, Anabella (Nancy Parsons)
  (1734–1814), 81, 106
Paterson, Mrs (*alias* Jackson), 105
Paulin, Thomas, 225
Pawn-shops, 230
Peep-o-Day Boys, 58
Pembroke, Henry Herbert, 10th Earl
  (1734–1794), 199, 221, 227
  see also Casanova
'People of Fascination', 156, 168, 182
'People of Fashion, The', 184, 237
  see also Fielding, Henry
Pepys, Samuel (1633–1703), 10, 26, 89
'Perdita' Robinson *see* Robinson, Mary
Perkins, Mary, 147–9
  see also Phillips
Perreaux, Daniel and Robert (?–1776),
  233
  see also Rudd
Petticoat, The (1716), 146

see also Gay, John

Pharaoh's Daughters, 135–43, 237
see also Faro houses, 135–43, 216

Phillips, Mrs Constantia Theresa
(1709–1765), 110, 144–9, 196
see also Cundums; Muilman; Perkins

Phoenix Theatre, the (1609–1642), 14

Piazza, the, 8, 10, 14, 16, 24, 28, 32, 37,
52, 75, 78, 94, 98, 114, 130, 138,
140, 184, 188, 201, 205, 223, 227,
234, 237 and *passim*

Piazza Coffee-House, the, 174, 188
see also Macklin

Piazza Tavern, the, 17

Pickpockets, 11, 19, 33, 205

Pigott, Adam, 17

Pillory, 32, 33, 65, 70, 121, 165, 232

'Pimpmaster-General', 98

'Pious Prelate, The' (1680), Nathaniel
Crew, Bishop of Durham, 18

Pit Passage, 214, 230

Pitt, Mrs George (Penelope)
(1728–1795), 'The Most Beautiful
Woman in all England', 81

Pizzoni, Count Giovanni Batiste
(1737–1789), Venetian
Ambassador, 1774–1778, 106
see also Wilkinson, Isabella

Plague, The Great, 15, 16

Platen, Countess von, 37

Playhouse Yard, 135, 137, 204

Playhouse Puncks, 15

'Pleading the Belly', 65, 227
see also Panel of Matrons

Pledwell (Plodwell) Mrs, 209

Plumbers Worshipful Company, 9

Poitier, Jenny (Mrs Joseph Vernon),
110

'Pollard Ashe, the', 166, 178
see also Ashe, Elizabeth

'Poor Fred', Frederick Louis, 68, 92,
125, 179
see also Prince of Wales

Poor Pensive Punck (1691), 15

Pope, Alexander (1688–1744), 26, 29,
111

Post Boy Tavern, the, 28
see also Buttons

'Posture Girls', 90–2, 227
see also Flagellants and the Rose
Tavern

'Posture Nan' (1762), 91

Potent Ally, The (1741), 146
see also Cundum

Powell, Harriet (1750–1779) *see* Lamb,
Harriet

Powell, Harriet (Jane) (?–1829), 217,
219

Powell, John, 8

Powell, William (1735–1769), 217

Pratt, Sir John, Lord Chief Justice
(1657–1725), 52

Prendergast, Mrs Sarah, 181

Press Gangs, 191–2, 208

Prince Regent, The, George, Prince of
Wales, 72, 100, 214, 219
see also Robinson, 'Perdita'

Prince of Wales, Frederick Louis
(1707–1751), 68, 92, 125, 179
see also 'Poor Fred'

Prior, Matthew (1663–1721), 45, 48
see also Sally Salisbury

Proclamations and Acts:
For Suppression of Jiggs (1612), 124;
Regulating Building (1626), 8;
Regarding Theatres (1737), 154;
Regarding Riots (1712), 35;
Against Indecency (1704), 33, 135;
Against Mascorades (1721), 136;
Against Prophaneness (1721),
136;
Against Vice (1712), 34, 135;
Against Vice (1787), 237;
Commencement of the Year
(1751), 166;
Against Discharge & Murder of
Bastard Children (1706), 70

Professional Stallions, 17

Public Advertiser, The, 182

Puffs, 136

Punch Bowl Tavern, the, 109, 179
see also Jews

Punishments
see also The Cage, The Pillory,
Whipping, Nose-Slitting

Puttana Errante, La, 102
see also Aretino

Quacks, 116, 160, 226

Queen Anne (1665–1714), 33–6, 42

Queen of the Garden, the (*c.* 1764),
Elizabeth Thomas, 93, 121

Queen of Clubs, The, 202
  see also Jane Lessingham
Queen's Head Tavern, the, 86
  see also Butler, Elizabeth
Queensberry, William Douglas, Duke
  of (1725–1810), 121
  see also 'Old Q'
Quin, James (1693–1766), 171

Rae, Martha (1740–1779), 102, 112, 172
  see also Hackman and Sandwich
Rake of Taste, The (1736), 67
Rake Reform'd, The (1718), by A. G.
  Gent, 90
Rambler Magazine, The, 201, 214, 220,
  231
Rann, Jack (*c.* 1750–1776), 233
Ranelagh Gardens, 167
Ranger, H., 103, 105
  see also Harris, Jack
Rapemaster-General, 70
'Rattlers' (Hackney Carriages), 206
Rawthnell, John, Rawthnell's Coffee-
  House, 88–9
  see also Royal Society of Arts
Red Cow, the, 24
Redshawe, Anne and Eleanor, 228
Register of the Ladies of Love (1607), 102
Rich, John (1682–1761), 94, 100, 132,
  157, 169, 171, 179, 184, 237
Richardson, 97, 102, 188
Richmond and Lennox, Charles
  Fitzroy, Duke of (1672–1723), 43,
  48
  see also Sally Salisbury
Rigby, Richard, MP (1722–1788), 81
Rigg, Francis 'Frankie', 62
Rigg, John and John Henry, 188
Riot in the Piazza, 37, 157, 161
Roach, Capt. David 'Tiger Roach'
  (?–1779), 115
Roach, Margaret, 233
  see also Rudd
Roberts, John, 121
Robinson, Miss, 181, 210
Robinson, Mary 'Perdita' (1758–1803),
  214, 219
  see also Prince Regent
Roche, Capt. David, 115
  see also Roach

Rochefoucauld, Duc de la (1747–1827),
  10
Rochester, John Wilmot, Earl of
  (1647–1680), 26, 140, 145
Rochford, Lord, 110
Rock, Dr Richard (?–1738), 116
Rodney, Admiral Lord George
  (1719–1792), 128
Rolleston, Samuel, 100
Rose Street, 67, 72
Rose Tavern, the, 80, 89–94, 98, 106,
  121, 125
Rosehill, Lady Christine and David
  Carnegie, Earl of (1749–1788), 212
Ross, David (1728–1790), 82, 84
Round Court and the Round House
  lock-up, 12, 119, 197
Rowbottom, Jack, 88
Rowlandson, Thomas (1756–1827),
  134
'Roxana Termagant', 74
  see also Bonnell Thornton
Royal Bagnio, 75
  see also Haddock; Harrington, Olivia
Royal Oak Lottery (1698), 135
Royal Society of Arts, 89
  see also Rawthnell's
'Royal Sovereign, the', 221–2
Rudd, Margaret Caroline née Young
  (*c.* 1740-post 1785), 233
  see also Perreaux; Roach, Margaret
'Rule-of-the-Roast', 56
Rules Restaurant, 12, 107
Rump Club, the (1727), 40
Russell family: Bedfords,
  John 1st Earl (1486–1555), 5; Francis
  2nd Earl (1527–1585), 4, 6;
  Edward 3rd Earl (1572–1626), 6;
  Francis 4th Earl (1593–1641), 6, 8,
  11; William 1st Duke (1613–1700),
  13
Russell, Master, Francis, 5th Duke
  (1765–1802), 231
Russell, Mr Jeames, 6
Russell Street, 10, 11, 16, 24, 29, 65–9,
  72, 103, 105, 126, 161, 178, 181,
  186, 188, 189, 212, 223–5, 234 and
  passim
Russian Ambassadors
  see also Matveyev, 34;
  Musin-Pushkin, 99

Rutland, John Manners, 3rd Duke
  (1696–1779), 108

Sadlers Wells Theatre, 82, 122, 124,
  125, 167, 211
St Albans, Charles Beauclerk, Duke of
  (1670–1726), 43, 48
St Clement's, 1, 122, 150
St Giles, 6, 21, 46, 70, 162
Saint Hilaries Teares (1642), 13
St James Chronicle, the, 148
St Martin-in-the-Fields, 6, 11, 17, 44,
  49, 73, 165, 188 and *passim*
St Martin's Lane, 1, 6, 11, 39, 71, 175
St Mary Axe, Bishopsgate, 231
St Paul's, Covent Garden, 10, 11, 19,
  29, 106, 107, 137, 165, 237
St Thomas' Hospital, 44
Salisbury, Sally née Pridden
  (1690–1724), 42–52, 54, 62, 76, 92
Salt, John, 35
'Salvators', 144–9
  see also Jacobs, J. and Phillips
Sam's Coffee-House, 141, 188
  see also The Hat & Beaver; Selthe
Sandwich, John Montague, Earl of
  (1718–1792), 56, 68, 81–2, 102, 112
Sanitation: Kennels; Sewers; Night
  soil; Chamberpots; Jakes;
  Gong-farmers; Schetynge-pans;
  and *passim*
'Santa Carlotta' *see* Charlotte Hayes
Sardinian Ambassador, 58
Sare, William (?–1723), 12
Satyre upon ye Players, A, by John
  Dryden, 15
Saunders, Elizabeth 'Betsy', 73, 122
  see also Haddock; Lemoy
Saville, Sir George (1726–1784), 172
Saxonia, Hercules, 144
  see also Cundums
'Schemers, the', 68
  see also Mohocks, etc.
Schetinge-pans, 10
Schulenberg, Countess, v.d., 37
Scourers, the, *see* Mohocks, etc.
Seaforth, Francis Mackenzie, Earl of
  (1754–1815), 198
  see also Lamb, Harriet
Secret History of the Green Room (1795),
  216

Sedan-chairmen, 160, 167
Selthe, Joseph (?–1779), 188
Sephardim, 35
  see also Jews
Sewers, 8, 10
  see also Sanitation
Seymour, Edward, Earl of Somerset
  (c. 1500–1552), 343
Shakespeare's Head Tavern, the, 16,
  52, 71–2, 78, 94–102, 106, 112,
  115, 118, 132, 188, 189, 196–8, 215
Sheridan, Richard Brinsley
  (1751–1816), 94, 100
Ship, the, marriage-shop, 231
Ship Tavern, the, 164
Shirelock, John, 2
Shute, Mother, *see* Mrs Cane
Shuter, Edward 'Ned' (1728–1776),
  122–7, 189
Siddons, Mrs Sarah (alias), 93
Sidmouth, Henry Addington, Earl of
  (1757–1844), 204
Slingsby, Lady Mary, née Lee, 15
Small, John, 17
Smart, Christopher, 112
Smollett, Tobias, writer (1721–1771),
  26
Snail Vendors, 160
Soap, 9, 10
Society for the Reformation of
  Manners, the, 19, 62, 192
Sodomy, 30–2, 164–5, 190, 206, 207
Somerset, Earl of, 3
  see also Seymour
Sommer, Charles, 114
'Sons of Circumcision', 187, 230
  see also Jews
Soup Shop Ale House, The, 86
Southampton St, 78, 94, 109, 114, 134,
  189
Southwell, Lord Thomas, 2nd Baron
  (1698–1766), 96
Sparre, Count Karl Gustaf
  (1688–1741), 227
  see also Flagellants
Spectator, The, 28
Spence, 'Lucky', 196
  see also Boswell
Spencer, Charlotte, The Hon. (Mrs
  Holden) (c. 1740–1789), 81, 212,
  231

Spencer, Hon. John (1710–1746), 79, 82, 130, 211
Spencer, John (1734–83), 1st Earl and Viscount, 82
Spencer, John George, Earl of (1758–1834), 177
Spiller, James (1692–1729), 32
Spiller's Head, the, 32
  see also Homosexuals
  see also Mollies houses
'Spindle Jack', 211
  see also Spencer, Hon. John
Spunging houses, 34, 120, 160, 173
Stacie (Stacey), Richard, Robert and John, 114, 116
Stafford, William Howard, Earl of (c. 1690–1732), 68
  see also Hell-Fire Club
Stanhope, Elizabeth 'Hell-fire', 68–70
  see also Dennison
Stanhope, Hon. John, 96
Star, the *see* Shakespeare's Head
Star Tavern, the, 161, 162, 199
Starvation, 190, 205, 208, 232
Statue of Queen Elizabeth, the, 225
  see also Paulin
Steele, Sir Richard (1672–1729), 26, 28
Steevens, George Alexander (?–1784), 58, 80, 232, 234
Stewes, *see* Bagnios, Bankside
Stock Exchange, The, 99, 156
Stow, John (1525–1603), 6
Strand, The, 1, 6, 9, 11–13, 29, 36, 107, 122, 131, 136, 148, 196, 211 and *passim*
Strawbridge, Mrs (c. 1720–1742), 178–9
  see also Bubb-Dodington
Streating, John, 114
Strype, John (1643–1737), 11, 13, 19, 88
Sturgess?, Mrs Mary (née Polly Jones), 198
Suffolk Street, Haymarket, 42, 99, 166
Sun Tavern, the, in Clare Market, 32
  see also Mollies houses
Sun Tavern, the, in Half-Moon Street, 171
  see also Quinn, James
Symonds, Elizabeth, *see* Gould, Elizabeth

Tabor, Isabella, 58
Talbot, Polly, 105, 121
  see also Harris
'Talking Flash', 62
Tankerville, Lady Camilla (?–1785), 70
Tarleton, Col. Sir Banastre (1754–1833), 220, 231
  see also 'Perdita' Robinson
Tatler, The, 21, 26, 28
Tavistock Court, 85, 225
Tavistock Row, 18, 85, 112, 225
Tavistock Street, 117, 134, 189, 198, 210, 225, 228, 234 and *passim*
Tawny Betty, 57
  see also King, Moll
Taylor, John 'The Oculist' (1757–1832), 120, 202
'Tea-pot Actor, The' (? John Palmer), 204
Theatre Royal, The, 14, 153, 154
Thieving Alley (Bow Street), 13
Thomas, Miss Elizabeth, *Queen of the Garden*, 93, 121
Thompson, Lady Dorothy, née Hobart (c. 1730–1798), 217
Thompson, Commodore Edward (1738–1786): *The Courtesan* (1770), 107; *The Demi-Rep* (1766), 109; *The Meretriciad* (1765 and 1770) (*q.v.*), 119
Thompson, Justice Sir William (1678–1739), 52
Thornhill, Sir James (1675–1734), 28, 100
Thornton, Bonnell, MA, MB (1724–1768), 74–5, 177, 220
  see also Haddock
Thornton, Mother Elizabeth (?–1798), 75
Three Chairs, the, 128
Three Hairs, the, 232
'Three Roses, the', 24
  see also Will's
Three Stags' Heads, the, 159
Three Tobacco Rolls, the, 33
  see also Mollies houses
Three Tuns, the, Drury Lane, 152
  see also Jennison
Three Tuns Tavern, the, in Chandos Street, 50
  see also Sally Salisbury

Thurlow, Sir Edward, later Lord Chief
   Justice (1731–1806), 189, 225
Tom and Jerry, 88
Tomkyns, Packington (?–1778),
   97–103, 115, 119, 188
Tom's Coffee-House, 29, 135
Tom's Tavern, St Martin's Lane, 29
Tothill Fields, 'Tuttlefields', 48, 72, 89
Town and Country Magazine, The, 108
Town-Pyrates, 12
Toy, Robert, 112
Tracy, Judge Robert (1655–1735), 52
Tracy (Tracey) Richard 'Beau' (*c.*
   1710–1756), 82
'Tradeing Justices', 152
   see also Smollett
Transportation, 149, 162
Treadmill, 19
Tricks of the Town (1743), 156
Trip Thro' the Town, A (1735), 36, 156
Tripolitanian Ambassador, 125
Tumbler's Arse, the, 67
Turk's Head Bagnio, the, in James
   Street, 159
Turk's Head Bagnio, the, in the
   Strand, 72, 75, 199, 209
Turk's Head Tavern, the, in Bow
   Street, 80
'Turnshite Alley' (Drury Lane), 5
Twigg, John (1729–1816), 85, 94–7, 134
Tybourne, The (Gallows), 1, 18, 126,
   160, 166, 233
'Tyburn Tickets', 160
Tyrawley, John O'Hara, Earl of
   (1682–1773), 174, 176, 178

Uffenbach, Baron Zacharias Konrad
   von (1683–1734), 36
Unicorn Tavern, The, 89
Upper Ossory, John Fitzpatrick, Earl
   of (1747–1813), 48, 216
   see also Ossory
Urwin, William, 'Will's' (ante
   1664–1698), 24
'Usquebaugh', 73, 225

Vandernan, William and family (ante
   1710–1751), 135–7
Vane, William Holles, Viscount
   (1714–1789), 172
Vaughan, Francis, 206–7

see also Homosexuals; Jones, Charles
Vauxhall Gardens, 167
Venables, John (?–1760), 114
Venetian Ambassador, 106
'Venus' Votaries', 201, 204
Vernon, Jenny and Joseph, 110
   see also Poitier, Jenny
Vincent, Elizabeth 'Priss' (1713–1790),
   115, 190, 198
   see also Hickey
Vincent, Mother, 69
Vincent, Richard, 188
Viper's Broth, 228
Voltaire, François (1694–1779), 107,
   227

Wallis, John, 42
Walpole, Sir Edward (1706–1784), 180
Walpole, Horace (1717–1797), 4th Earl
   of Orford, 57, 67, 103, 108, 132,
   141, 172, 179
Walpole, Sir Robert (1676–1745), 179
Wand'ring Whore, The, 102
   see also John Garfield
Ward, Edward 'Ned' (1667–1731), 32,
   165
Ward, John, 6
Warwick, Lady Charlotte, Countess of
   née Middleton (1679–1731), 26, 27
Water, 8–10
Water-closet, first, 10
Waterman, Elizabeth, 181
   see also Jacobs, Mrs; Jews
Weatherby (Wetherby), Elizabeth
   (?–1765), 93, 117–19, 124, 133,
   189, 234
   see also Ben Jonson's Head; Cooper,
   Lucy
Weemes (Wemyss) Elizabeth
   (*c.* 1725–1765), 93, 99, 121, 131,
   133
   see also Cooper, Lucy
Welch, Saunders (1711–1784), 132,
   157, 190
West, John and Anne, 30
West, Thomas (c. 1640–1722), 29, 30
Westminster, 'The West Munster', 1,
   166
   and *passim*
Westminster Bridge (1750), 167, 196
Westminster Fire Office, The, 29

Whale, Robert, 165
  see also Homosexuals
Wharton, Phillip, Duke of
  (1698–1731), 45, 68
  see also Charteris
Wheel of Fortune, the (*c.* 1698), 135
Whipping, 19, 56, 162
  see also Punishments
White Aprons, 19
'White Crow, the', Mrs Mary
  Corbyne, 214
White Hart Tavern, the, 234
White Horse, the, *see* Tom King
White Lion Tavern, the, 208
  see also Mollies houses
  see also Homosexuals
White Swan, the, Mrs Irvince, 214
White Wig (or White Peruke), the, 12,
  107
  see also Voltaire
White's Coffee-House, in Chandos
  Street, 12, 26, 135
Whore, The (1782), satirical poem, 221
  see also Fleming, Lady Dorothy
Whores' Club, the, 82, 98, 104
Whore's Curse, A, 62
  see also King, Moll
Whyburne (Wybourne), Mother
  Elizabeth (1653–1719), 41, 42–50,
  131, 144
Wife-selling, 19, 166
Wildman's Coffee-House, 107
Wilkes, John, MP (1727–1797), 82, 100,
  115
  see also La Charpillon
Wilkinson, Isabella (1735-post 1784),
  106, 211, 212
  see also Pizzoni

Will's Coffee House, 24–6, 29, 135, 178
  see also William Urwin, 178
William III (1650–1702), 19
Williams, Margaret, 162
Williams, John, *see* Fitzwilliam, Earl
Wilson, Benjamin (1721–1788), 57
Wilson, Mary, 228
  see also Flagellation
Winchester, Bishops of, 5
  see also Bankside Stewes
Woffington, Margaret 'Peg'
  (1714–1760), 93, 130, 154–6, 173,
  174, 184
Woffington 'Peg' (an *alias*), 174
Wood, Mother Sarah, 162, 231
Woods (Wood), Peter, 161–2, 199
  see also HMS *Grafton*
Woodward, Henry (1714–1777), 177
Worseley, Lady Dorothy Seymour
  (*c.* 1750-post 1808), 75, 214, 221
Worseley, Sir Richard Bt. (1751–1805),
  220, 221
Wortley Montague, Lady Mary
  (1689–1762) and Edward, 50, 68,
  178
Wren, Sir Christopher (1632–1723), 15
Wych Street, 1, 150
  see also Aldwych
Wyndham, Sir Charles, 78, 106
  see also Egremont
Wyndham, Hon. Charles Williams
  (1760–1828), 221
Wyndham, Lady Charlotte, 78

Yellow Cat, The, 105
York, James, Duke of, 144
York Street, 11
Yorke, Lt. Col. John (1749–1826), 82